The Horse in Sport

The Horse in Sport

William C. Steinkraus and M. A. Stoneridge

Foreword by

H.R.H. Prince Philip, Duke of Edinburgh

Stewart, Tabori & Chang / **Macdonald Orbis**

New York   *London*

in association with Channel Four Television Company Limited and Revel Guest for Transatlantic Films

Page 1: Polo at Cirencester Park, England.
Pages 2 and 3: Racing at Pompadour, France.
Frontispiece: The Water Crossing at Windsor, England.
Page 8: Steeplechasing in Virginia, U.S.A.

Text copyright © 1987 William C. Steinkraus and M. A. Stoneridge.
Credits for all photographs appear on page 272.

Library of Congress cataloguing-in-publication data
Steinkraus, William.
  The horse in sport.

  Includes index.
  1. Horse sports. I. Stoneridge, M. A. II. Title.
  SF294.2.S74 1987   798   87-9933
  ISBN 1-55670-014-8

British Library cataloguing-in-publication data
Steinkraus, William
  The horse in sport.
  1. Horse sports
  I. Title II. Stoneridge, M. A.
  798 SF294.2
  ISBN 0-356-14448-8

Quotes that appear in captions are from interviews in the Transatlantic Films television series with the following exceptions:
Pages 71, 83, and 238, provided by the authors.
Page 47, from *Guess I'm Lucky* by Woody Stephens with James Brough, 1985. Reprinted by permission of Doubleday & Company, Inc., New York.
Page 82, from *Champion's Story* by Bob Champion and Jonathan Powell, 1982. Copyright 1981 Bob Champion and Jonathan Powell. Reprinted by permission of G. P. Putnam's Sons, New York.
Page 245, from *Fox-Hunting* by the Duke of Beaufort, 1985. Reprinted by permission of David & Charles, Newton Abbot, Devon.

Editor: Madelyn Larsen

Picture research: Laurie Platt Winfrey

Design: J. C. Suarès

  Mary Cregan

Published in the United States of America in 1987 by Stewart, Tabori & Chang, Inc., 740 Broadway, New York, New York 10003.
Distributed in the United States of America by Workman Publishing, 1 West 39 Street, New York, New York 10018.

Published in Great Britain in 1987 by Macdonald Orbis, a division of Macdonald & Co (Publishers) Ltd, London & Sydney. A member of BPCC plc.
Macdonald & Co (Publishers) Ltd
Greater London House
Hampstead Road
London NW1 7QX

Published in France in 1987 by Editions Hologramme, 14 rue Ybry, 92200 Neuilly-sur-Seine.

Printed in Japan
87 88 89 90 91 10 9 8 7 6 5 4 3 2 1

First Edition

Contents

Foreword

The equestrian sports are unique among all the human sports in that they involve a direct partnership between horse and rider, or between horse and driver. There are many other sports involving animals in one way or another, but in none of them do man and animal compete as a team.

The dog has probably been man's companion for even longer, but only the horse among all the animals has helped man to fight, to move, to cultivate, and to play. This special relationship continues to stimulate a steady flow of literature on every aspect of equestrian activity. This book concentrates on the use of horses in sport.

But is another book really necessary? The answer is that things never remain the same for very long. The origins of some of the sports described in this book may be as old as time, but their practice is constantly changing and evolving. People have been driving horses for thousands of years, but international rules for combined driving competitions were only developed about fifteen years ago. Polo is not quite the same game that the Persians used to play. There have been subtle changes in the game even during the last thirty years.

Modern agriculture has changed the hunting scene, and modern technology has invaded the racing business, so that every now and then, it is a good idea to make a record of the state of the art. Contemporary enthusiasts always like to read about their sport, and future generations will be able to see how their ancestors enjoyed themselves in this era.

This is a splendid book and I am sure that it will give much pleasure to present and future generations who are lucky enough to be able to take part with horses in sport.

Philip

H.R.H. Prince Philip, Duke of Edinburgh
President, 1964–1986
Fédération Equestre Internationale

Flat Racing

Pounding hooves, pounding hearts. Spine-tingling moments that may mean triumph and fortune for some, disappointment and despair for others. Drama played in scenery that is often spectacular: rolling hills or desert dunes, snowcapped mountains, or (as at Longchamp) bright green turf, dark green foliage, and in the distance the soaring filigree of the Eiffel Tower.

Does any other sport attract and enthrall such a diversity of enthusiasts as Thoroughbred racing? Where but on a racecourse mingle modest citizens and international aristocrats, oil sheikhs and merchant princes, banking barons, shipping magnates, entertainment czars, perhaps the Queen of England herself?

Horse racing as we know it today originated in England during the seventeenth century, and its development is inseparable from that of the Thoroughbred horse. The word *Thoroughbred* does not designate simply a purebred animal, as some believe. It refers to a particular breed of horse, systematically selected for speed and stamina, with a conformation and temperament specifically designed for racing.

In previous centuries, the horse's principal usefulness to man was as a war steed. A medieval knight fully equipped for battle needed a horse with weight-carrying ability more than speed. Cold-blooded Northern breeds filled the role perfectly until the Crusades revolutionized warfare and European armies recognized the advantage of the smaller, fleeter Arabian mounts. With national security and foreign conquest in mind, the English imported Eastern stallions and bred them to native mares, eventually producing the Thoroughbred.

In the era when Britannia ruled the waves and was primarily a naval power, horses were bred increasingly for sport and transport. During the reign of Henry VIII, races were organized at Chester. James I "discovered" Newmarket in 1605; he used the region as hunting grounds and built the first permanent racecourse there. For Charles I, Newmarket was a frequent seat of residence; from there he issued the decree that started the Civil War in 1642.

But it was during the Restoration (1660–1688) that horse racing as we know it was born. Charles II, the Merry Monarch, "Father of the British Turf," loved horses, loved racing, loved pleasure. He also loved Nell Gwynn, for whom he built a house near his royal palace in Newmarket. He rode in flat races himself (the only "royal" to do so until Princess Anne made her debut as an amateur jockey in 1985), founded the Newmarket Town Plate (the oldest English race still run), and was the arbiter and authority in racing matters.

They're off! A big field has just left the gate at Pimlico and all the horses have broken well, but within the next furlong their respective abilities and the racing strategies of their jockeys will soon separate them.

Pages 12–13: Leaving the gate is a critical moment of a horse race. The starter's aim is to spring it open only when all of the horses are standing squarely and have an equal chance; but even so, many a race has been lost before the running even began.

Among George Stubbs's sixteen portraits of the great racehorses of his day is this famous painting of Eclipse (1764), a great-great-grandson of the Darley Arabian and ancestor of the vast majority of modern Thoroughbred racehorses.

His successors inherited his interest: William III founded the Royal Stud at Hampton Court; Queen Anne ordered a racecourse to be built on Ascot Heath, near Windsor Castle, in 1711 (a course that still belongs to the Crown and is graced by the royal family's presence *en masse* during the Royal Ascot meeting in June); the Duke of Cumberland, a son of George II and an expert rider and breeder (Herod and Eclipse were among his products), helped found the Jockey Club.

Queen Victoria was quite "amused" by racing and donated the first purse (in 1860) for the Queen's Plate Race, Canada's equivalent of the Kentucky Derby combined with Royal Ascot; it is a brilliant social occasion as well as the supreme three-year-old event for Canadian horses. Her eldest son, the Prince of Wales (later Edward VII), was an assiduous racing man as well as an inveterate gambler. King George VI was Britain's leading owner in 1942, largely due to Sun Chariot, a filly he leased from the National Stud. The present Queen Mother's horses also appear in flat races (though more often in steeplechase), while Queen Elizabeth II is as knowledgeable as any racing professional. A highly successful owner after her accession to the throne in 1952 (leading all others in 1954 and 1957), her familiar purple, gold braid, scarlet sleeves, black velvet cap with gold fringe appeared less frequently in the winner's circle during the 1960s. In the 1970s there was a return to form thanks to two fine fillies: Highclere, who won the 1974 1,000 Guineas race at Newmarket, then the Prix de Diane at Chantilly in the royal presence, and Dumferline, who must have been a monarchist at heart: she won the Oaks and the St. Leger in 1977, the year of the Queen's Silver Jubilee.

Three of the Eastern stallions imported to England between the 1680s and the 1720s proved to be prodigiously prepotent. All Thoroughbred horses descend from them: the Byerly Turk, the Darley Arabian, and the Godolphin Barb. In fact, all modern Thoroughbreds can be traced back to three descendants of these founding sires, other lines having since died out: Herod, a great-great-grandson of the Byerly Turk, whose line survives in France (largely due to the imported 1851 Derby winner, The Flying Dutchman, and the predilection of the Aga Khan) but is almost extinct elsewhere; Matchem (born in 1748, a grandson of the Godolphin Barb, whose last champion direct descend-

Horse racing in England in the early 19th century. This old print highlights its contrasts with the modern sport: a radical difference in riding style; small fields, often match races; ladies discreetly watching from carriages, instead of cheering exuberantly in the stands.

Just after the start, the field has broken cleanly. In the next few strides the varying riding strategies will begin to emerge, some jockeys heading for the "front end," others determined to lie off the pace and count on a late run.

ant was 1964 Derby winner Santa Claus); and Eclipse (born in 1764, the day of a solar eclipse), appropriately the most phenomenal of the three. Horse of the Year awards in the United States are called Eclipse Awards in memory of him.

Eclipse made his racing debut at age five, as was customary at the time, and won all of his twenty-seven races by enormous margins. "Eclipse first, the rest nowhere" is a famous phrase of racing history. He was also a brilliant and prolific sire, fathering some four hundred foals. In his direct line figure eighty-two of the first hundred winners of the Kentucky Derby, thirty-six winners of the Arc de Triomphe race—compared to seven for Herod and two for Matchem (but Eclipse descendants also are more numerous by far).

All modern Thoroughbreds also descend from forty or so of the two hundred "royal mares" registered in the General Stud Book compiled by James Weatherby in 1793 and updated every four years, listing the pedigrees of every Thoroughbred in England. There is a difference of opinion as to the origin of the royal mares. Were they native English stock? Were some of them French? (King Henri IV of France is known to have made a gift of fifty Norman mares to Elizabeth I.) In any case, *Thoroughbred* is a somewhat misleading term, since the breed is a blend of English and Oriental bloodlines, subsequently inbred.

Modern Thoroughbreds measure between 15 and 17 hands high at the withers (a "hand" being 4 inches/10 cm), considerably more than the foundation sires, who were all under 14.2 hands and would be considered ponies today. They weigh between 900 and 1,200 pounds/ 408 and 545 kg (since muscle weighs more than flesh, the heaviest may be the fittest, not the fattest). All of them share the same birthday, the Jockey Club has so decreed: January 1. Exceptions are those born in the Southern Hemisphere, where seasons are reversed; the Thoroughbreds have their birthday on August 1. A Thoroughbred racehorse is called a "filly" or "colt" through its three-year-old season, after which it is called a "mare" or "horse" (or "gelding" if unsexed).

Thoroughbreds vary in size and shade. Though never piebald, they are sometimes spotted—like The Tetrarch, a Herod descendant called "The Spotted Wonder." Born in 1911, he was a fabulously fast racer who sired the Aga Khan's brilliant foundation mare, Mumtaz Mahal, as well as two of the most famous fillies in racing history, Sceptre and Pretty Polly. Arab horsemen had a prejudice against four white feet, although some splendid racehorses have had them, including unbeaten Flying Childers, immortalized by James Seymour in a famous painting; Sea Bird II, who won the Derby and the Arc de Triomphe in 1965 with sensational finishing runs, and excelled as a sire as well as a racer. As an example of the prepotency of their early founders, almost all gray Thoroughbreds descend from the Alcock Arabian, the rest from the Brownlow Turk.

Man o' War (1917) was a legend in his lifetime due to his dynamic presence, his fabulous racing record, and the arrogant ease with which he produced prodigious speed.

Nearco (1935), bred by the Italian "wizard" Federico Tesio, was a Thoroughbred owner's dream come true. Undefeated as a racer (here he has just scored his fourteenth straight victory in the 1938 Prix de Paris), he was also extraordinarily successful as a sire.

Early flat racing in America, as depicted in this print of an 1823 match race on Long Island, was rustic indeed, yet these events attracted enormous crowds.

Hyperion (1930), bred and raced by Britain's most successful owner-breeder ever, the 17th Earl of Derby, was a sweet-tempered little horse who won the 1933 Epsom Derby in record time and led the English stallion list six times.

Buckpasser (1963), a rather plain dark bay, was flawless in conformation and action. Here he is winning the Hopeful Stakes at Saratoga, a victory that helped make him the world's first two-year-old Thoroughbred millionaire. Unable to compete for the Triple Crown due to a hoof injury, he was nevertheless voted Three-Year-Old of the Year as well as Horse of the Year in 1966.

Most Thoroughbreds are still bred with racing in mind: about 50,000 a year in the United States, 3,500 in France, and 10,000 in Great Britain. During their early training, more than half of them will be found to lack speed, stamina, soundness, or racing temperament and will be converted to some other equestrian use. Many unsuccessful flat racers have excelled as steeplechasers; many Olympic jumpers are Thoroughbreds who were unable to earn their oats at the racetrack.

Thoroughbred blood brings speed, courage, refinement, "class," one might say, to most other equine strains. It has contributed to the creation of the American Saddle Horse, the American Quarter Horse, the German Hanoverian and Trakehner, the Irish Hunter, and the Argentine Polo Pony. Because of their value to breeders, Thoroughbred mares are very rarely "altered," but unsuccessful racing colts often are gelded, an operation that tends to promote growth and calm intractable temperaments. Although gelded racehorses are barred from many Classic events for three-year-olds, a number of them have had sensational careers: Kelso, the richest horse in the world during his lifetime, winner of thirty-nine out of sixty-three races, Horse of the Year from 1960 through 1964; Forego, a big bay who won thirty-four of fifty-seven races and was Horse of the Year from 1974 through 1976, despite recurrent leg problems and his reputation as a rogue; John Henry, the first unanimous choice as Horse of the Year in 1981, again in 1984; now retired, he had earned all-time world-record winnings in eighty-two races by the age of nine. Geldings have held many records of purses and numbers of races won. With no breeding prospects, they are retired only when they become unsound or lose interest in racing, whereas successful "entire" colts often are assigned to lucrative stud duties at the end of their three- or four-year-old season, thus enjoying a short racing career and a long sex life.

While the Thoroughbred horse was being perfected by seventeenth- and eighteenth-century English breeders (most of them nobles and wealthy landowners), racing was a means of measuring the breed's progress. It was also a popular diversion, increasingly invaded by scoundrels and rakes. Scandal was rife. Bookmakers absconded with the receipts; horses were "got at" (surreptitiously administered soporifics or a bucket of water before a race); drugs commonly were used to stimulate mediocre runners; older horses were disguised as younger ones. In 1791 the Prince of Wales himself was implicated in a famous incident involving his gelding Escape and his jockey Sam Chifney (inventor of "the waiting race"). When Escape's running was flagrantly inferior to his normal form, Newmarket stewards barred Chifney from racing, whereupon the loyal Prince refused to race, or even to appear at Newmarket.

Chantilly in June, when the French Derby and Prix de Diane are run, is a rendezvous of international racegoers, but all year long, Chantilly and its environs is the principal location for training Thoroughbreds in France. One of the leading trainers established there is Criquette Head: ". . . There is much more money involved in racing than ever before, but it doesn't change my way of training. Whether I'm given a horse that isn't worth much or one that cost four million dollars, I'll try to make the best of him. . . . It's very important to get the right jockey for the right horse. Piggott could ride any kind of horse with no problem, and my brother Freddie sometimes gets on a horse he's never seen before the race. But, like people, each horse has his own character, and it's important for us, the trainers, to tell the jockey what to do, how to ride, depending on the way the horse feels."

Pages 18–19: Glorious Goodwood! At this lovely rural course, one of the oldest in England, fashionable Goodwood Week with its famous Goodwood Cup is a high spot on the British Racing Calendar.

Around 1752, a group of horse-racing aristocrats founded the Jockey Club in Newmarket. (The word *jockey* then meant simply "horseman"; no professional jockey has ever been elected to this exclusive circle.) They compiled the Rules of Racing, maintained the Thoroughbred stud book, and published the Racing Calendar in association with the Weatherby family, which still acts as agent for administrative matters concerning racing in England. They registered racing silks, licensed owners, trainers, and jockeys, and appointed stewards to ensure the integrity of the sport. When a famous fraud was perpetrated in the 1844 Derby and the winner, Running Rein, turned out to be not a colt but a cunningly disguised four-year-old named Maccabeus, the Jockey Club was there to expose the plot and disqualify the impostor. It has remained the ruling body of racing in Great Britain, with headquarters still in Newmarket and London offices in Portman Square. The only phase of racing to escape its autocratic control is betting, the domain of the Horserace Betting Levy Board. The Board, which took over management of the National Stud in 1963, distributes a portion of betting revenue to owners, breeders, and tracks.

The development of the railways during the nineteenth century made the racecourses at Newmarket, Ascot, Epsom, York, Doncaster, Chester, and Goodwood accessible to the general public. The Goodwood Cup was such a national event that Parliament adjourned for the day to permit its Members to attend. There was no stigma attached to racing or to wagering on the results. Not only royalty but also eminent statesmen participated in the sport—a tradition revived by Winston Churchill, who enjoyed modest success with Colonist II. An earlier Prime Minister, the Earl of Rosebery, won the 1894 Derby with Ladas, and one of the most popular Derby wins in history was that of Persimmon in 1896, owned by the Prince of Wales—who won it a second time with Minoru in 1909, when he was King Edward VII.

From the end of the nineteenth century, the British racing scene became increasingly international. Leading English owners—Lord Derby, Lord Woolavington, Lord Durham, Lord Rosebery, Lord Berner, Lord Dewar, Lord Portland, the dukes of Westminster, Bedford, Grafton, Norfolk, Richmond, Cumberland, and their peers—were joined by more exotic ones: Baron Meyer de Rothschild (founder of the banking dynasty), J. B. Joel (a South African diamond millionaire, who was still an active racing owner in his nineties), Prince Batthyany (a Hungarian nobleman who lived in England, was elected to the Jockey Club, and won the 1875 Derby with Galopin, the sire of St. Simon, one of the greatest nineteenth-century Thoroughbreds—Hyperion, Nearco, and Ribot were all inbred to him).

American owners also came to England and Ireland, sometimes in their oceangoing yachts, to buy, train, and race. Pierre Lorillard helped make racing history when his horse Iroquois won the 1879 Derby, ridden by American jockey Tod Sloan in a revolutionary "crouch" seat. "A monkey on a stick!" they said. But soon the British jockeys were all following his example. The Wideners and Vanderbilts brought American horses and jockeys to England too. A wealthy American sportsman, James Foxhall Keene, won the Ascot Gold Cup of 1882 with Foxhall. Then, in 1913, the British passed the Jersey Act, a protectionist measure that virtually banned the import of American Thoroughbreds. American owners withdrew or transferred their stables to France.

In 1921, the Aga Khan III thought the time was ripe to move his racing and breeding operations from India and challenge the Europeans. He did so on a grand scale and soon ranked among the leading owner-breeders in England, along with Lord Derby, whose Hyperion and Gainsborough were practically unbeatable. The Aga Khan's best racers were Blenheim, Bahram, Mahmoud, Tulyar, and the temperamental Nasrullah, who was also his best sire; his best filly was Mumtaz Mahal, who in retirement produced marvelous broodmares like herself, including Mumtaz Begum. During the 1930s, the portly spiritual leader's horses, mainly descendants of Mumtaz Mahal, finished first and second in four Classic races.

During World War II, the Racing Calendar was drastically reduced and Classic events were transferred to Newmarket. But when life returned to normal, so did racing. One of the leading postwar English owners was Sir Victor Sassoon, whose silks finished first in the Derby four times in eight years, carried by Pinza (1953), Crepello (1957), Hard Ridden (1958), and St. Paddy (1960), a record never equaled.

The Jersey Act was repealed finally in 1949, whereupon a new contingent of American owners arrived, among them Oxford-educated Paul Mellon (whose mother was British). His beautiful little Mill Reef won twelve major races before a leg fracture curtailed his racing career. In a gesture typical of that fine philanthropist, Mellon sent his champion to the National Stud rather than to more lucrative breeding assignments in the United States. Mill Reef's success as a sire was sensational, as has been that of his 1978 Derby-winning son, Shirley Heights, who sired another Derby winner, Darshaan, for the present Aga Khan. In 1985, the year before his death (at age eighteen), Mill Reef and his progeny accounted for over half the revenue of the National Stud.

Another American arrival was platinum millionaire Charles Engelhard, leading owner in England in 1971, thanks to some wonderful horses: Ribocco, Ribero, and Nijinsky (English Triple Crown winner in 1970, the first in thirty-five years). Nijinsky had been trained in Ireland by Vincent O'Brien, who was beginning to specialize in foreign owners and to engage Lester Piggott to ride his best horses—a combi-

Kelso (1957) was so slow to develop that he was gelded, and then he achieved a long and brilliant career as well as immense popularity. His eight racing seasons included five Jockey Club Gold Cup victories, five Eclipse Awards as Horse of the Year, fifteen speed records equaled or bettered, and a new money-winning record. His jockey here is a confident Ismael Valenzuela.

22

nation that already had proved its success with Raymond Guest's Sir Ivor, who was trained by O'Brien and ridden to victory by Piggott in the 1968 Derby, the 2,000 Guineas, and the Washington International.

A flamboyant Texas oil man, Nelson Bunker Hunt, dominated the English owners' list during 1973 and 1974. One of the first to establish a global racing empire (over a thousand horses in Europe, the United States, and Australia; stud farms in Kentucky and New Zealand), his American-bred, French-trained Dahlia, daughter of his co-owned 1968 Arc winner Vaguely Noble, took the international lifestyle in her stride: she won top races in five different countries, including the 1973 Washington International and the King George VI and Queen Elizabeth Stakes in 1973 and again in 1974.

Among more recent American owners on the British scene are the Bertram Firestones, who purchased the Aga Khan's Irish stud farm and divide their racing activities between the United States and Europe, their racehorses between themselves: he owns the colts and she the fillies—including Genuine Risk, the first filly to win the Kentucky Derby in sixty-five years (in 1980), her only predecessor being Regret (in 1915).

During and since the 1970s, Thoroughbred breeding and racing have become so costly that in England, as elsewhere, the number and importance of private stables have steeply declined. While illustrious names maintain their presence on a more modest scale, the most powerful English owner in the 1980s has been Robert Sangster, a football pools magnate, who built a racing conglomerate in the image of a multinational corporation. Paying top prices for well-bred yearlings, and with the collaboration of a master trainer (Vincent O'Brien) and leading jockeys (successively Lester Piggott, Pat Eddery, Steve Cauthen, and Cash Asmussen), Sangster keeps hundreds of racehorses in the care of some forty trainers around the world. In 1982 he accomplished the unprecedented exploit of winning the Epsom Derby, the Irish Derby, and the French Derby all in the same year.

Other innovations have altered the traditional British racing scene: tote betting, television, the licensing of women trainers and jockeys, commercial sponsorship of races, racehorse and stallion syndication. But the most striking feature of present-day racing is the presence of the Middle Eastern "oil princes." While their Thoroughbred interests are worldwide, many of them prefer to race in England, where they were educated; many historic English and Irish horse farms have been purchased by them. Most prominent among these lavish investors and shrewd horsemen are the Maktoums of Dubai: Sheikh Rachid al-Maktoum and his four sons, princes Maktoum, Mohammed, Hamdan, and Ahmed (four of the opening-day races at the 1985 Goodwood meeting were won by members of the family, while the 1985 1,000 Guineas turned into an all-Dubai affair with the winner owned by

Sheikh Maktoum al-Maktoum, the two runners-up by his brothers Mohammed and Hamdan). Rivaling the al-Maktoums are the al-Sabahs, members of the ruling family of Kuwait, and Prince Khaled bin Abdulla of Saudi Arabia.

Smaller stables still manage to survive and succeed: Lord Howard de Walden, Chairman of the Jockey Club and also active in steeple-chasing, is owner of the 1985 Derby winner Slip Anchor and of an outstanding miler, Kris, who has become the leading syndicated sire in Britain. Moon Madness, owned by Lavinia, Duchess of Norfolk, won the 1986 St. Leger. But the Arab presence is increasingly conspicuous: Sheikh Mohammed was the Leading Owner in England in 1985, his brothers Hamdan and Maktoum fourth and sixth; Prince Khaled was second, and a lone Englishman—Lord Howard de Walden—was third. This may be no more than historic justice, when one remembers that it was the Byerly Turk, the Godolphin Barb, and the Darley Arabian who founded the Thoroughbred and started it all.

In Ireland, just across the Irish Sea, the Thoroughbred found an ideal breeding ground and nursery. It is not merely that horses were essential to Ireland's agricultural economy; to the Irish people horse sports are a national pastime and horse breeding a passion for which they seem to possess an uncanny instinct.

The Emerald Isle was virtually an English colony from the twelfth century until the Irish Republic achieved independence early in the twentieth century. Much of its best land was confiscated or accorded by the Crown to English landlords; aristocratic English Thoroughbred fanciers of the seventeenth and eighteenth centuries founded stud farms in Ireland to complement their establishments at home.

While English and Irish Thoroughbreds were thus closely related, the latter soon made a name for themselves. At the same time, Irish farmers utilized Thoroughbred blood to improve their native breeds, the Irish Draught Horse and the Connemara Pony. By the end of the nineteenth century, the Irish Hunter (part Draught, generally three-quarters or seven-eighths Thoroughbred) was considered the finest in the world. The Connemara-Thoroughbred mixture also produced exceptionally game and agile sporting animals.

During the 1840s, the disastrous potato famine led to a massive emigration which reduced the Irish population by almost half. Among those seeking fame and fortune as well as survival in foreign lands were many Irishmen whose expertise as breeders, trainers, and riders was welcomed in England, Europe, America, even farther afield. Although no longer so urgently motivated, the emigration of Irish horsemen and horses has continued ever since.

The fact is that the Irish themselves have always had a predilection for jump races, undoubtedly a consequence of their tradition of fox hunting, which is not only a national pastime, but also an important activity for the protection of the farmers' livestock. Flat racing in Ireland was a minor sport until the end of World War II. The Racing Board was founded only in 1954.

Today, in addition to countless informal racing events throughout the land, twenty-eight official racecourses hold 250 meetings a year, mostly mixed, but with year-round steeplechase and hurdle races far outnumbering flat events. Most Irish trainers run mixed stables.

Thoroughbred racing in France is closely related to racing across the Channel. As in England, selective horse breeding was promoted by the Crown for military purposes. The first royal stud, the Haras du Pin, was built by Louis XIV, who was continually engaged in wars.

As in England, horse racing was a popular pastime of the court from the middle of the eighteenth century. Nobles imported English Thoroughbreds and raced them on the Champ de Mars, where a track was built by Count d'Artois, brother of Louis XIV. Although Louis XVI disapproved of racing because of the gambling involved, his pleasure-loving queen Marie Antoinette appointed Prince Lambesc to be her Master of the Horse and raced her horses there. So popular were these events that the French revolutionaries later attempted to organize "patriotic races."

Studying the form: a familiar and endlessly fascinating activity throughout the racing world.

25

Napoleon was more interested in breeding than in racing, since his military campaigns required an unlimited supply of horses. In 1805 he founded the *Administration des Haras* to promote breeding, using native mares and Arabian and Spanish stallions. It would have been unthinkable to breed to enemy English Thoroughbreds.

The post-Napoleonic era was, on the contrary, marked by a craze for anything English. In 1833, during the reign of Louis Philippe, Lord Henry Seymour, an English sportsman and dandy who lived in Paris, helped his friend the Duc d'Orléans to found the *Société d'encouragement pour l'amélioration des races des chevaux en France*, patterned after the English Jockey Club. Still the governing body of French racing and breeding, it is now part of the Ministry of Agriculture. It runs a jockey school, owns tracks and training grounds, and is totally distinct from the "social" French Jockey Club.

In 1836, the Duc d'Aumale founded the Prix du Jockey Club (the French Derby) at Chantilly, where a track had been built by the Prince de Condé in front of the luxurious stables near his château. A believer in reincarnation, the Prince expected to return to earth in the form of a horse and wished to ensure his comfort. The first winner was Rank, a colt belonging to Lord Seymour. A few years later, a race of equivalent prestige for fillies, the Prix de Diane, was inaugurated at Chantilly.

The Longchamp course was opened in 1857 to replace the swampy Champ de Mars. Every year the Prix du Cadran is run there in memory of its predecessor, the "cadran" referring to the ancient clock on the façade of the Military School at the end of the Champ de Mars. In 1863, the Grand Prix de Longchamp was run for the first time. The next year, summer racing was established at Deauville on the Normandy coast, where a racecourse was built by the Duc de Morny, bastard brother of the reigning Emperor Napoleon III. The region has become the hub of Thoroughbred breeding in France; Deauville, the summer capital of Thoroughbred racing. Its August meeting is a fashionable international event, complete with polo and yearling sales, the most important on the Continent.

As the art of the time attests, racing had become a popular sport, still dominated by but no longer restricted to the aristocracy. Its popularity soared when a sensational racing event occurred in 1865: Gladiateur, a French horse, won the Epsom Derby. It was a thrilling race. After trailing by 20 lengths, he finished 2 lengths in front of his closest rival in a tremendous spurt of speed. He received a hero's welcome on his return to his native land—hailed as "the avenger of Waterloo," no less—and proceeded to win the Grand Prix de Paris. His statue stands at the entrance of the Longchamp racecourse.

In 1866, the Ministry of Agriculture divided the administration of French racing into three parts: flat racing, steeplechasing, and trotting —all under its control. Racing thus became a nationalized industry,

Though racing has become increasingly informal and democratic, a top hat and boutonnière are still de rigueur for gentlemen attending Classic races at elegant European venues.

quite unlike the situation in Great Britain and the United States, where it is a private industry.

During the Belle Epoque after the War of 1870, horse racing was fashionable, gambling widespread. A wave of British trainers emigrated to France: they included the Palmers (the first "public trainers," who filled their stables with horses belonging to a number of different owners), the Carters, Cunningtons, Bartholomews, and Heads—whose descendants are still prominent in French racing. During the nineteenth century there were also many famous horses for whom major races are named, among them Jouvence, Monarque (the sire of Gladiateur, he too won in England as well as in France), Dollar, Fille de l'Air, and Vermeille.

The Jersey Act of 1913 may or may not have succeeded in its aim of protecting the integrity of the English Thoroughbred—probably not, because it was later repealed. But it provided new blood for French racing. American owners like Pierre Lorillard, William K. Vanderbilt, and Ralph Beaver Strassburger came to France as did American jockeys. Even without this influx, French racing was enjoying a heyday with some legendary horses running for some legendary owners: Edmond Blanc, owner of the Jardy Stud, with his horses Ksar (winner of the Arc in 1921 and 1922, but especially renowned as a sire), Quo Vadis, Ajax, Camargo, Flying Fox, and Teddy; Count Evremond de Saint-Alary with Omnium II and Brûleur; Baron Edouard de Rothschild with Sardanapale and La Farina.

French racing resumed after the interruption of World War I on a very cosmopolitan note with the presence of Englishmen (such as Lord Derby), Greeks, Americans, Argentinians (such as Martínez de Hoz), and the Aga Khan. But Edmond Blanc retained his place as leading owner-breeder until he died in 1920. This was the year in which the Prix de l'Arc de Triomphe was founded at Longchamp to become the climax of the French racing season, the unofficial European Championship, the model for similar international races in other lands.

Edmond Blanc's preeminent place in French racing was inherited by Marcel Boussac, a textile magnate and dedicated racing man who dominated the French racing scene from his first success in 1922 until the 1950s. In 1950, he was leading owner not only in France but also in England. Many great horses carried the familiar orange silks and gray cap, among them Tourbillon, who won fifteen races and produced such fine offspring as Djebel, Corrida, and Pharis, a black beauty famous for his thrilling final runs from far behind the field. Stolen by the Germans during the Occupation, Pharis was later recovered and returned to stud; but Corrida, Boussac's best mare, was never seen again. Business disasters caused the crash of Boussac's empire. When he died in 1979, his horses were purchased by the young Aga Khan, his stud farm by Stavros Niarchos. During his years of glory, Boussac had

won the Prix du Jockey Club twelve times (among 140 Classic victories). The only owners who could rival him were Baron Edouard de Rothschild (with Brantôme), Pierre Wertheimer (with Epinard), and Léon Volterra (with Phil Drake and later Topyo, surprise winner of the 1967 Arc de Triomphe at odds of 80 to 1).

After having spurned the Germans' efforts to maintain a semblance of racing during the Occupation, the French welcomed the "liberated" sport. While the Boussac stable resumed its dominance, new horses and owners rose to challenge it: Baron Guy de Rothschild, leading owner of 1950 with Vieux Manoir and Exbury, a courageous, extremely popular little horse who won the 1963 Arc; Jean Stern with Sicambre; Pierre Wertheimer with Vimy and the 1956 French Derby winner Lavandin; English-born Mme. Jean Couturié with Right Royal; Daniel Wildenstein, an international art dealer, with Allez France, daughter of the great Sea Bird II; and François Dupré with Match II, Tantième, Tanerko, and Relko.

Dupré, a hotelier by profession, owned the Hotel George V (still a favorite rendezvous of the racing set), but his passion was racing and breeding. Like the Italian genius Federico Tesio, he believed in international crosses and imported Dan Cupid from the United States to infuse new blood into the French Thoroughbred. The transatlantic outcross produced at least two genuine champions: Bella Paola and Sea Bird II, whom some consider the finest French Derby winner ever (in 1965, by 2 lengths, and in a canter at the finish).

In 1954, the Tiercé, a government-sponsored betting scheme offering tremendous possible gains, swept France and provided welcome funds for racing, since a portion of the profits was allotted to generous breeders' bonuses and to some of the richest purses in the world.

During the 1950s and 1960s, French horses excelled everywhere. Three French fillies took the first three places in the 1956 English Oaks: Mme. Léon Volterra's Sicarelle, Boussac's Janiari, and Prince Aly Khan's Yasmin. Between 1947 and 1957, five French-trained horses won the Epsom Derby. Then for some mysterious reason French racing fortunes declined; in 1970, every French Classic race was won by a foreign horse. At the same time, economic and social pressures were causing the big traditional private stables to disappear. Boussac's and Dupré's were taken over by the young Aga Khan IV; others, like those of Baron Guy de Rothschild and Léon Volterra, reduced the scope of their racing activities.

Today, only a few French owners (Wildenstein, Wertheimer) maintain operations vast enough to compete with the mammoth challenge of the Arab oil princes, of Robert Sangster (British), Stavros Niarchos (Greek), the Aga Khan (best described as international), Mahmoud and Moustapha Fustok (Lebanese-born Saudi Arabians), Serge Fradkoff (a Swiss diamond merchant), William duPont de Nemours and the

Exercising horses in the early morning mists of Newmarket may seem lonely and bleak, but it is probably the high point of the day for these English "lads," who spend most of their time attending to stable chores, perhaps dreaming of becoming another Lester Piggott.

30

Bertram Firestones (American), and a few wealthy Japanese (less prominent since the 1970s). Most French owners compete with no more than half a dozen horses entrusted to trainers like John Cunnington, Hubert d'Aillières, Patrick Biancone, the Pélats, and François Boutin. Most French trainers, as in England and America, work for a number of patrons.

In the New World, the British colonists built their new lives, as British colonists were wont to do, around the traditions they had left behind—and one of these was horse racing. As early as 1665, the British Governor of New York, Col. Richard Nicholls, founded the first American racecourse on Long Island.

In 1730, the first Thoroughbred racehorse was imported from England by a Virginia tobacco planter. Bulle Rocke, a son of the Darley Arabian, was too old to race but still capable of performing as a stud. He was followed in 1750 by Janus, a descendant of the Godolphin Barb and the foundation sire of the American Quarter Horse. But the most influential early imported Thoroughbred was the 1780 Derby winner Diomed. Although his racing days were over (he was twenty at the time), he performed ten years of stud duty and is one of the forefathers of the Lexington line, unfortunately now extinct. The legendary mid-nineteenth-century sire fathered no less than six hundred foals, 236 of them winners; his incomparable breeding career spanned twenty-one years, during sixteen of which he was the Leading Sire in America.

Since the Colonial wilderness consisted of dense woodlands rather than plains, races were run over laboriously cleared straight tracks. Many were no more than a quarter of a mile (400 m) long, a condition that encouraged the development of the American Quarter Horse breed, and gave it its name. Racing and breeding were at first concentrated in the South and East. Many leading Thoroughbred establishments are still located in Maryland, Virginia, Pennsylvania, New York, but especially in Kentucky, where soil and climate are ideal for raising horses.

The Civil War nearly brought racing to a standstill. Many horses had been given to the cavalry; most of them were killed in battle. In the North racing was revived in 1864 at the Passaic County Fair Derby in New Jersey. That same year the Travers Stakes was inaugurated in Saratoga, New York, promoting the charming spa town to a major racing summer rendezvous, rather like Deauville in France, complete with steeplechase, polo, and bloodstock sales.

In 1867, the Belmont Stakes was inaugurated in New York. The first of the Triple Crown races to be founded, it is the last to be run since it is also the longest: originally 2 miles/3.2 km, now 1½ miles/ 2.4 km. The other two races were founded soon after in the South: the Preakness (1873) in Maryland, named after a famous son of Lexing-

31

American racehorses in training might be envious if they knew of the idyllic conditions of European training grounds. In contrast, they generally work out at dawn or even earlier (under lights) on the enclosed oval of a dirt training track, like this one at Saratoga.

Morning workouts take place on the Heath at Newmarket rain or shine, heat or cold, under the watchful eye of the trainer (often mounted on a pony), who judges his horses' potential and condition by observing them in action: walking, galloping, breezing— usually in "sets" but also in trials against other colts of established merit.

Every trainer has pet remedies, sometimes closely guarded secrets, for treating injuries and keeping his horses in condition. A common method is some form of hydrotherapy, like this horse bath at Newmarket.

After the intense effort of a workout or a race, the horses are given a comforting bath, as here in the stable area at Saratoga. At the same time they're being carefully examined for signs of swelling, heat, or soreness in the legs, since it is these on which a race-horse's career, perhaps his very life, depend.

ton; and the Kentucky Derby (1875), conceived as an equivalent of the Epsom Derby. Only eleven horses have won all of these events for three-year-olds: Sir Barton (1919), the Canadian-owned, Kentucky-bred, ill-tempered son of a blind stallion and a seventeen-year-old mare—the Derby was his maiden race; Gallant Fox (1930); Omaha (1935); War Admiral (1937), a son of Man o' War; Whirlaway (1941); Count Fleet (1943)—he won the Belmont by 25 lengths in record time but cut himself during the race, which was his last; Assault (1946); Citation (1948), the first Thoroughbred millionaire. Then came a long suspenseful wait until Secretariat, a big playful Bold Ruler son, achieved the exploit in 1973, winning the Belmont by 31 lengths and setting a world record for 1½ miles/2.4 km on a dirt track. He was followed by Seattle Slew in 1977, the first undefeated Triple Crown winner, and Affirmed in 1978. Pensive (1944) and Tim Tam (1958) failed by the narrowest margin, since they won the Derby and the Preakness, but finished second in the Belmont. Swale, a brilliant Seattle Slew son, won the 1984 Derby, lost the Preakness, won the Belmont—and then mysteriously died a few weeks later.

By the end of the nineteenth century, racing in America had become sufficiently important and sufficiently disorganized (every track had its own rules) for a group of prominent racing men to found the American Jockey Club in 1894. Just as exclusive and aristocratic as its British model (its first Chairman was August Belmont II, its present one Ogden Mills Phipps), it was equally omnipotent in racing matters for many years. Today, however, while it still controls the stud book, registers horses and U.S. racing colors, maintains records, and appoints stewards, it has turned over many licensing and regulating tasks to various state racing commissions. Race track managements have created their own governing body, the Thoroughbred Racing Association, which has a security branch, the Thoroughbred Racing Protective Bureau.

World War I did not interrupt American racing. Indeed, the sport was more popular than ever because of radio broadcasts and perhaps even more because of an extraordinary horse: Man o' War. An imposing presence with his fantastically extended stride and bright chestnut coat, he was called "Big Red" by his adoring public and his famous groom, Will Harbutt, who proclaimed to one and all that Man o' War was "de mostest hoss." His record was almost perfect: twenty races, nineteen of them easily won by an average of 9½ lengths, generally carrying top weight. In eight of his eleven three-year-old races, he broke either a track or a world record. He was retired to stud at the end of that season, a national celebrity. Never bred to more than twenty-five mares a year (forty or more is the usual number today), he headed the sire list only once, in 1926. But his influence was profound and his name figures in the pedigree of outstanding racers throughout

33

the world: Match, Relko, Reliance in France; English Derby winners Never Say Die and Sir Ivor; Kelso, Forego, Seattle Slew, and John Henry in the United States. Not only did he transmit speed and stamina—especially to his sons War Relic, 1929 Kentucky Derby winner Clyde Van Dusen, and 1937 Triple Crown winner War Admiral—but also jumping ability. His son Battleship was the first American horse to win the Grand National Steeplechase at Aintree.

Seattle Slew, ridden by French-born Jean Cruguet, is about to win the 1977 Kentucky Derby, the first step toward his Triple Crown. After proving his excellence at the racetrack, he became an equally outstanding sire.

In 1925, winter racing was inaugurated at Hialeah Park in Florida, in 1934 at Santa Anita Park in Southern California (where the equestrian events of the 1984 Olympic Games were held). Thoroughbred racing became a year-round activity.

During the 1930s, the photo-finish camera, the mobile starting gate, and legal betting with the totalizator all contributed to create a racing boom despite the economic crisis—perhaps as a distraction from it. Another innovation was stallion syndication, when Leslie Combs II organized a group of shareholders to purchase Louis B. Mayer's Beau Père for $100,000, a fabulous sum at the time. Who could have imagined that this would one day revolutionize the Thoroughbred industry?

Racing was severely reduced after the United States entered World War II, owing to lack of fuel and manpower, but it was officially banned only during a few months from January 1945 until V-E Day, May 8. Those wartime years produced some unforgettable racehorses, including Whirlaway (1938), the chunky chestnut winner of the 1941 Kentucky Derby and Belmont Stakes, noted for nonchalant starts and breathtaking finishes; and Stymie (1941), a mischievous, ordinary-looking colt, whose indomitable will to win made him immensely popular.

When racing returned to normal after the war, there was Citation (1945), a paragon of a Thoroughbred. "A Cadillac!" said his jockey, Eddie Arcaro. And then Tom Fool (1949), a horseman's horse, a real "pro"; Native Dancer (1950), a striking steel-gray winner of twenty-one out of twenty-two races and, after injury curtailed his career, a superior breeder, siring Raise a Native (who sired Majestic Prince) and Kauai King (who avenged his father's unlucky single defeat in the Kentucky Derby by winning it in 1966). When his filly Natalma was bred to a Nearco son, Nearctic, she produced Northern Dancer, the most important Thoroughbred sire of modern times. Already Native Dancer's influence had spread to Europe through his daughter Hula Dancer and his son Dan Cupid.

The most famous racers of the 1950s were Swaps and Nashua, the former a homebred Californian, the latter a Kentucky aristocrat. Their rivalry thrilled the nation, including nonracegoers, and culminated in a match race won by Nashua. (But there were doubts as to Swaps's soundness that day, and we will never really know which colt was the better.)

Along with every other sector of the economy, racing boomed during the postwar years. Many new tracks were built, and new owners appeared. While traditional dynasties continued at the fore—Whitneys, Woodwards, Belmonts, Phippses, Mellons, Guests, Wideners, duPonts, Klebergs, Strawbridges—they were joined by newcomers: self-made millionaires like Elizabeth Graham (Elizabeth Arden cosmetics), Charles Engelhard (platinum), Nelson Bunker Hunt (Texas oil), movie moguls, and real estate developers.

And with them came a new crop of Thoroughbred champions: the great gelding Kelso and his arch-rivals Carry Back and Gun Bow (Elizabeth Graham's best); Round Table, a cocky little Californian whose race earnings were second only to Kelso's before he became a high-ranking sire and passed on the bluest of blood (his sire was Princequillo, his dam Knight's Daughter, bred by the Queen of England); 1969 Kentucky Derby winner Majestic Prince, and that year's Belmont winner Arts and Letters; Buckpasser; Secretariat (considered by some the horse of the century); Ruffian, an immensely popular filly who won ten out of ten races before losing the eleventh, a match race against the Kentucky Derby winner Foolish Pleasure in 1975, during which she fatally shattered a leg bone; Riva Ridge, Forego (another great gelding), and Seattle Slew—a Cinderella horse if there ever was one. Purchased for $17,500 as a yearling by two young couples new to racing, Slew became the first undefeated Triple Crown winner in 1977, then, syndicated with a capital value of $24 million, he became a champion sire.

Affirmed and Alydar were two great rivals whose neck-and-neck duel in the 1978 Belmont Stakes, a thriller all the way, ended in victory for Affirmed as well as a Triple Crown. Spectacular Bid might have inherited it in 1979, if he hadn't stepped on a safety pin on the morning of the Belmont. Genuine Risk was one of two fillies to win the Kentucky Derby (1980), followed by second places in the Preakness and the Belmont. Indomitable, indestructible John Henry, Conquistador Cielo (1983 Horse of the Year), All Along . . . the story of American racing is not so much a series of events and dates as a parade of great horses.

During recent decades, Thoroughbred racing in the United States as elsewhere has become not only more democratic (though more costly), but also more international. The Washington D.C. International, founded in 1952, anticipated the trend. And Dahlia, a star of the 1970s, was the prototype of the modern equine jet-setter: she was bred in the United States, sired by an English stallion out of an American mare, owned by a Texan, trained in France by a trainer of Hungarian-Turkish descent who had begun his career in Egypt, and she raced (and won) all over the world.

The trend continues. What is true of racing in England and France

Pages 36–37: A brilliant spectacle? A thrilling, fleeting moment? A moving example of teamwork between horse and man? A horse race is all this . . . and more.

35

tends to be true of racing in the United States, except for minor details and the fact that everything (except jockeys) is apt to be on a bigger scale. American-organized breeding syndicates offer irresistible bids for the cream of European racers, while Arab, European, and other foreign buyers bid for the best American yearlings—which often are sent to Europe to be trained and raced there. Only an exceptional individual American owner can surpass their offers—like Allen Paulson, who is reputed to have invested $100 million of his aerospace fortune in bloodstock since 1982.

Unable to match the prestige of historic English and French Classic racing events, American racing men and track managements appeal to foreign owners by offering million-dollar races. Begun in 1984, the innovative Breeders' Cup Day attracts foreign champions and television sponsors by distributing $10 million in seven races on a single day!

From its modest beginnings on hand-hewn tracks, the American racehorse has become the most valuable animal in the world. A share in Seattle Slew, theoretically representing one-fortieth of his value, was sold in 1985 for $2.7 million. But that same year, horse racing lost its long-held place as America's leading spectator sport. It is a paradoxical situation: more successful than ever as an industry, has Thoroughbred racing in the United States passed its peak of popularity as a sport? Or is it evolving into a different kind of sport?

The racing season is not a haphazard series of events, but a coordinated schedule providing increasing challenges over increasing distances as colts and fillies mature and older horse reach their peak of form.

Racing Secretaries try to attract as many entries as possible to their meetings by scheduling events in which horses at every stage of development will have a chance to win. This is accomplished first by restricting entries in each race to a certain sex and age, then by setting "race conditions." Three different categories are designed to handicap older or better horses by obliging them to carry greater weight, and to improve the chances for younger, less successful runners by means of weight allowances. (Every extra pound/450 g on the horse's back is considered the equivalent of a fifth of a second or a half-length.)

Weight-for-age conditions mean that weights are allotted according to the Jockey Club "scale of weights," which has changed very little since it was drawn up in the nineteenth century by Admiral Henry John Rous, a famous figure in racing history. His table takes into account the horse's age and sex, the distance, and the time of year.

Allowance races take into account the horse's record in terms of money won, the less successful being given weight allowances.

In *handicap* races, the track handicapper distributes weights ac-

In spite of close historic links, French and English Thoroughbred breeders and owners are keen rivals. The easily identified British contingent flocks to France to support its entries in the Arc, the French Derby, and the Prix de Diane—led by the Queen herself in 1974, when her own Highclere won this prestigious event for three-year-old fillies.

Standards of decorum at American racetracks might seem excessively relaxed to some European racegoers, but to these Saratoga fans cheering their favorite horses, that doesn't bother them a bit.

cording to some complex formula perhaps of his own invention—but today more likely the output of a computer.

Other denominations of races refer to a form of purse rather than to conditions. *Stakes* races, for example, are usually for same-age horses under equal weights. As their name suggests—short for "sweepstakes"—they offer the richest purses and generally the greatest prestige. Costly entry fees, often paid in installments, are divided among the winners. The merits of sires and broodmares are measured by the number of stakes winners they've produced.

Owners and trainers are just as concerned with weight as are the handicappers; they try to bring their horses to the most important races with the least possible weight, and spend hours poring over the Conditions Book issued for each track meeting.

Two years is the minimum legal age for a Thoroughbred racing debut, 5 furlongs the legal minimum distance (a furlong being an eighth of a mile, or 220 yards/200 m, traditionally the length of a furrow in a field). Race distances increase as the season progresses.

At three years, the horse is challenged with increasingly demanding tests of speed and stamina. The Classic three-year-old events are the most prestigious on the Racing Calendar. Run under the Jockey Club weight-for-age scale, their lists of past winners comprise a veritable *Who's Who* of racing. English racing has five Classics. The *2,000 Guineas* (1809) and *1,000 Guineas* (1814) are both run over a straight one-mile/1.6 km course at Newmarket, the latter reserved for fillies. The *Epsom Derby* was co-founded by Lord Derby and his friend, fellow-owner and Jockey Club director Sir Charles Bunbury, in 1780. The name of the 1½ mile/2.4 km race was decided by the toss of a coin: Bunbury lost the toss but won the inaugural race with Diomed. The *Oaks*, a 1½ mile/2.4 km race for fillies, was founded at Epsom in 1779 by the same Lord Derby, who named it after his nearby country estate (and won the inaugural race with Bridget, a daughter of Herod). The *St. Leger*, the oldest of all and open to both sexes, has been run at Doncaster since 1776 over a 1¾ mile/2.8 km course.

Very few colts have won the British Triple Crown (the 2,000 Guineas, the Derby, and the St. Leger). Among the most memorable are Flying Fox (1899), Rock Sand (1903, an ancestor of Man o' War), Gay Crusader (1917), and Gainsborough (1918). The latest was Nijinsky in 1970. The likelihood that there will be others diminishes as racehorses increasingly specialize in certain distances, whereas the Triple Crown events, ranging from 1 to 1¾ miles/1.6 to 2.8 km, require versatility.

Ireland has its Classics, counterparts of the English prototypes: the Irish 2,000 and 1,000 Guineas, the Irish Derby, the Irish Oaks, and the Irish St. Leger. All of them are run at The Curragh, a vast horse training and racing establishment (originally a cavalry camp, founded in 1646) in County Kildare, not far from Dublin.

In America, flat tracks are literally flat, but in Europe the final drive to the finish is often uphill, as here at Ascot—a real test of stamina and courage.

The French, who emulate the British in many Thoroughbred matters, created their version of the English Classics: the Poule d'Essai des Poulains and the Poule d'Essai des Pouliches are counterparts of the 2,000 and 1,000 Guineas; the mile-and-a-half Prix du Jockey Club (1½ miles/2.4 km) corresponds to the Epsom Derby and is often referred to as the "French Derby"; the Prix de Diane corresponds to the Oaks. The latter two are run at Chantilly in June, during the most elegant meeting of the year. The Grand Prix de Paris was founded in 1863 to match the English St. Leger, but it has been eclipsed in importance by the Grand Prix de St. Cloud, and the "French St. Leger" is now the Royal Oak at Longchamp in October. The Prix Vermeille corresponds to the English Oaks for three-year-old fillies.

American equivalents would be the Triple Crown races and three important events for three-year-old fillies: the Kentucky Oaks, run the day before the Derby, equal in prestige to the 1,000 Guineas; the Coaching Club American Oaks; and the Mother Goose Stakes.

The consecration of a champion, the aspiration of every trainer and owner, is to win "the Derby," be it Kentucky, Epsom, French, Irish, German, Italian—not overlooking the Derby races in Australia, New Zealand, South America, and elsewhere, all of them highlights of their respective racing seasons.

Races for horses three years old and upward bring together the cream of several crops. The distances are longer: 1¼ miles/2 km in England's Champion Stakes and Eclipse Stakes; 1½ miles/2.4 km in the King George VI and Queen Elizabeth Stakes, the Prix de l'Arc de Triomphe, the richly endowed Japan Cup, and the Preis von Europa in Germany; 2 miles/3.2 km in Australia's Melbourne and Sydney Cups; and a challenging 2½ miles/4 km in the Ascot Gold Cup. To society as well as racing fans these are events "not to be missed." The Ascot Gold Cup fills the Royal Enclosure to overflowing; the Prix de l'Arc de Triomphe attracts racegoers from all over the world, including thousands of British who cross the Channel to cheer English and Irish entrants.

Needless to add, it would be impossible to fill the schedules of Ireland's three major courses, sixty racecourses in England, some 272 in France, and over a hundred in the United States exclusively with superior horses competing in historic events. The usual seven or nine races scheduled at intervals of a half hour or so (the races themselves lasting from just over a minute to two and a half minutes) consist mostly of sprints and longer races, seldom longer than 1¼ miles/2 km, sometimes dignified with a name but more often listed simply as the "first race," "second race," and so on.

Many of these are *claiming races* ("selling races" in England, "reclamer" in France), the most modest category of all, although they account for 70 percent of all horse races in America. Special rules are

Tattenham Corner, the treacherous final turn on the undulating 1½-mile course at Epsom Downs, is often the decisive point in the Epsom Derby. Second from the left among the leaders in this closely bunched field is Teenoso, the 1983 Derby winner, ridden by Lester Piggott.

designed to deter owners from entering a good horse against inferior competition. A price is specified in the race conditions, representing the value of the horse. At the end of the race, it may be claimed for that price if a sealed bid has been deposited with the stewards by one or more owners with entries in a prior race of the meeting. When there is more than one equal bid, they are "thrown into a hat" and drawn by lot; if there is no bid, the owner keeps his horse. Obviously, promising colts are not entered in claiming events. But many honest horses have changed hands in them. One in thousands turns out to be a genuine bargain: Stymie was claimed for $750 and went on to win almost a million dollars. Today, however, claiming prices range from $5,000 to $100,000 as a rule. There is always the hope that a horse will improve under new management—and some of them do.

A more recent racing term merits explanation: *pattern races*, or—in America—*graded stakes*. In order to attribute a relative value to major racing events throughout the world, an international list of a hundred races was compiled in the early 1970s, divided into groups according to importance from Group I at the top to Group III—which could hardly be said to be "at the bottom," because winning even a Group III race is a guarantee of quality.

Nowadays many owners prefer to retire their successful colts to stud at the end of their three-year-old racing season rather than risk their reputation in all-age handicaps, thereby exchanging one risk for another. The owner may profit from stallion syndication, but the colt who was fantastic on the racecourse may prove a failure as a sire. The "glorious uncertainty of the turf" prevails even beyond the finishing point.

Training a racehorse is a science and perhaps an art, because intuition and talent are involved—the intuition and talent not only of the trainer, but of a team of collaborators: stable and racing grooms, jockeys, veterinarians, blacksmiths, and, of course, the breeder, who began it all. In this age of specialization, there are few remaining owner-breeders, even fewer who are trainers too, and nobody to compare with Lord Derby (of Epsom Derby fame) who bred, owned, trained, and sometimes rode his own horses.

Early in the morning on Newmarket Heath in England (owned by the Jockey Club), on the 700-acre/280-hectare training grounds at Chantilly in France (owned by the *Société d'encouragement*), on the racetracks at Saratoga, Santa Anita, and Belmont Park, on private farms in the Kentucky Bluegrass country, in Ocala, Florida, at commercial training grounds like Fair Hill, Maryland, in all these places one can witness the enthralling spectacle of racehorses in training. The typical Newmarket trainer (with binoculars, often mounted on a pony or retired racehorse, accompanied by his head lad) plans a campaign

Beautiful women and fancy hats are a tradition of Royal Ascot in England, Chantilly and Longchamp in France, where elegant, well-groomed creatures parade outside as well as inside the paddock.

Watching a horse race requires intense concentration and a good pair of binoculars. The horses are identified by numbers corresponding to their post positions, but even more easily by the distinctive owners' silks worn by the jockeys.

45

for each horse depending on its stage of development and its racing engagements. Some are jogged, some merely walked, other galloped. Unsaddled youngsters are led by lads mounted on older horses. Daily walking and trotting is followed by work, some of it uphill, designed to develop wind and stamina. Later, slow gallops in groups of three or four give them the "feel" of racing, arousing instincts that have been bred in them for generations.

With possibly a hundred horses worth millions of dollars in his care, the trainer must be not only an excellent horseman but also a good businessman, a clever strategist, and a psychologist. He has to have the self-discipline to rise at dawn, the energy to supervise morning workouts, attend races in the afternoon, and exercise diplomacy in the evening with his owners (most adroitly with owners whose horses have failed to win that day) before making a final round of the stables to ensure that all is well. It is then that he may finally be able to turn to one of his major tasks: a careful study of the Conditions Book to select races for which the horses in his charge are eligible and which they have a good chance of winning.

A surprising number of individuals have possessed all of the required aptitudes, many of them having inherited family talent and traditions. One of the outstanding English trainers of all time was the Hon. George Lambton, younger brother of the Earl of Durham,

Superstar jockey Angel Cordero, after a winning effort riding Chief's Crown at Saratoga in the 1985 Travers Stakes, salutes the steward and requests permission to dismount. He'll throw his whip to his valet, since it is not included in the gear with which he weighs in and out.

Eminent Hall of Fame trainer Woody Stephens gives instructions in the paddock to jockey Eddie Maple. Stephens has saddled five consecutive winners of the Belmont Stakes, an impressive, unprecedented achievement:

". . . Speed used to be less important when races were longer and horses were bred and trained for endurance and stamina. The average distance got shorter when racing programs stretched from six or seven to nine or ten races a day. Almost everybody now looks for a quick turnover of his money: owner, trainer, gambler, speculator, track management. Put it all together, and you know where the present emphasis on speed comes from."

who brought respectability to a profession that had previously been considered slightly shady. A leading amateur jockey before becoming Lord Derby's private trainer, he masterminded the careers of many great horses, including Sansovina, Diodem, Phalaris, Corrida, and Hyperion.

Fred Darling (1884–1953), son of a successful trainer, prepared seven Derby winners. Austrian-born Frank Butters (1878–1957) started with Lord Derby, then trained the Triple Crown winner Bahram and Derby winner Mahmoud for the Aga Khan. In the 1932 St. Leger, four Butters-trained horses finished among the first five!

Sir Cecil Boyd-Rochfort (1887–1983) won many races for his royal patron King George VI. His Newmarket establishment was inherited in 1969 by his assistant and stepson Henry Cecil, son-in-law of another royal trainer, Sir Noel Murless (nine times the leading trainer in England and mentor to many top trainers of the younger generation). Henry Cecil soon headed the list himself—four times by 1984—handling the horses of an exclusive group of leading owners, many of them foreigners.

Major Dick Hern trained Highclere for his "landlady" (Queen Elizabeth II), as well as Brigadier Gerard (defeated only once in eighteen races) and Lady Beaverbrook's Petoski, stunning victor of the 1985 King George VI and Queen Elizabeth Stakes—a race Hern supervised from a wheelchair, to which he has been confined since a hunting accident. Another of the Queen's trainers is Ian Balding, who managed the brilliant, abbreviated career of Mill Reef. Since few owners employ a private trainer anymore, many (like the Queen herself) entrust their horses to several public trainers. Some trainers seem to have a special gift for developing fillies, for example, or for straightening out recalcitrant colts, even for succeeding especially well with the progeny of a certain sire.

Other important Newmarket establishments are run by Clive Brittain, whose luxurious yard includes an equine swimming pool; Tom Jones, who has many Maktoum horses in his charge; Michael Stoute, the Aga Khan's trainer in England; Jeremy Tree, Guy Harwood, and Bruce Hobbs (whose yard is in King Charles's royal stables). The only village to rival Newmarket in the number of racing stables is Lambourn, which produces many of England's top steeplechasers. But Peter Walwyn, among others, trains flat racers there. A cousin of the famous steeplechase trainer Fulke Walwyn, he holds the twentieth-century record for winners during a single season in England: 120 in 1975.

Some trainers have turned from steeplechase to flat racing, the most illustrious being Vincent O'Brien (born in Ireland in 1917), an ex-jump rider and trainer whose flat racing record is no less than fabulous: he managed the careers of Sir Ivor, Nijinsky, Roberto, The

47

Minstrel, Caerleon, and El Gran Señor; he has scored five Derby wins (he built a replica of the Epsom Derby course at his Ballydoyle Farm in Ireland). Some racing men believe O'Brien to be the greatest trainer that Ireland, perhaps the world, has ever produced—even greater than Paddy Prendergast (1909–1980), who was preeminent during the postwar years and has since become a legend.

Many English jockeys retire from racing to become trainers, the most successful so far being Harry Wragg, who rode three Derby winners. His son Geoffrey took over his Newmarket stables in 1982 and enjoyed immediate success by saddling the 1983 Derby winner Teenoso. Geoff Lewis, who rode Mill Reef into the winner's circle many times, has yet to hit his stride as a trainer. Luca Cumani, son of a top Italian trainer, won more foreign money than any of his English colleagues in 1983, largely due to Tolomeo's victory in the Budweiser Million in America.

Will Lester Piggott excel as a trainer as he has done as a jockey? He opened Eve Lodge in Newmarket when he retired in 1985, with a list of top owners.

Ireland's major racecourses—The Curragh, Phoenix Park, Leopardstown, Fairyhouse, and Gowran Park—are rich in tradition but offer less in the way of prestige, purses, and opportunities than can be found in England, Europe, and America. And so, many successful Irish-bred and Irish-educated horses, trainers, and jockeys still venture to other lands for important races or for lifetime careers.

Many of them have indeed found fame and fortune abroad. Trainer Peter Gilpin, who managed the brilliant careers of 1906 Derby winner Spearmint and the sensational filly Pretty Polly, moved his operations from The Curragh to Newmarket, as did the late Aga Khan's trainer, Richard Dawson. Pat Eddery is one of many riders who have been persuaded to move from Ireland to England, where he has been leading jockey several times since 1974.

On the other hand, the late, great Paddy Prendergast maintained his base in Ireland while making frequent forays onto English tracks where he earned the Leading Trainer laurels from 1963 through 1966. His sons Paddy, Jr., and Kevin are leading trainers in Ireland. His protégé Vincent O'Brien supervises worldwide breeding and training operations, while Vincent's son David manages a successful Irish establishment. The younger O'Brien's achievements have included the victories of Assert in the 1982 Irish and French Derbies, of Secreto in the 1984 Epsom Derby, and of Authaal in the 1986 Irish St. Leger. While Authaal, his sire Shergar (who had only one season at stud before he was kidnapped), David O'Brien, and jockey Christy Roche (the leading flat jockey in Ireland) are all as Irish as can be, Authaal's owner is Sheikh Mohammed al-Maktoum.

"My Old Kentucky Home" is the theme song that traditionally announces the running of the Kentucky Derby, the most famous horse race in America and the first jewel in the Triple Crown.

Racing action is already intense at the first turn at Churchill Downs, where the Kentucky Derby has been run since 1875. The historic racecourse attracts worldwide attention only during Derby week, but Thoroughbred breeding and training are year-round activities in the Blue Grass State.

48

It is thus often difficult to attribute a nationality to a racehorse, to give credit where credit is due. But there is no denying the prominence of Irish names in the pedigrees of many champions (like Pretty Polly in the ancestry of Nasrullah), in the lists of leading trainers and jockeys, and among the personnel of Thoroughbred establishments throughout the world. Racing men everywhere recognize and admire Ireland's contribution to horse sports—and especially to Thoroughbred flat racing—a contribution felt far beyond the shores of that green island.

French trainers, many of English or Irish ancestry, also tend to create dynasties: Frank Carter, supreme during the 1930s; John Cunnington, Sr., who trained not only many winning horses during the 1940s, but also many present leading French trainers; Richard Carver, E. Bartholomew, Freddy Palmer, Geoff Watson during the 1960s; Willy Head, the most successful patriarch of all: his son Alec is a leading trainer, Alec's wife a leading owner; son Freddy is a leading jockey; daughter Christiane ("Criquette"), who inherited his stable in 1984, soared to the top of the trainers' list in record time.

The Pélat family is another remarkable racing clan: René Pélat was associated with the most glorious years of the Del Duca stable;

Flat races in Europe are run on grass, and none is greener than Ireland's. In America, where most track surfaces are covered with dirt (often a carefully composed mixture of dirt and other elements), grass racing is more of a specialty and there are relatively few major events for "grass horses."

Racing takes place rain or shine, and when it rains some horses run better than others. Some even do their best in mud or on a "sloppy" track like this at Saratoga (firm underneath with water on top). Why this should be so is one of the many unsolved mysteries of racing.

Noël, Pierre, and Jean-Pierre are prominent among the younger generation. Robert Pollet continues in the footsteps of his father, Etienne, trainer of Vaguely Noble. François Mathet (three Arc winners to his credit) trained for the Rothschilds, for whom only the best was good enough. Maurice Zilber trains for Nelson Bunker Hunt, and has won the Washington International four times. Alain de Royer-Dupré is in charge of the Aga Khan's French racing string.

Leading French trainer in number of races won is François Boutin, whose patrons include Niarchos and the Firestones. The leader in money won (much of it earned by Wildenstein horses) is one of the youngest: Patrick Biancone, who represents the third generation of a training family of Italian origin. His brother Pierre is also a trainer, his wife and uncles close collaborators; even his grandfather contributes his experience to the highly successful, very international Biancone enterprise.

In the United States, as abroad, leading trainers now manage vast operations and supervise the horses of a number of different owners, whereas before World War II the most famous (far more famous than they are today) were associated with a single stable, sometimes with a single champion racehorse.

One of the legendary training figures of the twentieth century was Max Hirsch, who started out as an exercise boy in Texas at the age of ten, became a jockey at fourteen and a trainer at nineteen. He worked for Robert J. Kleberg's fabulous King Ranch (as big as a small nation) until his death, at age eighty-eight, in 1969.

Ben Jones (aided by his son H. A. Jones) trained the amazingly versatile Citation to Triple Crown victory in 1948 for Calumet Farm and its owner Warren Wright. James E. "Sunny Jim" Fitzsimmons trained at William Woodward's Belair Stud during the glorious era of Gallant Fox, Omaha, and Nashua, before ceding his place to Frank Whitely, Jr., and moving on to Wheatley Stable where he died, at age eighty-eight, in 1967. (Could early rising, horse lather, and racetrack nerves be the recipe for longevity?)

Bill Winfrey, son of trainer Carey Winfrey, brought out the best in Alfred G. Vanderbilt's fragile-legged colt Native Dancer. Eddie Neloy assumed the training of Buckpasser for Ogden Phipps and was the first American trainer to break the $2 million winnings barrier—by a wide margin.

During the 1940s, racehorse training became rather a fashionable career, with the arrival from Argentina of Horatio Luro, trainer of Northern Dancer (whose son El Gran Señor was named after the dapper South American). John M. Gaver, an erudite Princeton graduate, managed the champion handicap career of Tom Fool for the Whitneys' Greentree Stable.

In America as elsewhere, horse-training talent seems to run in families. John Veitch continues the tradition of his father Sylvester; John Nerud, breeder-trainer-owner of Tartan Farm, home of Gallant Man, Intentionally, and Dr. Fager, was succeeded by his son Jan. Lucien Laurin, who trained and campaigned the great Secretariat for Mrs. Penny Tweedy, passed on his secrets to his son Roger. Leroy Jolley and John Gosden are also sons of famous trainers.

With racing a year-round, coast-to-coast activity, training farms are found all over the United States, with the concentration still in Kentucky and the East. Jack Van Berg, like his Hall of Fame father Marion H. Van Berg, started out in the Middle West. Eight times leading trainer in number of races won, he has trained more winners than anyone in the history of racing. D. Wayne Lukas, a former Quarter Horse specialist (the mighty Dash for Cash was among his twenty-three champions), trains top Thoroughbreds in California with his son Jeff; he has won the Santa Anita Derby three times and, in 1984, set a record for money won. Charlie Whittingham, another Californian, is the all-time leading trainer of stakes winners. A Hall of Famer since 1974, he started in the 1930s as assistant to Horatio Luro; at the age of seventy-three in 1986, he hoisted fifty-four-year-old Bill Shoemaker into the saddle of Kentucky Derby winner Ferdinand, and also won the Arlington Million with Estrapade. His son Michael trains top horses too.

Secretariat (1970)—here making his move to victory in the 1973 Preakness, ridden by Ron Turcotte—has been called "the horse of the century." He captured the Triple Crown in triumphant style, breaking a track record in each race and winning the Belmont Stakes by 31 lengths.

Another memorable Triple Crown winner (1978), another fabulous racing stride— Affirmed, ridden by Steve Cauthen (who soon afterward moved to England and reached the top of the jockey list there, just as he had in the United States): ". . . It took three years for me to adapt my style to the European way of riding. English tracks are where they laid them out two hundred years ago, and the humps and bumps are still there. Some courses are left-handed, others run to the right. Some have odd turns and unusually long straightaways. In Europe, the horses often come to the finish line running uphill, so stamina is important and rating your horse is critical. . . . In America, racecourses are flat, left-handed, usually dirt instead of grass, and one mile around. Everything is more hyped up. Instead of running on six cylinders, they're running on eight!"

Some trainers seem to possess a special talent for handling certain types of horses, even for winning certain races. The accomplished veteran Woody Stephens, for example, who managed Northern Dancer's racing career, won his fifth straight Belmont Stakes in 1986 with Danzig Connection. His previous win with Creme Fraiche in 1985 was remarkable for being the first time a gelding won the Classic event since they were made eligible for it.

Is training, along with other sectors of racing, becoming internationalized? During the mid-1980s, the Frenchman Patrick Biancone ranked among the leading trainers in America as well as in France.

While these and other consistently successful experts attract the leading owners and win the annual awards, one must not forget the dedicated horsemen who never earn Trainer of the Year titles, much less a place in the Hall of Fame; who never get the chance to train a Classic hopeful, even less a potential Triple Crown winner, but who continue, year in, year out, to make the most of less talented racehorses. They are the unsung heroes who play a vital role in the world of Thoroughbred racing.

The jockey enters the racing scene in the saddling enclosure half an hour before the race, when he is "given a leg up" on the horse he is to ride and receives instructions from the trainer and owner. As with all performances, this is but the tip of the iceberg.

The jockey has become perfectly familiar with the course (even the most experienced do not disdain to test the going of a course they may have ridden countless times). He may already be familiar with the horse he is to ride. (Lester Piggott worked with Shergar, the Aga Khan's kidnapped Derby winner, during three weeks of early-morning training gallops before the colt's first race.) Though the jockey may look like a youngster, he probably has years of experience with Thoroughbred racers behind him.

Because of the importance of weight in a horse's racing performance, the essential attribute of a jockey is lightness, which generally implies smallness (although Piggott measures 5 ft 8 in/1.73 m). In order to remain within the standard weight allowances, a jockey has to keep his weight down to just under 110 pounds/50 kg, often through strenuous diet, sauna sessions (perhaps in an overheated sports car on the way to the track), laxatives, diuretics, and regurgitation. Sometimes the strain is too much. Fred Archer, the greatest English jockey of the nineteenth century, shot himself at the age of twenty-nine when he could no longer make the weights. Sometimes jockeys simply outgrow the limit and become exercise riders, or in the best of cases, trainers.

Race riding may seem rudimentary compared to other equestrian disciplines. Two-year-old racehorses are kindergarten babies compared

53

to dressage horses or show jumpers. The jockey communicates by means of his hands (acting on the bit through rubber-covered racing reins), his whip, at times his voice. Flat jockeys ride with their weight poised evenly over the horse's back in a crouch seat; they use their legs more for balance than communication. During a race, the message is usually restricted to controlling speed by lengthening the stride ("rating"); if necessary, steadying, balancing, encouraging, stimulating the horse, steering, aiding change of lead around a turn. Sprints are relatively simple to ride, but races of a mile or more with several turns, perhaps uphill and downhill stretches, require considerable jockey skill.

The jockey must be very strong despite his small stature, especially in the upper body, which has to withstand a pull that has been measured as 150 pounds/68 kg on each arm. He must possess exceptional aerobic fitness, rapid reflexes, a sense of pace (keen enough to distinguish between a second or two over a mile distance), anticipation, courage, nerve, and judgment. He needs the latter two qualities not only in order to ride the race, but sometimes to disobey his orders when the race is not going the way the trainer expected it would.

But usually jockeys are expected to follow the trainer's instructions —which take into account the horse's ability, condition, and temperament—the distance, track conditions, competition, and future plans for the horse. Generally speaking, there are only two racing strategies: taking the lead at once and trying to hang onto it; or playing a waiting game, saving the horse's energy for a burst of speed at a calculated distance from the finish. Many horses have a predilection for one or the other. The "waiting race" is more common in Europe than in America, where most races are shorter and most horses run "against the clock."

What is the importance of the jockey in a horse's performance? It's hard to say, because the best jockeys get the best horses to ride and score the best results. While the best jockey in the world cannot perform a miracle with a mediocre horse, an inexpert rider may fail to exploit the possibilities of a good one. Races are run at such a speed that instinctive reflex is bound to take over at crucial moments. Jockeys of talent and experience are apt to make the right move at the right moment.

In England, Lester Piggott is such a celebrity that his retirement as a jockey at the end of 1985 was front-page news. The grandson of a steeplechase jockey, son of a rider-trainer, he won his first Derby (the first of nine) at the age of eighteen on Never Say Die in 1954. Along with a record twenty-nine Classic victories, he won the Arc de Triomphe three times, the Irish Derby four, the German Derby three; he was Champion English Jockey eleven times. A ruthless competitor, he was noted for his conscientious training rides, his keen perception of a horse's personality and possibilities. When a reporter asked him after

54

One seldom sees a jockey hilarious in the paddock before a race, especially when wearing the Queen's silks! Willie Carson is sharing a joke with trainer Maj. Dick Hern, while receiving final orders. Most often, strategy has already been decided, and the last-minute advice may be no more than to "bring him home safe."

No diet faddist suffers more from the tyranny of the scales than a flat race jockey—especially one as tall as Lester Piggott, who is weighing in here after a race (in Europe, since he's sitting in a chair to be weighed, whereas in the U.S. jockeys stand on the scales).

one of his Derby victories, "When did you feel you were going to win this race?" he replied, "Three weeks ago."

In his lifetime, Lester Piggott is already as legendary as his famous predecessors. Among these are Steve Donoghue (an idolized Derby specialist—six wins!), champion English jockey for ten years straight from 1914 to 1923; Sir Gordon Richards, the Queen Mother's choice until he retired to become a trainer after winning fourteen Classics in twenty-nine years, during twenty-six of which he was England's top jockey; and Harry Carr, who rode nine Oaks winners during a span of ten years.

Who will be Lester Piggott's successor? Will it be Willie Carson (esteemed for his riding technique and his indomitable will), Pat Eddery, Walter Swinburn (five-time Epsom Derby winner), the American expatriate Steve Cauthen? (Piggott himself selected Tony Ives to be his stable jockey.)

In France, the same question may arise. There is a reigning champion: Yves Saint-Martin, and a number of talented jockeys eager to succeed him.

Saint-Martin is not only the best French jockey of the past two decades, but perhaps the best that France has ever produced. After winning the first of his fifteen Cravaches d'Or as leading jockey of the year in 1961, only two years after making his racing debut at seventeen, he has scored over three thousand victories including three Arc de Triomphes—one of them a famous ride on Allez France in 1974 with a two-week-old hip fracture—five Prix de Diane, nine French Derbies, and the international event of the 1984 Breeders' Cup races, in which he beat the 1983 Horse of the Year All Along by a neck, riding the Aga Khan's Lashkari, a 50-to-1 shot.

During most of the 1970s and 1980s, Saint-Martin has remained at or near the top, fighting off the challenges of his leading rival, Freddy Head, and the experienced French riders who always pose a threat— Maurice Philipperon, Alfred Gibert, Alain Lequeux, Alain Badel, Henri Samani, Guy Guignard, young Eric Legrix—as well as the elite of British and American jockeys who come to France to compete in major international races.

In the United States, where Americans have been growing bigger and heavier, very few are born as small nowadays as Bill Shoemaker (the most successful jockey in history, he weighed only 2½ pounds/1.1 kg at birth); English-born Johnny Longden (who rode over six thousand winners between 1927 and 1966, then turned to training); Eddie Arcaro (one of the shrewdest turf strategists ever, winner of five Kentucky Derbies and two Triple Crowns); Bill Hartack (an effective, tempera-

Being draped in a blanket of roses was no novelty for Bill Shoemaker after his winning ride on Ferdinand in the 1986 Kentucky Derby. He'd won the race three times before. In fact, since his first win at Santa Anita in 1951 as a nineteen-year-old apprentice, he's set a record as a jockey that may never be equaled: ". . . Techniques have changed since I began riding back in 1949. South American riders have strongly influenced the general style. Jockeys ride with much shorter stirrups and sit up higher and closer to the horse's neck than they used to. Shorter stirrups raise the legs, making the body more compact. And the more compact the rider, the less he moves during a race, the better he can help the horse to carry the load on his back. As in every other sport, the techniques of race riding have improved, and so have riders generally."

mental rider, esteemed by his peers); and Ron Turcotte (who was forced into retirement by a paralyzing injury). French-born Jean Cruguet, Eddie Maple, Pat Day (leading rider in races won from 1982 through 1984), Chris McCarron (John Henry's regular rider), and Gary Stevens, a fast-rising star from the West, still make the weights.

But the American jockey list is dominated by Latin Americans, led by the Panamanians. Manuel Ycaza was one of the pioneers, followed by Braulio Baeza (a flawless rider, champion from 1965 to 1968, again in 1975, turned trainer in 1978), Jacinto Vasquez, Jorge Velasquez, Ismael Valenzuela, Laffit Pincay, Jr. (who broke Shoemaker's long-standing hundred-million-dollar money-won record in 1985). Meteorically successful José Santos is the son of a Chilean jockey-trainer. Superstar Angel Cordero, Jr., leading jockey in 1976, 1982, and 1983, three-time Kentucky Derby–winning rider, was born in Puerto Rico, where his father was a trainer and jockey.

At the same time, some talented American jockeys have moved to Europe. Steve Cauthen, "The Kentucky Kid," won the Triple Crown on Affirmed as an eighteen-year-old apprentice, then raced to the top in England, where he was leading rider in 1984 and 1985. Texas-born Cash Asmussen was lured to France by Stavros Niarchos, but even before collecting his Cravache d'Or as leading rider of 1985 he had moved to Ireland as first jockey for the Sangster-O'Brien team. Californian Darrell McHargue divides his time between Europe and America. Jorge Velasquez was recently engaged to ride in France for Mahmoud Fustok. Leading jockeys move from stable to stable and from country to country these days as in a game of Musical Chairs.

Professional women jockeys were finally permitted to compete alongside the men, after a long battle, only some twenty years ago. Oddly enough, they seem to have been accepted more kindly by their fellow riders than by trainers, owners, and bettors. And yet there are some very good ones: in England, Lorna Vincent, Franca Vittadini, Elain Mellor (wife of champion steeplechase jockey Stan), and Gay Kellaway (who rides for her trainer father). In the United States, Diane Crump was the first in 1969; Robyn Smith (now Mrs. Fred Astaire) was the first woman, in 1975, to ride an American stakes winner; Abigail Fuller has won stakes races at Belmont and rode her father's Mom's Command in the filly's 1985 American Oaks victory to become the sixth distaff Triple Crown winner in history. In France, Darie Boutboul became a national celebrity due to her achievements as a lady jockey; currently prominent is Caroline Lee, a deceptively delicate-looking Irish rider.

They're off! After taking their positions one by one in the starting gate, sometimes accompanied by another rider on a lead pony, the horses are "under starter's orders." He presses a switch, the gate springs open. The race is on.

The mobile electronic starting gate is a great improvement over the elastic tape of former times, although it was adopted in England only in 1965. The jockey's principal preoccupations at the start are to break well, establish the horse's balance and stride at once, "place" him according to the distance, the size of the field, the going, the horse's temperament, even its mood—not forgetting the trainer's orders.

A familiar sight on English and Irish racecourses is the "tic-tac man," who uses rapid coded hand signals to transmit betting information from his vantage point in the stands to the book-maker (or "turf accountant") on the grounds.

Cameras along the course record the entire race on film, which may be consulted by the stewards if there is a protest. A photoelectric beam at the finish line triggers other cameras to record the crucial moment. (Oddly enough, there have been many more dead-heat finishes since these devices have been used than there ever were before.)

As the horses leave the track, they are met by their grooms, probably by their trainers, certainly if they are winners by their happy owners. Testing for drugs is done on a random basis, so some horses may have to furnish a sample of blood or urine. Back at their stables, they are bathed, then walked, rubbed, their legs bandaged; all the time they are watched for signs of injury, heat, or swelling, especially in the legs and feet. Racing is a stressful activity for these immature animals, who are in constant risk of straining a tendon or cutting a foreleg with an overstriding hind foot, to cite only the most common injuries.

The jockey, in the meantime, has been weighed out. He makes a quick change into the silks prepared by his racing valet (or one he shares with several other riders), then with his saddle over his arm he returns to the saddling enclosure to join a new team of horse, trainer, and owner.

The trainer may also have to turn his attention at once to another horse and owner. Only after his racing day is over will he have time to visit the stables and give instructions in view of the day's results and the horses' condition. That night he'll have a mass of paperwork to do, maintaining or scratching horses from their next engagements after consulting the owner, who always has the final say.

Every win affects the horse's eligibility for future events. Some races require an entry fee, sometimes far in advance, paid in installments. Many entry lists close months before the race, and for this reason horses are entered in more races than they actually run. And there are often far more entries than the course can handle. As accepted entries are withdrawn, others are drawn by lot from an "also eligible" waiting list. But many are left behind. In the 1982 Epsom Derby, for example, 288 horses were listed in the original entry list drawn up at the end of 1981. When the last payment was due four days before the race, most of them had dropped out at various "forfeit" stages, and thirty-eight were left. The number dwindled to twenty when final declarations were made, and on the morning of the race only eighteen remained. (All that forfeited money was added to the pool.) On the other hand, late entries pay huge premiums. The owners of Wild Again had to pay $360,000 to enter him in the inaugural Breeders' Cup race for three-year-olds in 1984. (A good investment, as it turned out; he won the race and collected a purse of over a million dollars.)

The owner, if his horse has won, experiences a thrill, he'll tell you, that is beyond compare. The thrill may be his principal reward, although he'll receive about half of the purse money a few weeks later, the rest going to the three runners-up, and a percentage to the trainers, jockeys, and grooms. If he bred his winner, he may qualify for a generous bonus. Nevertheless, racing is an expensive hobby. Five percent of owners, it is said, win 80 percent of the purses, while more than half win nothing at all and only 25 percent of American racehorses earn enough to pay for the expenses they incur. Success stories like that of Spectacular Bid, a $37,000 yearling who won almost $3 million as a racer and then was syndicated as a stallion for $22 million, are exceptions to the rule. The vast majority of racehorse owners lose money, unless they are supported by a profitable breeding operation or are extremely lucky.

Speaking of luck, what about the bettors? Betting on horse races has probably existed as long as racing itself and is supervised as never before. Only in England and Ireland is the majority of wagering still done through bookmakers in off-track betting shops as well as at the track, where bookies set up shops and their "Tic Tac men," wearing battered hats and white gloves, roam the stands, communicating orders through a code of rapid hand signals.

A Frenchman, Joseph Oller, invented the "pari-mutuel" system in 1865 when his winning bet on the Grand Prix de Paris was not paid off. The sum wagered on a race is divided among the winners, after "take-out" deductions have been made for the benefit of the government, the track, and the racing industry. The British "tote" system is similar, but has not replaced the bookmakers. In the United States, on-track betting is generally pari-mutuel.

The traditional wager is for a horse to "win, place, or show"—that is, finish first, either first or second, or among the first three. Modern variations offer greater returns: the French Tiercé (selecting the first three horses), Daily Doubles (selecting the winners of two specified races on the same card), Exactas, Quinellas—and the rest. While many bettors never have set foot on a racecourse and may not even be interested in horses, few racegoers can resist the temptation of placing a bet.

Whether one approves or not, betting is an element of horse racing and a vital source of revenue for a spectacular, enthralling sport that could not survive without it.

Will this expensive yearling at the Keeneland Sales turn out to be a future champion? It will take another year at least before this handsome little fellow will be put to the test on the racecourse, perhaps to fulfill high hopes, perhaps to disappoint. Much of the drama and fascination of Thoroughbred racing is due to "the uncertainty of the turf."

Steeplechasing

The idea of racing horses over a course studded with obstacles originated among Irish and English fox hunters, an indirect result of the mid-eighteenth-century Enclosure Acts which permitted the fencing in of agricultural land by various kinds of barriers. Till then, fox hunting had involved jumping only over streams and ditches; now the horses had to clear a wider variety of larger obstacles as they followed the hounds from field to field.

Natural rivalry led to match races. The first recorded one took place in Ireland in 1752, over a distance of 4½ miles/7.2 km between a church in Buttevant and another in St. Leger, church steeples being the most obvious landmarks in open country. Ever since, the sport of racing over jumps has been known as steeplechasing.

Quite rapidly, it spread throughout Ireland and England and to many other parts of the world—especially where horse racing was popular, tracks had been built, and British colonists and cavalry had imported their sporting pastimes. But nowhere did it become as widespread as in the British Isles, where leapers (to the Irish) and 'chasers (to the English) are also called "the Winter Kings," not because the Queen Mother is a leading owner and supporter, but because steeplechasing takes over after the flat racing season comes to an end in the autumn. Elsewhere, it is mainly an adjunct to flat racing (as in France), a rather elite activity for the hunting set (as in the United States), and almost everywhere a family tradition.

From the beginning of the nineteenth century, steeplechasing developed simultaneously in the countries where it is still most widely pursued, as can be judged from a few historical milestones:

1807 The Irish Racing Calendar referred to steeplechase racing for the first time.
1821 The first formal hurdle race was run at Bristol, England.
1829 Steeplechase was introduced in France at Saint-Germain-en-Laye, then in the Bois de Boulogne.
1835 First recorded French hurdle race.
1836 First steeplechase at the Aintree track in Liverpool.
1839 First running of the Grand Liverpool Steeplechase, later to become the Aintree Grand National. Its first winner was a great one: Lottery. One of the Grand National's most fearsome obstacles, Becher's Brook, acquired its name when Captain Becher (who had won the 1839 event) fell into the deep, water-filled ditch and later remarked that water without brandy was a most unpleasant beverage.
1843 First North American steeplechase in London, Ontario, Canada.
1844 First recorded hurdle race in the United States at Hoboken, New Jersey.

Cheltenham is the capital of English steeplechase racing, and its permanent course is a test of quality second to none. Desert Orchid and Charcoal Wally (9) clear one of its typical brush fences in the 1986 Arkle Challenge Trophy, named for the immensely popular Irish 'chaser who won the Cheltenham Gold Cup three straight times (1964–66).

Compared to steeplechasing on major tracks, American hunt race meetings, such as this at Radnor, Pennsylvania, are more informal, more closely related to the fox-hunting scene. They are run over timber fences in a convivial atmosphere and at rural venues where the permanent facilities may consist of no more than a paddock and a judge's stand at the finish line.

1845   The first Steeplechase Calendar was published in Ireland, incorporating the Marquess of Waterford's Rules of Steeplechasing.

1861   Steeplechase racing was inaugurated at Cheltenham in Berkshire, today the Mecca of the English sport.

1863   Prince Murat founded the *Société générale des steeplechases* to govern the French sport, with headquarters at Vincennes.

1865   First recorded American steeplechase race in Paterson, New Jersey, over twenty-seven varied obstacles.

1866   Founding of the English governing body, the National Hunt Committee.

1874   The Grand Steeplechase de Paris, the richest jumping race in the world, was inaugurated at Auteuil, where a hippodrome dedicated to steeplechase was built in 1873 to replace the Vincennes course (requisitioned by the army during the War of 1870). The race, as well as two later runnings, was won by Baron Finot, who hitched his racers among the carriage horses that took him to the elegant course, noted for lovely landscaping and its innovative grandstand.

1891   Thomas Hitchcock, Sr., and August Belmont II founded the Steeplechase, Hunt and Pony Racing Association, which later became the National Steeplechase and Hunt Association (NSHA), the governing body in the United States.

By the turn of the century, steeplechasing was already an established, regulated international sport with a distinctive personality: more "cliquey," more "horsey," less pretentious, less costly than flat racing; less influenced by profit motives due to lesser financial rewards; more a vocation than an industry.

While all kinds of jumping races are commonly called "steeplechase," the term actually describes only one of three kinds of races which are defined by the nature of the obstacles in each case: hurdles, brush, or timber (the last type also called "point-to-point").

Hurdle races are where young jumpers begin their racing career, usually in the autumn of their three-year-old year in the United States, often a year later in Europe. The obstacles resemble sheep hurdles: thin rails packed with gorse against the take-off side and inclined in the direction of travel. In America nowadays, the base may be of padded metal, the gorse a plastic imitation. In France, they are heavier and more solid at the base, although of the same height (3 ft 6 in/1.1 m) and slope (45 degrees), making it easy to brush through without overturning them. Speed is more important than clean jumping in a hurdle race, and the pace is faster than in other jump events—up to 40 miles per hour/64 kph. Racing over hurdles is often a consolation career for Thoroughbreds who have failed to make the grade in flat racing.

Brush races are what most people imagine to be the entire sport of steeplechasing. The rules require at least twelve fences during the first 2 miles/3.2 km, six in each succeeding mile, one ditch fence (the most awesome) in each mile, and one water jump in each race. Originally

Pages 64–65: The Irish Grand National steeplechase at Punchestown is a national event that attracts international attention, not only because of its famous double bank, shown here, but also because of its connection with the Irish Sweepstakes. The festive occasion thus satisfies two Irish passions: horses and betting—and sometimes a few drinks may be taken too.

comprised of fences imitating hedgerows, famous courses like those of Cheltenham, Aintree, Auteuil, and Punchestown include variations within the rules that present formidable challenges to horse and rider. The famous Chair Fence at Aintree, for example, consists of an 18 in/ 46 cm take-off rail in front of a 6 ft/1.83 m wide open ditch 2 ft 6 in/ 76 cm deep, preceding a narrow 5 ft 2 in/1.53 m fence; its 12 ft/3.66 m water jump requires a leap of at least 14½ ft/4.42 m. Brush races are usually 2 to 4 miles/3.2 to 6.4 km long, inevitably ending with a straight run-in to the finish line: 500 yards/457 m in the Aintree Grand National. In the United States, brush fences tend to be less varied and more softly built and the pace is faster. Irish courses are like the English, except for the peculiarity of natural banks, as on the Punchestown course. French steeplechase courses, as at Auteuil, are often run over a figure-eight pattern at breathtaking speed.

A view of the paddock during the 1935 Maryland Hunt Cup where upwards of 30,000 spectators gathered to watch America's classic steeplechase event.

Point-to-point races are more directly related to the fox-hunting scene. Since a steeplechase has to be sanctioned by the NSHA, entries are restricted to registered Thoroughbreds. In point-to-points, hunting experience with a recognized pack is the usual qualifying requirement. Often a proving ground for horses and riders in England, they may be an end in themselves for American sportsmen, who call them "timber races," because their obstacles are versions of post-and-rail fences. There may also be a stone wall with a rail or two on top. These require precise jumping, especially in the United States; elsewhere the obstacles are more varied, often more forgiving. The French equivalent of the point-to-point is the cross-country jump race, similar to the final day of the three-day event. Some point-to-points are restricted to amateurs, regular members of a hunt; others are open to professional jockeys "acceptable to the Committee" as well as to qualified amateurs.

The racing card during a steeplechase meeting at a major track includes hurdle and brush races for various grades of horses according to age and past winnings, and in Europe sometimes according to breed: Thoroughbred, non-Thoroughbred (AQPS, or *autre que pur sang*), Anglo-Arab. As in flat racing, there are maiden and claiming races, allowances and handicaps, and weight-for-age events. Hunt race meetings, generally run over one or two days, consist of a series of hurdle, brush, and flat races; perhaps a race for ladies, one for hunt club members, one for farmers, a pony race, in addition to the major steeplechase event. The Maryland Hunt Cup and the Aintree Grand National are unusual in that they are the only event of the day on which they are run.

Blockade was one of several Man o' War sons to inherit extraordinary jumping ability as well as speed. Here he is about to score the last of his three victories in the Maryland Hunt Cup (in 1940), with J. F. Colwill in the saddle and Or Else, ridden by Sidney Watters, Jr., close behind.

Most of the early steeplechase owners were also prominent in flat racing. In 1883, the Meadowbrook Hunt Club on Long Island presented a series of steeplechase events that attracted many of the leading names in American racing to the sport: the Whitneys, Belmonts, Clarks,

The first fence of the Aintree Grand National in 1929. Such a huge field fighting for a place on so relatively narrow a course caused so much disaster that the track eventually was widened and the number of entries limited.

Battleship, another Man o' War son, in the lead at Becher's Brook the second time around the Aintree Grand National course in 1938. Not only was he first at the finish, he was also the first American-owned, American-bred horse ever to win the challenging event.

Wideners, Foxhall Keene. Today most major stables specialize in one form of horse racing or the other, although a few owners (and many trainers) maintain a steeplechase string along with their flat racers: Guy de Rothschild and Daniel Wildenstein (the leading owner) in France; Paul Mellon, the Strawbridges, Clarks, Bert Firestones, Will Farish in America; Robert Sangster, J. B. Joel, and the Queen Mother in England. Family stables of owner-trainers, even owner-trainer-riders of the same clan, still exist in the steeplechase world, but have practically disappeared from Thoroughbred racing. While some of the most illustrious flat-racing dynasties have vanished or retired from racing, many American steeplechase families are still active in their third or fourth generation and show no sign of stopping there.

Steeplechase trainers also seem to inherit a passion as well as an aptitude for discovering and developing talented jumpers. Their special technique often consists of knowing how to convert a flat racer into a good steeplechaser. Many of their pupils already have received basic training on the flat; many are more mature than the flat trainer's colts and fillies, more developed physically and mentally—for better or for worse.

Irish trainers are past masters in the art. Between 1946 and 1955, seven Grand National winners were Irish; three of the others were Irish-trained. One of the world's leading trainers, Vincent O'Brien, started out as an amateur steeplechase rider, then became a steeplechase trainer in 1944. He persuaded his first client to buy a bargain jumper who had failed to pass two vet tests, but whose aspect and ancestors appealed to him. It was Cottage Rake, winner of three straight Cheltenham Gold Cups (1948 to 1950) and later an outstanding sire. During the next decade, O'Brien trainees won three Grand Nationals in a row and a fourth Gold Cup, whereupon he switched to training flat racers in 1959, establishing an equally brilliant record—and still succumbing to the temptation of a gifted jumper from time to time. Other Irish trainers, like Tom Dreaper, devote their lives to 'chasers and nothing but. For Anne, Duchess of Westminster (long a leading owner), Dreaper trained Prince Regent (whose wartime record of eighteen wins included the 1946 Gold Cup and the Irish Grand National), as well as the unforgettable Arkle.

Like Vincent O'Brien, many ex-riders, amateur and professional, have become successful steeplechase trainers in England and Ireland. For example, Toby Balding manages a mixed stable in Newmarket. The late Peter Cazalet was always near the top of the steeplechase trainer list, with over 1,100 wins to his credit—including 250 with the Queen Mother's horses. During a weekend houseparty at Windsor Castle in 1948, his great friend and collaborator Lord Mildmay, an accomplished amateur jockey, persuaded Her Majesty to buy her first jumper, Manicou, in partnership with her daughter, then Princess Elizabeth. After winning their first two events, the Princess took up flat racing like her father, while her mother remained a loyal 'chasing supporter.

Fulke Walwyn has been a top trainer since the 1960s; his skill and strategy contributed much to the careers of Mandarin and Mill House. The late Fred Rimell and Fred Winter share the distinction of leading the National Hunt list four times as a jockey, four times (to date) as a trainer.

There have also been many successful steeplechasing fathers and sons: trainer Keith Piggott (Lester's father) was himself the son of Ernie Piggott, rider of three Grand National winners. Top Dublin trainer Tom Taaffe sired two outstanding jockey sons: Tos and Pat. The latter won every major steeplechase in Great Britain and rode Arkle throughout his great career before opening a training establishment of his own in 1970.

Women trainers are far more prominent in steeplechase than in flat racing. The first to train a Grand National winner was Jenny Pitman with Corbière in 1983. Mercy Rimell and Monica Dickinson are also leading trainers. In America, Janet Elliott trained Census, the top winner of 1978, and missed the Leading Trainer title in 1984 by the narrowest of margins.

In France, Maisons-Laffitte, outside of Paris, is to jumpers what Chantilly is to flat racers: the principal place for training. Many leading flat trainers also work with hurdlers and steeplechasers: the Pélats (Georges Pélat being the dean of them all), André Fabre, Robert Collet, Bernard Sècly, Patrick Biancone. Others specialize in jumpers: Jack-Hubert Barbe (leading trainer 1983 to 1985), Patrick Rago, Jean-Paul Gallorini, Joël Rémy, René Cherrvau.

In the United States, the scene is slightly different, if only because steeplechase activity is more regional, concentrated in the Southern and Atlantic states: Maryland, Virginia, the Carolinas, and Pennsylvania (but also in Georgia, Tennessee, Kentucky and spreading elsewhere). The closest equivalents to Lambourn would be Camden and Aiken in South Carolina, Southern Pines in North Carolina, Unionville in Pennsylvania. Throughout these areas are scattered stables small and large, many of them multigeneration operations of illustrious steeplechasing families: the Smithwicks, Aitchesons, Fenwicks, Woolfes, Houghtons, Bosleys, Meisters, and Walshes (now in its fourth generation). The mentor of many top trainers, still among the leaders himself, is W. Burling "Burly" Cocks, whose protégés include Mike Smithwick, Ronnie Houghton, and English-born Jonathan Sheppard, who runs a public stable in Unionville and has been leading trainer in America thirteen times since 1970 in number of races won, and since 1973 has been the country's top money-winner.

Among the horses in this big field during a hurdle race at Cheltenham, the fastest may become hurdle champions; others may proceed to steeplechase and compete over higher, wider, more varied obstacles at slightly slower speed.

As the horses are saddled in the paddock at Cheltenham, racegoers gather at the rail to observe their condition and behavior and (they hope) to spot a winner.

Wherever they happen to come from or settle, steeplechase trainers are an individualistic, ingenious lot. All of them have their own techniques, their special secrets of feed, conditioning, and exercise. Many believe in lots of roadwork, hunting, cross-country rides. In England they still give the horses a daily "strapping" with a hay wisp (a sort of vigorous equine massage). Some Americans still swear by free unmounted jumping in a "Hitchcock pen," invented by the legendary all-round sportsman Thomas Hitchcock, Sr. Some strengthen their horses' legs with long gallops on a sandy ocean beach or in the latest therapy aid: an equine swimming pool.

Steeplechase jockeys also often inherit a family tradition and passion. They almost have to, in order to accept such high risks and relatively low rewards.

The line between professional and amateur is less of a barrier than on the flat, where amateur jockeys can compete only in a few "gentleman" and "lady" rider events. Amateur jump jockeys, on the other hand, have often held their own against the pros.

Sir Harry Llewellyn of show-jumping fame finished second in the 1936 Grand National, the year of Sir Anthony Mildmay's famous bad break. This intrepid, aristocratic horseman was in the lead on Davy Jones and seemed a certain winner when his rein snapped on landing after the next to last fence and the horse ran off the course. Veteran

Charles ("Charley") Fenwick, Jr., scion of an illustrious American steeplechasing family, rides Cancottage toward a third victory in the Maryland Hunt Cup in 1983. It was one of four for Charley, who also won the 1980 Aintree Grand National (on Ben Nevis, another of his victorious Hunt Cup mounts): ". . . The Hunt Cup and the Grand National? They're similar in some ways, but very different too. The Hunt Cup demands a more precise jumper because of the solid fences, and the course gives you no let-up at all, no place to coast. The National requires perhaps more speed, because the course is flat, and surely more racing luck, because you're running against thirty or forty mostly professional riders instead of six or eight amateurs. You stick to your basic riding style and length of leather, but you can sit up a bit more over Maryland's timber than at Aintree, with all those drops. All in all, I'd cherish both wins equally, if the National didn't involve so much more luck and enjoy so much higher a profile around the world."

six-time Australian three-day event Olympic rider Bill Roycroft (member of the gold medal team in 1960, and the bronze in 1976) could also hold his own among the pros. In 1965, at the age of fifty, he rode his home-trained Olympic mount Stoney Crossing in the Cheltenham Gold Cup, finishing third to the immortal Arkle and his great rival Mill House. One month later, Roycroft rode the same horse to finish sixth in the Badminton three-day event, having ridden another horse a few days earlier to finish sixth in the Grand National. The Duke of Albuquerque, a Spanish grandee and ardent horseman, celebrated his fifty-seventh birthday in 1976 by riding two steeplechase winners at Leicester.

An amateur American rider, Tommy Crompton Smith, made Aintree history by winning the Grand National on American-bred, American-trained Jay Trump in 1965. George Sloan, joint Master of Foxhounds of the Hillsboro Hunt in Tennessee, scored another American first when he won the title of Champion Amateur Steeplechase Rider in America in 1977 and its English counterpart the following year.

Most steeplechase jockeys are professionals, however, and leading amateurs generally end up by joining their ranks. When age or injury forces them to hang up their saddles, many are so addicted to the sport that they remain as trainers. These include all-time great British jockeys like Bryan Marshall, who rode two Grand National winners for Vincent O'Brien, then retired to train other jockeys; beloved Stan Mellor, who scored a record-setting thousandth win in 1972, was awarded an MBE (Member of the British Empire, an honor given by the Queen), and now trains National Hunt hopefuls at Lambourn; Fred Winter (another MBE), also a trainer now, famous for winning on Mandarin with a broken bit in the Grand Steeplechase de Paris, and for turning Hallowe'en into a champion when no other jockey could stay on him; Dick Francis, who rode the Queen Mother's horses for Peter Cazalet, was Champion Jockey in 1953, then retired to write bestselling novels with a racing background; the Molony brothers, Tim and Martin, both now training in their native Ireland, where the late Dan Moore (uncle of the American Smithwicks) prepared and managed the dramatic career of Escargot for owner Raymond Guest; his son Arthur, who carries on the splendid family tradition.

John Francome started as a Pony Club member and retired in 1985 after ten years at or near the top of the leading jockey list. F. B. Rees, a stylish, strong Irish rider, has led the list five times since 1973. (Five may be his lucky number: he once rode five winners at Perth on the same day.) "Johnjo" O'Neill mounted a record number of winners (149) during his first freelance season in 1977 and retired at the top in 1986. The most likely candidate to join this admirable roster is Richard Dunwoody, who rode West Tip to victory in the 1986 Grand National when he was barely twenty-two.

In France, the consistently successful steeplechase riders include Didier Mescam, Alain Chelet, Daniel Leblond, Michel Chirol, Patrick Sabarly, Roger Duchène, Dennis Bailliez, Patrick Lemaire, Jean-Claude Dessaint, and Gérard Dubroeucq (a phenomenon, since he is also a leading trotting driver). A brave girl, Béatrice Marie, joined their ranks in 1982.

In the United States, two of the outstanding steeplechase riders between the two World Wars were amateurs, superior all-round horsemen, and as gentlemanly as a gentleman rider can be: Pete Bostwick and George Strawbridge, Jr. Many Hitchcock winners were ridden by another outstanding amateur, Rigan McKinney. Among his leading rivals was Dooley Adams, a professional, son of a pioneer woman steeplechase trainer, Clara Adams.

Post–World War II leaders included Johnny Harrison, William H. "Billy" Turner, Jr. (who became even more famous as the trainer of Seattle Slew), D. M. Smithwick of the prolific Irish-American steeplechase clan, Ben Griswold, Joe Aitcheson (twenty-two years at the top and seven times the leading jockey), Tommy Walsh and Raymie Woolfe, Jr., both sons of leading trainers. Stars of the following generation include Janon Fisher, Jeff Teter, Jerry Fishback, John Cushman, Charlie Fenwick, Jr. (four Maryland Hunt Cup victories, three Virginia Gold Cups, a Grand National win with Ben Nevis in 1980), Louis "Paddy" Nielson III, George Sloan, Tommy Smith, and Jonathan Sheppard. Future steeplechase riding laurels may be divided between D. M. "Speedy" Smithwick, Jr., Ricky Hendricks, and Bernie Houghton (leading American steeplechase rider in 1985 at the age of twenty-two).

The most visible difference between flat and steeplechase jockeys is their height and weight. Steeplechase jockeys can tip the scales at 150 pounds or more, about 68 kg, and still come within the usual allowance of 165 pounds/75 kg, in amateur races, although they must not exceed 145 pounds/66 kg, including saddle and clothing, in major track events. Many steeplechase riders are 5 feet 6 to 10 inches tall, or 1.68 to 1.78 m, like John Francome in England, Michel Chirol in France, Jerry Fishback in America. Lester Piggott, who stands 5 feet 8 inches/1.73 m, won twenty of fifty-six races over hurdles. Daredevil Dave Dick, a famous English rider before World War II and now a Thoroughbred breeder, is 6 feet tall, or 1.83 m. Bruce Hobbs, already a gangly seventeen-year-old when he won the 1938 Grand National with Battleship, grew to 6 feet 3 inches/1.91 m.

Their riding styles also differ visibly. While hurdle races are ridden almost like the flat variety in a forward "crouch" seat, steeplechase requires another technique. In order to remain over the horse's center of gravity, not too far ahead of it, steeplechase jockeys traditionally sit in a less forward position, adjusting it according to circum-

Richard Earnshaw parts company with Badsworth Boy, who has missed his takeoff stride while leading Weston Rose, ridden by Peter Scudamore, top winning English jump jockey of the 1986–87 season. Surprisingly, as here, serious harm seldom results. An essential skill of steeplechase riders is knowing how to fall and roll free—and, if injured, how to be patient until they are fit to ride and risk their necks again.

72

stances. They use their legs more, ride with longer stirrups and longer reins—although the trend is closer to flat-racing style, relying more on balance than on leg contact. Sometimes, to help a horse avoid "pecking" on landing after a jump, regain its balance, and resume a gallop stride, they lean backwards, in the style of those quaint eighteenth-century hunting prints. Like flat jockeys, they steer, adjust speed by inducing the horse to lengthen or shorten its stride, and signal the horse to change the leading leg of its stride in order to facilitate sharp turns and avoid one-sided fatigue over the long course.

Steeplechase jockeys devote more time to schooling their horses. They too walk the course they are to ride, study it for danger spots, pick the shortest, safest route. During the race they try to judge the best take-off spot, in order to meet each obstacle in stride, with sufficient impulsion. Sometimes this involves simply refraining from interference—not as easy as it sounds! They also try to "rate" their horses, saving sufficient energy for a spurt of speed at the final run-in. And all the time there is the preoccupation of avoiding fallen horses and riders, loose horses, and treacherous footing.

Even when undertaken by experts, steeplechase riding is a high-risk activity. One out of every ten rides ends in a fall. Most jockeys are stitched up and wired together. But very few abandon the sport because of anything so banal as another broken bone. The only thing they fear is fear itself, losing their nerve. Joe Aitcheson seemed impervious to pain; he sometimes had to be assisted into the paddock and hoisted into the saddle—and then rode a winning race. Fulke Walwyn retired from riding only after a second skull fracture put him in a month-long coma—whereupon he became a successful trainer, failing to figure among the top six only eight times during the next thirty-three years. Fred Rimell, four-time champion jockey between 1938 and 1946, stopped riding only after he'd broken his neck twice in eight months, whereupon he too became a leading trainer. John Francome was almost killed at Cheltenham in 1985 when his foot got caught in a stirrup during a spill and the frightened horse began to bolt. He retired a few months later.

Steeplechase horses usually start out in three- or four-year-old hurdle races before advancing to steeplechase the following year. American horses are raced younger and more frequently than English and Irish 'chasers.

Some horses are specifically bred or selected for jump racing; others may reveal an unsuspected talent during a local hunt race meeting; still others may be trained for jumping simply as a last resort. A certain temperament and conformation often indicate jumping ability. Some horsemen place their faith in the presence of a "jumping bump" on the hindquarters; all appreciate soundness, intelligence, a steady

Pages 75–76: The "Winter Kings"—like this string of English 'chasers trained by John Thorne—exercise daily, even when there's snow on the ground. Only when the course is frozen hard, or when falling snow interferes with visibility, do the stewards cancel racing for the day.

temperament. Not surprisingly, Thoroughbreds dominate the sport—although the first two horses in the 1986 Grand Steeplechase de Paris at Auteuil were non-Thoroughbreds (AQPS). Hurdlers often come straight from the flat. But steeplechase and timber horses require more jumping training, strength, and stamina. Four years is the minimum legal age for a steeplechase debut, five or six is more customary.

Hunt races (corresponding to timber races, or point-to-points) generally are open to all breeds, but qualification requirements often limit them in practice to Thoroughbreds or horses with a high percentage of Thoroughbred blood. Races specifically restricted to non-Thoroughbreds (AQPS) and Anglo-Arabs are popular in southwestern France, at Pau and Pompadour, site of an ancient National Stud and a beautiful permanent jumping course with its finish line in front of a magnificent historic château.

While many disappointing flat racers have been converted into superior steeplechasers, seldom does the opposite occur. But as always with men and animals, there are exceptions: Brown Jack, a famous Irish gelding born in 1924, had won seven hurdle races when his jockey, the great Steve Donoghue, suggested that he try his luck on the flat. Too old for the three-year-old Classics, he won the Goodwood Cup, and finished first in the Queen Alexandra Stakes at Royal Ascot six years in succession! In America, a "reformed" steeplechaser named Azucar was winner of the inaugural Santa Anita Handicap, outrunning Equipoise, the 1931 Kentucky Derby winner Twenty Grand, and the Preakness winner Mate.

It is far more customary for Thoroughbred racehorses to be converted to steeplechase, however, if only because there are few flat races for horses over four or five years old. Once the decision has been made, male horses usually are gelded. If they avoid serious injury (and a surprising number of them scramble to their feet after a spectacular crash, unharmed), they can compete until the age of ten or twelve, though normally reaching a peak around the age of eight. Nevertheless, four twelve-year-olds won the Grand National between 1962 and 1977; and a nineteen-year-old once finished that grueling course—not among the winners, but still, quite an achievement at such an age.

The steeplechase season starts at the end of summer and lasts through the spring. In Ireland, hunt racing, as they call it, is a popular national sport, noted for its enthusiastic, informed public and aggressive racing. Small courses and local meets abound, and there are twenty-seven permanent steeplechase courses. Major events take place at Leopardstown (site of the Irish Sweeps Derby and the Leopardstown Chase), Fairyhouse (where the Irish Grand National is run), and Punchestown (scene of the Grand Steeplechase).

Preceding pages: A brush race at Fair Hill, Maryland, where hunt racing and training take place on the former estate of William duPont, Jr.

"He was sublime," says this plaque at Aintree in memory of Red Rum, one of its most beloved heroes. His Grand National record of three wins, two times runner-up, is indeed awesome.

In England, too, there are numerous provincial point-to-points, fifteen mixed tracks, and forty-five courses exclusively devoted to jump racing. The Derby of steeplechase is the Cheltenham Gold Cup; the King George VI Steeplechase at Kempton Park is a great event, as are several at Sandown. But the most famous steeplechase race in England, probably in the world, is the Grand National, run since 1839 at the Aintree course in Liverpool.

Grand Nationals exist in other lands, including a formidable one in Japan, but to the general public "Grand National" means Aintree, and Aintree Grand National is practically synonymous with steeplechase. To the racing fraternity, however, it is more a thrilling spectacle than a true test of quality like the Gold Cup. A handicap race (rather than weight-for-age), its flat, triangular, left-handed course is studded with enormous obstacles which the horses have to cover twice in order to total a distance of 4½ miles/7.2 km. Sheer luck, good or bad, is an ever-present factor, if only because the huge field (recently restricted to forty horses) competing for a place on the relatively narrow course (recently widened) tends to result in many falls at the very first fence, posing the additional danger of fallen and loose horses as well as deteriorating footing. Is it surprising that behind the name of almost every past winner there lies a dramatic tale?

Moifaa won in 1904 after being shipwrecked on a desert island on the way to England from his native New Zealand (among the horses he defeated was sixth-placed sixteen-year-old Manifesto, making his farewell appearance). Rubio (1908) was a California-bred flat racing discard who pulled a hotel bus for three years before being trained for 'chasing. Master Roberts (1924) had pulled a plow. It was the only race that Tipperary Tim (1928) ever won in his life—by beating American champion Billy Barton; and he did it with a tube in his windpipe to compensate for a defective respiratory system. Foinavon was a lucky winner in 1967, when twenty-eight horses fell at the twenty-third fence and he was too far behind to be bothered by the mass debacle. So unexpected was his 100-to-1 victory (the third win in his life) that neither his owner nor trainer had taken the trouble to attend.

On the other hand, sheer merit and perseverance accounted for the wildly cheered win of Escargot, owned by Raymond Guest, a former U.S. Ambassador to Ireland and an active flat racing owner. He also had two Derby winners, Larkspur in 1962 and Sir Ivor in 1968. Steeplechase Horse of the Year in America in 1969, Escargot returned to his native land to win the Gold Cup in 1970 and 1971. He fell during his first Grand National effort in 1972, finished third to Red Rum in 1973 and second to him in 1974, and finally won the race in 1975 at the age of twelve.

After Battleship in 1938 and Jay Trump in 1965 (in a close finish with "Fearless" Freddie, the pride of Scotland), a third American-owned (but British-bred and -trained) horse won the Grand National in 1980: Ben Nevis II, ridden by Charlie Fenwick, owned by his father-in-law. Undefeated in twelve American jump races, including two Maryland Hunt Cups, he was unable to score a win in twelve English races, then triumphed at Aintree.

In France, steeplechase is characterized by high-class horses, some of whom also race on the flat, and extreme speed. Its moment of glory is at Auteuil after Longchamp closes in the autumn. Major events include the Grande Course des Haies and Prix du Président de la République (hurdles), the Grand Steeplechase de Paris, Prix Montgomery, and Prix de la Haye-Josselin (steeplechase). Other important meetings are held at Enghien and Maisons-Laffitte. Winter racing over jumps as well as on the flat continues at Cagnes on the Côte d'Azur, and at Pau in the southwest with snowy Pyrenean mountain peaks in the distance. Throughout the land sixty-four tracks are used exclusively for steeplechase and 140 for mixed schedules; over two thousand jump races are run each year.

In the United States, every racing category, it seems, must have its Triple Crown. The steeplechase triad consists of the Grand National, America's oldest stakes race over fences, founded in 1898, now run at Foxfield, an ultramodern course in Charlottesville, Virginia. Next comes the Temple Gwathmey at Belmont Park (the most important Thoroughbred racetrack to feature steeplechase, along with Saratoga, Monmouth Park in New Jersey, and Delaware Park in Maryland). The final event, the Colonial Cup at Camden, South Carolina, is the climax of the steeplechase season in December.

A number of festive, fashionable events highlight three dozen or so annual hunt race meetings. The richest is also the youngest, the Breeders' Cup, inaugurated in 1986, patterned after the Thoroughbred racing model. Others include the Virginia Gold Cup, My Lady's Manor, the American Grand National, the Middleburg Hunt Cup, the Radnor Hunt Cup, the New Jersey and Pennsylvania Hunt Cups. But the most historic and prestigious is the Maryland Hunt Cup. Noel Laing, a great rider of the 1930s, said that the Aintree Grand National was the hardest race to win, the Maryland Hunt Cup the most difficult to ride. The first three finishers, in fact, automatically qualify for the Aintree race.

It has been run since 1896 at Glyndon, Maryland, over a permanent course 4 miles/6.4 km long and 100 ft/30.5 m wide over undulating terrain. The 4 miles are studded with timber fences up to 5 ft 3 in/1.60 m high. Open to riders "acceptable to the Committee," it is considered a jumping race rather than a running race, and the field is small, with seldom more than eight starters. Jay Trump won in 1964 by beating only four other horses. (He also won it in 1963 and 1966.) Before becoming a Hall of Fame trainer, D. Michael Smithwick rode

Two famous jumps on two famous steeplechase courses: Becher's Brook at Aintree, and the rivière at Auteuil. Two different riding techniques to cope with them: a backward-leaning seat to aid the horse's balance when landing on the steep drop jumps for which the Aintree course is famous; and at Auteuil a more forward position with short stirrups and no knee grip at all—a perfect example of the modern style of jump riding.

more Maryland Hunt Cup winners (six of them) than anyone in history. Six horses have won it three times, all of them outstanding champions: Princeton, Blockade, Winton, Pine Pep, Jay Trump, Cancottage.

Steeplechase racing exists in many other countries, generally on a fairly modest scale: in Germany at Baden-Baden, in Scandinavia, Australia, New Zealand, and behind the Iron Curtain. The Grand Pardubice Steeplechase, an annual international event in Czechoslovakia since 1974, is the Central European equivalent of the Grand National: a 4 mile/6.4 km course over pastures and farmland with thirty-one jumps, including the world's biggest steeplechase fence, the Taxis Ditch (6 ft/1.83 m high and 22 ft/6.71 m wide overall). Falls are commonplace, but most riders remount to finish the race — often behind a Russian winner.

In short, wherever there is fox hunting there is apt to be hunt racing; and wherever there is horse racing there is apt to be steeplechasing. But nowhere is it as widespread and popular as in the British Isles.

Wherever equestrian sports exist, there are also horses of exceptional talent, bravery, or character who have endeared themselves to the public and earned a niche in history. Steeplechase has its share.

French racing men revere the memory of Wild Monarch and of Lutteur III, the only French horse to win the Aintree Grand National (in 1909) when he was five years old with merely one year of jumping experience; of Héros II, indeed the hero of Auteuil during the 1920s, winner of the Prix du Président de la République under the top weight of 163 pounds/74 kg. The postwar heroine was Hyères III, who outjumped and outran the best colts of her time to win the Grand Steeplechase de Paris in 1964, 1965, and 1966, a remarkable achievement for a mare.

Should Mandarin be considered French or English? He was a gallant little horse, English-bred, French-trained and -owned, who raced mostly in England. But it was at Auteuil that he won the 1961 Grand Steeplechase de Paris even though his bit had broken at the fourth fence with twenty-two left to clear. It was a memorable feat by horse and rider (Fred Winter), who had only his knees and weight to act as brakes and steering gear around the double figure-eight course — and the sportsmanship of his fellow jockeys, who took no unfair advantage. There have been a number of similar exploits before and since, but none was more sensational nor more widely praised.

The first American steeplechase horse to become a national hero was Battleship, a Man o' War son whose dam was French. He succeeded on the flat, then in hunt races, finally in steeplechase, winning the Belmont Grand National, the most important jumping race in America. His owner, Mrs. Marion duPont Scott (a magnanimous patron and expert owner-breeder) then sought new fields for him to conquer.

82

Bob Champion, a leading English steeplechase jockey (now a trainer), dreamed of riding Aldaniti in the Aintree Grand National when, in 1979, he was stricken with cancer and the horse developed tendon trouble. Both of them overcame their maladies and all odds, and in 1981 they won the event, adding an inspiring chapter to the dramatic annals of the world's most famous steeplechase race:
". . . People make a lot of fuss about the so-called heroic courage of jump jockeys, which is nonsense. We all know the risks and we accept them. Nothing can match the thrill of riding good horses at speed over fences — nothing! I don't see that courage has anything to do with it. It's simply a job we all enjoy doing."

W. Burling ("Burly") Cocks, here instructing his rider at Far Hills, New Jersey, 1986, is a veteran American Hall of Fame trainer of steeplechase horses (and horsemen):
". . . Training steeplechase horses is a lot different from training runners, because the 'chasers not only have to run, they need to be able to jump just as fast as they can run. If they don't have a talent for jumping, it takes a lot of patience to develop enough skill to get by; and if there's jumping blood in the pedigree, it sure saves time working in the corral and schooling over little fences. Even so, you can plug along with the ungifted ones and only start them later in the year, and sometimes in the end they put it all together and you can't tell the difference between them and a real natural."

Why not the Aintree Grand National? No American horse had ever won it; none in fact had ever entered it, for it was no simple matter to ship a valuable, delicate Thoroughbred across the Atlantic then. (Sea-sickness is bad enough for humans, but it can be fatal to horses because they are unable to regurgitate.) Battleship was at the starting line of the 1938 Grand National, mounted by Bruce Hobbs, son of trainer Reginald Hobbs, then a seventeen-year-old apprentice jockey (now one of the leading flat race trainers in England). And he won the race—one of the few stallions, one of the smallest (15.1½ hands), and the first American-bred horse ever to do so.

Elkridge was the most famous American steeplechaser during the 1940s. A slender bay nicknamed "The Iron Horse," he won thirty-one races during eleven years of competition, falling only once when a piece of brush got caught in his girth and tangled with the following fence to bring him down.

Neji, a Man o' War grandson through his dam, bred by Mrs. Scott, owned by Mrs. Ogden Phipps, and trained by her brother, Pete Bost-wick, raced only on major tracks and never finished lower than third in forty-nine races between 1954 and 1960, carrying as much as 176 pounds/80 kg. He was one of six Bostwick-trained horses to be voted Steeplechaser of the Year.

Bon Nouvel, Mrs. T. A. Randolph's Smithwick-trained champion of 1964 and 1965, made a remarkable comeback to top the list again in 1968.

Jay Trump was not only the hero of a typical American success story, but also a dream come true for Tommy Crompton Smith. Born into a famous horse-minded Maryland family, Smith's youthful ambition was to win the Aintree Grand National with an American horse, bred and trained in America, ridden by an American (himself). And Jay Trump helped him do it in 1965.

Café Prince, a Sheppard-trained, Strawbridge-owned horse, was Steeplechase Champion in 1977 and 1978. Between 1979 and 1984, Zaccio, Horse of the Year in 1980, 1981, and 1982, earned more money than any other steeplechaser in American history. His remark-able contemporary, Cancottage, specialized in winning the Maryland Hunt Cup—three times (1980, 1981, and 1983). He is also an exam-ple of the dynastic character of American Hunt racing: owned by Mrs. Miles Valentine (a long-time leading owner); partly trained by her daughter, Mrs. Jill Fanning; ridden in his first two Hunt Cup tri-umphs by her granddaughter, Joy Slater Carrier. Three generations of expert equestriennes!

But no horse had ever won the Steeplechase Triple Crown until Flatterer, in 1983. An ex-flat racer, jointly owned by William L. Pape (President of the NSHA), bloodstock agent George Harris, and Jona-than Sheppard, he was Horse of the Year in 1983, 1984, and 1985. In

1986 he flew to France and finished second in the French Champion Hurdle at Auteuil against the best Europeans; a few months later, he won the Colonial Cup at Camden for the fourth straight time.

In England and Ireland, many steeplechase horses are better known than flat racers, if only because their careers are so much longer. Idols of the 1880s were Cloister and Manifesto. The latter competed in seven Grand Nationals, won it twice (1897, 1899), finished third three times, fourth once, and sixth in 1904, aged sixteen.

Easter Hero, a bold little Irish-bred Gold Cup winner (1929), retired from steeplechase at his prime, then went fox hunting with his owner, "Jock" Whitney, until the age of twenty-eight.

Golden Miller was the first 'chaser in history to win both the Cheltenham Gold Cup (five times!) and the Aintree Grand National (1934), under top weight and in record time. Incredibly sturdy and sound, he was owned by Miss Dorothy Paget, a wealthy patron of equestrian sports who was famous for her eccentricities and sentimentality where her horses were concerned.

Mill House, a massive, precocious jumper of noble allure, won the Gold Cup three times in succession during the 1960s, and seemed invincible until he met Arkle.

Red Rum led a rather melodramatic life with a happy ending. He started modestly, purchased for the virtually minimum sum of 400 guineas at the Dublin sales. After winning three out of ten minor races on the flat, he was sold as a jumper prospect. Eight wins out of forty-nine tries was not enough to satisfy his owner, who resold him at the age of seven. His poor record was due to chronic lameness. After a fourth change of ownership, he ended up in the backyard stable of trainer "Ginger" McCain, who patiently nursed him back to health. When Red Rum returned to racing, free at last from infirmity and pain, he made the most of his uncanny jumping ability: twelve wins in his next nineteen tries. Among them his Grand National record is unique. He won it by a narrow margin in 1973, then in a canter in 1974; after placing second in 1975 and 1976, he tried again in 1977, aged eleven, and won it for the third time, setting an Aintree record unlikely ever to be beaten.

Like many outstanding steeplechasers, Red Rum was bred in Ireland. But to the Irish, the most fervent fans of all, one great 'chaser eclipses all others: an Irish-bred, Irish-trained, Irish-ridden horse, a gangly bay with shiny black tail and points, large eyes, and huge ears; unusually hardy, resourceful, and independent like all true Irishmen. His name was Arkle. The only horse of his generation that could come close to him was Mill House. Their dramatic duels culminated in the 1964 Gold Cup, in which Arkle stole the lead from Mill House at the last fence and produced a typical, incredible burst of speed to win by

Like many trainers, Jenny Pitman likes to exercise her string of horses — including 1983 Grand National winner Corbière and outstanding steeplechaser Burrough Hill Lad — on the beach at Brean Sands, preferably right after the tide has receded.

five lengths—with the third-placed horse some 25 lengths behind. Many racegoers say that Mill House's heart was broken that day. Arkle won the race again in 1965. When he won it for a third time in 1966, with Mill House absent, it was by 30 lengths! Like his valiant rival and many other high-class 'chasers, he was never entered in the Grand National. Never did he fall during a race. A fractured pedal bone caused him to retire, and when severe, incurable arthritis made his life an agony, he was put down in 1970. But he is still present at Cheltenham, scene of his finest triumphs, where his statue reigns over the parade ring.

The most poignant Gold Cup victory since Arkle defeated Mill House occurred in 1986, when Dawn Run, a hurdle champion (eighty-four wins in France, Ireland, and England) and a filly to boot, won by a length. She made up for her lack of steeplechase experience with sheer heart that brought cheers to the throats and tears to the eyes of all who witnessed her gallant feat. Tears were shed again at Auteuil a few months later, when she broke her neck in a fatal fall during the French Champion Hurdle.

Notwithstanding its star performers, its thrills and spills—perhaps partly due to the latter, and to the facts that steeplechase horses tend to run true to form and betting is less profitable—jumping races are on

the wane everywhere but in Ireland and England. There, it is an active sport with devoted owners and trainers, addicted jockeys, and faithful supporters. In France, it is a popular provincial activity, a traditional adjunct to urban flat racing, filling the hiatus between flat meetings and providing events for the nationalized betting industry. In America, hunt race meetings thrive and expand, while major track steeplechase has diminished. Increasingly a world apart from the flat racing community, it depends more on wealthy patrons and corporate sponsorship than on betting revenue and big purses (although they've improved).

Far from being a poor relation of flat racing, steeplechasing is a major horse sport with a personality all its own: cheerfully sociable, rather bucolic, as competitive as any but still very sporting. To the owners, trainers, and riders who participate, true horselovers all, there is no other sport that can compare.

The famous Chair Fence of the Aintree Grand National course is one of its most formidable—especially when nine horses attempt to clear it at once, each in his own manner, sometimes without a rider.

If horses run in the snow, play polo in the snow, trot under harness in the snow, why shouldn't there be steeplechasing in the snow? There is, in St. Moritz, during its Winter Festival, and nowhere is 'chasing more spectacular!

Show Jumping

High-jumping was an important early form of show jumping, and impressive heights were scaled. Here the American Thoroughbred Heatherbloom and Dick Donnelly jump 8 ft 2 in/2.49 m in 1902.

In much of the Western world, the activity that best exemplifies equestrian sport in the minds of the public is show jumping. This popularity is due to the fact that show jumping probably enjoys the highest aggregate of spectator values, and especially the fact that it is almost uniquely well suited to the medium of television. Some recognizable form of show jumping has existed for well over a century, and the sport has been widely based at least since the 1920s in many countries. However, the explosive growth of show jumping as we know it today traces only to the early 1950s and closely parallels the powerful rising trend of television viewing. More households saw more coverage of the show jumping from the last Olympic Games, World Championship, and World Cup than have ever before been reached by this most accessible of equestrian disciplines.

What makes show jumping so attractive to the nonhorseman? To start with, of course, it shares the appeal of all equestrian sports—the innate beauty, excitement, and highly prestigious associations that characterize almost all of the sporting activities in which horse and man collaborate. But beyond that, the action takes place in an area and at a speed that are ideal for the television camera to cover perfectly, and it is easy to understand as well as diverting to watch. Though the sport has many subtleties and complexities, and a good measure of unpredictability, its obvious virtues are just that, and they combine to generate high levels of spectator excitement and enjoyment, whether the event has been experienced on the spot or watched on the television screen.

Finally, show jumping is a relatively "safe" sport to broadcast in this hypersensitive era. True, there are some who consider it a violation of animal rights. But generally, both the equine and the human competitors seem to enjoy what they're doing, and injuries to either are uncommon and rarely serious. Intrusions of mere bad manners are rare enough, let alone violence, yet somehow show jumping is seldom bland or even only moderately entertaining, and the big occasions, when everything works right, are absolutely riveting. Realistically, show jumping is the only equestrian discipline to have been successful enough on television to have even been threatened, at least in England, with the ill that only success can breed: overexposure. It is probably the only nonbetting sport to have achieved this level.

There is no reliable birthdate for show jumping, but it is safe to say that it was an uncommon sport a century ago, and didn't even exist a century before that. Of course, horses have always had some capacity to

Gilles Bertran de Balanda, a second-generation member of the French jumping team, competing with his most successful collaborator, the sensational stallion Galoubet, at Calgary in 1981.

jump—though it must be considered limited compared to that of many other animals, from house cats to deer—and no doubt early horsemen began negotiating simple natural obstacles (fallen logs, ditches) as soon as they learned to ride. However, for many centuries there was no practical reason for breeders or trainers to concern themselves with the horse's latent jumping ability; its potentials for speed, for pulling, for weight-carrying, and for training entirely on the flat were of far greater importance. Prior to the Enclosure Acts of the eighteenth century, even the fox hunter had little need to jump obstacles in order to stay with hounds; any "leaping" in the equitation of 1600 was done without obstacles, like the "airs above the ground" performed by the Spanish Riding School of Vienna.

The principal formulator of the modern "forward seat," Federico Caprilli of Italy, schooling his high-jumper Meloppo at the Turin Horse Show in 1902. This was the first true international show-jumping competition.

By the second half of the eighteenth century, however, the only way to stay with hounds in most countries was by jumping, and by the first half of the nineteenth century, it was not only expedient, it was the height of fashion to do so. The accounts of hunting exploits in Leicestershire by the famous sporting chronicler "Nimrod" (C. J. Apperley, 1777–1843) are replete with jumping feats, as are the innumerable hunting prints and paintings of the time. Since Georgian sportsmen were also much addicted to wagering, it hardly seems unlikely that jumping "in cold blood"—to use the fox hunter's traditional deprecation for jumping fences other than in pursuit of hounds —developed to settle disputes (and bets) as to which "thruster" had the best jumping horse.

There are many claimants to the distinction of having presented the first organized "leaping contests," as they originally were called. They seem sometimes to have been included at horse fairs and agricultural fairs well before 1850, but the documented introductions are all later than this date—Paris in 1866, Dublin in 1868, Islington's first Royal in the following decade, New York's National as late as 1883. Most early competition was either over a single high jump (bars with a hedge) or a single broad jump over water (also with a hedge as a take-off), and some impressive fences were jumped, especially considering the fact that most riders leaned backwards as the horse left the ground. A horse named Leo, ridden by a whip from the Rockaway Hunting Club, jumped 6 ft 6 in/1.98 m in the class for qualified hunters on the closing night of the 1884 National Horse Show in New York, and by 1891 the record was 7 ft 1 in/2.16 m. The American Thoroughbred Heatherbloom jumped 7 ft 10½ in/2.40 m at Richmond, Virginia, in 1902 with Dick Donnelly up, and while schooling at home in White Plains, New York, topped 8 ft 2 in/2.49 m, a height that would qualify as a record today if it were performed under the conditions stipulated by the Fédération Equestre Internationale (FEI).

Jean Cariou of France, the very first Olympic show-jumping champion, with Mignon at Stockholm in 1912. He competed in all three equestrian events and had to endure a jump-off for his victory.

Though high-jump competitions were unquestionably the glamour events of the Victorian horse shows, there were other forms of jumping

Maj. Harry D. Chamberlin was the leading U.S. horseman and theorist between the two World Wars. He jumped this bank with Nigra in the 1928 Olympic Games in Amsterdam.

Pierre Jonquères d'Oriola of France was the first civilian Olympic show-jumping champion, with Ali Baba at Helsinki in 1952. He repeated his triumph at Tokyo in 1964, a unique double.

competitions as well. A course of permanent natural fences was included in the Royal Dublin Society's new showground at Ball's Bridge in 1881, and by 1900 a very wide variety of fences, ditches, and banks was being jumped by civilian and military horsemen in many countries. Show jumping failed to gain a spot at the first modern Olympic Games in Athens in 1896, but four years later it was an exhibition sport in Paris, waiting in the wings.

The wait proved longer than expected. The first big international competition came to Turin in 1902, followed by the introduction of international jumping at Olympia, London, in June of 1907 and in New York's Madison Square Garden the following November. Even so, it was not until 1912 at the Stockholm Olympics that show jumping became a main attraction. A French officer, Jean Cariou, and his horse Mignon prevailed over thirty other competitors from eight nations on this occasion, beginning four decades of utter domination of the Olympics by the military, a pattern that was not to be broken until another French rider, winegrower Pierre Jonquères d'Oriola, won with Ali Baba at Helsinki in 1952.

Though the cavalry schools of the world effectively excluded civilian riders from participation in the Olympic Games prior to World War II, they promulgated a technical revolution in jumping technique that emancipated the jumping horses of the world from the old "leanback" school of riding, at least as far as the show ring was concerned, and made possible the negotiation of infinitely more complex and more interesting show jumping courses. The revolution was spearheaded by the great Italian officer, Captain Federico Caprilli (1868–1907), whose *sistema* was the first rational codification of forward riding and the so-called "forward seat."

Sweden won the team competition (Nations' Cup) at the Stockholm Olympics and proved it was no fluke by winning again at Antwerp in 1920 (following the suspension of Olympic competition occasioned by World War I) and at Paris in 1924. From then on, no single nation dominated the Games: Spain beat fourteen other nations at Amsterdam in 1928, and no team finished the competition in the Depression-stricken Los Angeles Games four years later. Germany's powerhouse prevailed as expected over seventeen other nations in Berlin in 1936, but the margin of victory was surprisingly narrow.

Individual awards in the first six Olympics were divided evenly among six nations. After Cariou's victory for France in 1912 the winners included Lt. Tommaso Lequio from Italy in 1920, Lt. Alphonse Gemuseus from Switzerland in 1924, Capt. Frantisek Ventura from Czechoslovakia in 1928, Baron Takeichi Nishi from Japan in 1932 (but riding a French horse), and Oberleutnant Kurt von Hasse from Germany at Berlin in 1936. Two of the strongest prewar teams never won an Olympic medal. The team from Imperial Russia anchored by Capt.

93

Current "anchor man" of the British team is Yorkshire's John Whitaker, individual silver medalist at the 1980 "Alternate Olympics." Here he and Ryan's Son show how Hickstead's huge Derby Bank should be negotiated: ". . . My strategy is to win, but you can't always win. I've won going first in a competition, and I've won going last. Sometimes when you go first and put up a good time, you can force others into making mistakes. Of course, if you go last, you know what you have to do, and if you have to go hell-for-leather, you do it. The main thing is, you have got to be clear and as fast as you can, not just as fast as you can. The clear bit is the important thing. . . . When I'm riding Ryan, I don't think about what I'm doing, or what I'm going to do, he's already done it. . . . But sometimes you misjudge something and get a bit too far off or a bit too close. Then—and that's the difference between a good 'un and a bad horse—the good one will help you out."

Alexander Rodzianko, a pupil of Caprilli himself, was only fifth at Stockholm, while the powerful Irish team of the 1930s coached by Rodzianko's brother Paul, an equally famous Caprillist, never competed in the Olympics.

After World War II a new set of national powers in show jumping emerged as the military domination of the sport weakened and then vanished with the mechanization of most of the world's cavalry. Mexico's military trio of riders won at London in 1948, as did its leader, Col. Humberto Mariles, in the individual classification, but the French civilian rider Jean d'Orgeix won the bronze individual medal. In 1952 at Helsinki, however, civilians won half of the medals, led by individual gold medalist d'Oriola and a victorious British team that featured Cheshire farmer Wilf White and Welsh colliery owner Harry Llewellyn and his famous Foxhunter. Newspaper accounts of the British win further aroused an English enthusiasm for horse sports that had already been inflamed by the exploits of a lovely young rider, Pat Smythe, and watching show jumping "on the telly"—BBC Television—became a new national pastime. Pat Smythe herself won a team bronze medal in the Stockholm Olympics of 1956 (the equestrian events having been moved from Melbourne because of Australian quarantine restrictions on horses); women had been ineligible for the event in prior games. The real story from Stockholm, however, was the reemergence of a dominant German (West German, now) show-jumping team, led by individual gold medalist Hans Günter Winkler and his brilliant mare Halla.

The story has often been told how Winkler painfully and seriously tore a groin muscle as Halla incurred her only fault in the morning round of the competition. Somehow she seemed to sense his exquisite pain in the afternoon, for the mare who ordinarily became upset by the slightest rough move simply ignored Winkler's obvious distress, and jumped one of only two clear rounds of the entire day to seal the victory. The individual silver and bronze medals went to the brothers Raimondo and Piero d'Inzeo of Italy, who were both to move up a notch when the Olympics came to Rome four years later. Germany won the team gold at Rome, and repeated in Tokyo in 1964, where the individual gold medal also went to a repeat winner, the only one in Olympic show-jumping history: Pierre Jonquères d'Oriola of France, this time riding Lutteur B.

Mexico City in 1968 saw North American teams break the European domination of the coveted Olympic gold medal, Bill Steinkraus with Snowbound winning the individual gold ahead of England's Marion Coakes with the remarkable 14.2-hand pony Stroller, and Canada accounting for the Nations' Cup ahead of France. West Germany returned to the fore at Munich in 1972, with Graziano Mancinelli of Italy annexing the individual gold medal, but lost out to France in the team competition at Montreal in 1976. Three sensational clear rounds

—the only clear rounds of the entire competition—earned the individual gold medal for Alwin Schockemöhle of West Germany with his horse Donald Rex at Montreal to mollify any German disappointment with the team result.

Jan Kowalczyk of Poland and the host Russian team accounted for the gold medals in the boycott-stricken Moscow Games, which saw only seven nations represented. But it was a different story at Los Angeles in 1984, where even the absence of the Russian bloc failed to dampen enthusiasm for an all-American sweep of the show-jumping gold medals, Joe Fargis and the wonderful little mare Touch of Class just nosing out their teammates, Conrad Homfeld and Abdullah, with a brilliantly stylish display of precision jumping.

Of course, there was more to show jumping between the two World Wars than the Olympic Games, just as there is now. Professionals were excluded from the Olympics (though a prewar cavalry officer, whose livelihood also depended directly on horses, was considered a gentleman and an amateur). There were few show-jumping professionals on the Continent, but many of the luminaries of the English-speaking show-jumping world were thus ineligible for Olympic and for most international competition: Donald "Curly" Beard, Tommy Glencross, Sam Marsh, and Phil Blackmore in England; Jack Prestage, "Cappy" Smith, Mickey Walsh, and Danny Shea in the United States, to name only a few.

Though this situation remained unchanged in the years immediately following World War II, there was a considerable relaxation of strictures during the 1960s and 1970s; it became easier to retain or to recover amateur status, and professionals became eligible to compete virtually everywhere except in the Olympics, including the World Championships. Such current stars as David Broome, Harvey Smith, and Malcolm Pyrah of Great Britain, Eddie Macken of Ireland, Nelson Pessoa of Brazil, Rodney Jenkins and Bernie Traurig of the United States, and Gilles Bertran de Balanda of France have competed as professionals in recent years, and represented their countries with great distinction. A further relaxation of the International Olympic Committee's rules in 1986 now makes it possible for professionals to regain their amateur status, even for the Olympics, provided that they do so only once; previously the professional "taint" had been considered ineradicable.

Show jumping undoubtedly owes much of its popularity to the relative ease with which the layman can understand its scoring, in contrast to other kinds of horse-show judging. One need not appreciate the beauty of a well-turned hock or pastern to distinguish the winner from the also-ran in jumping; it is mostly a question of observing which horse and rider knocked down the fewest fences or equaled the best score in the shortest elapsed time. Simple though the rules may be in

94

Hans Günter Winkler was the winner of a record five Olympic equestrian gold medals, one of them the 1956 individual title at Stockholm with Halla. Here he rides Torphy, the horse on whom he won his last team gold medal, at Munich in 1972.

A brilliant and versatile stylist, the Carabinieri officer Raimondo d'Inzeo (Italy) won two World Championships and the 1960 Olympic championship, edging out his gifted brother, Piero. Here he rides his last great horse, Bellevue, at Hickstead in 1969.

England's (and Wales's) David Broome, the 1970 World Champion, also accounted for three European titles, the last two with Mister Softee (seen here) in 1967 and 1969: ". . . If you've got your partnership working well and the horse is listening to you, you know where every foot is on the ground. . . . It's my job to have the rhythm right and the pace right, and to have him in the right shape, for if one of these things is wrong, he can't jump. . . . After that, it's up to him to carry me over. To me, the jumping part is terribly easy; it's the approach that's difficult."

concept, however, in practice they have developed quite an intimidating complexity. They are, after all, quite arbitrary. Should the knockdown of a fence be scored as 4 faults or as 2? Should there be a difference between knocking it down with front legs or with hind? Should the initial refusal or "disobedience" count as 2 faults or as 3, and how should subsequent refusals and falls be penalized? Different generations have tried different answers to these questions, and formerly it was common for each individual horse show to impose its own formula. It became a primary goal of the various national federations and the international governing body of the sport, the Swiss-based FEI, founded in 1921, to regularize and standardize the judging of show jumping and other national and international equestrian competitions, and they have succeeded in creating order (if not simplicity) out of chaos.

Today the vast majority of jumper competitions around the world are scored with a penalty of 4 faults for any knockdown of a fence, whether by front or hind legs, and any foot in a water jump or on the tape defining its limits; 3 faults are scored for the first refusal or disobedience, 6 for the second, and elimination for the third; and 8 faults are scored for a fall of horse or rider. Time faults are incurred at a rate of ¼ fault per second in excess of the allowed time, which is cal-

culated by dividing the length of the course by a stipulated speed appropriate to the size of the fences and other conditions of the class. (In jump-offs over a shortened course, the penalty is raised to 1 fault per second.) The only significant exception to this generalization occurs in certain speed competitions, which are judged under a scoring table in which faults are translated into seconds and added to the competitors' elapsed times, and in puissance competitions. The latter are true tests of jumping power in which speed is never a decisive factor, the competitors jumping off over higher and higher fences (one usually a spread and the other an imitation stone wall) until a result is obtained.

Horse shows usually include a variety of different types of competitions. There is a broad distinction between classes in which speed over the course is a dominant consideration in the first round, and those that emphasize precision over somewhat bigger fences (such as the puissance) or a combination of the two. The competition with the largest prize money, the Grand Prix, is usually a one- or two-jump-off class. This means that horses having jumped without fault in the first round come back and jump again over a shortened course on which the fences have been raised and widened. Then, in either the first or second jump-off (depending upon the conditions of the particular class), time is used to separate horses that are tied with the same number of jumping faults. In practice, this means that in order to win a

Thinking about the last competition, planning for the next one, and just plain waiting occupy a large part of the show jumper's day. John Whitaker at the Dublin World Championships, 1982.

96

Derby courses like the historic one at Hamburg's Klein Flottbek stress natural obstacles and lots of them. The Hamburg Birkenoxer is typically massive and big and remains a formidable challenge today, more than half a century after it was first constructed.

Left: Youthful Norbert Koof (Germany) glows with pleasure after winning the 1982 World Championship with Fire II at Dublin. The third successive German World Champion, Koof had won the European Junior Championship just ten years earlier.

major Grand Prix, you must ride like blazes over a very big course and leave all the fences up. It is a breathtaking feat both to perform and to observe!

Riding being essentially an individual sport, most show-jumping competitions are individual contests. Aside from the odd relay class or change-of-pace "rescue" relay, which are "fun" classes in the speed category, there is only one serious team class in show jumping, and it is so serious that the show must be specifically authorized by the FEI to conduct it. In principle, only one show per nation can offer an official Nations' Cup, or Prix des Nations (although the United States and Canada, with their vast distances from coast to coast, are permitted two), and only in a Nations' Cup does a rider officially represent his nation.

The Nations' Cup is basically a two-round competition for teams of four riders, with only the best three scores to count in each round. There is a jump-off over a shortened course if two or more teams are tied on faults at the end of the two rounds, and then, in the event of equality of faults, the aggregate time of the best three riders determines the winner. Originally, a Nations' Cup was the only show-jumping competition in the Olympic Games, with only three riders (all scores to count) and both an individual and a team classification. Since 1972 the Olympic event has been a standard Nations' Cup for four-rider teams; since 1968, the individual Olympic gold medal has been

won in a separate competition. The competition for the individual Grand Prix is also a two-rounder, but here, unlike the Nations' Cup, the two courses are not identical; the second is higher and shorter, and entirely different fences are used.

The show-jumping World Championship occurs only in a four-year cycle, like the Olympics, but takes place two years later. As in the Olympics, there are both team and individual titles at stake, but the formula is quite different, since time and space are not quite so precious as they are within the framework of an Olympics. There are four competitions; the first two determine the team champions, the last two the individual championship. Nations with full teams start four riders in the first competition, which is an FEI "Table C" (faults translated into seconds) over a big speed course (5 ft 3 in/1.60 m maximum height). It seems odd to start a championship with a speed class, a type of competition ordinarily reserved for horses of more limited scope, but there are two reasons for doing so: first, there is the intention to provide for a greater test of equestrian versatility for the individuals than is possible in the Olympics; second, Table C enables the clever rider to compensate for an unlucky fault by saving time, and thus not dropping too far down in the classification after only one round.

The second competition in the World Championship is a straightforward Nations' Cup, and the World Champion Team is that with the

The lovely and skillful Janou Lefèbvre Tissot (France), seen here with Rocket at Lucerne in 1974, was twice a Ladies' World Champion (1970, 1974) before the separate title was merged into the Men's.

Six times a U.S. Olympic rider (and since then a winning chef d'équipe), Frank Chapot was equally successful in puissance competitions (especially with the giant San Lucas, seen here) and against the clock (riding anything):
". . . Training the horses is very difficult, because a jumper is a very delicate mixture of "chicken" and bravery. The jumper has to be scared enough not to want to hit the jumps, but still brave enough to go down to them and try to jump them. If the trainer puts too much chicken in the mixture, the horse won't go at all. But if you put in too much bravery, the horse knocks everything down; he just doesn't care. So that's what training is—trying to find that very delicate balance. If you've luckily done it right, and the horse's stride is synchronized with the rider's eye, that's when everything works."

Not every good rider gets an opportunity to represent his country, and not every promising horse makes it all the way to Grand Prix competition. This young American unsung hero (Michael Dorman) represents countless others who constitute the backbone of show jumping around the world.

lowest total number of faults for the best three competitors in each of the three rounds that have been jumped at that point. After a day's rest, individual competitors go on to a two-round competition like the Individual Grand Prix in the Olympics, and at that point scores are totaled and only the best four individuals proceed into the finals, where they all start from scratch on an even footing.

The World Championship final is something of a Musical Chairs in which each finalist rides first his own horse and then the horses of the other three finalists over a short course of moderate difficulty—eight obstacles including a double and a treble with a maximum height of 5 ft/1.50 m. (The rider returns to his own horse if a jump-off against the clock is required after the scores for each rider have been totaled, but this has been rare.) The formula is an interesting one, and the final is unquestionably fascinating for the public. It has often been criticized on several grounds, however. It seems curious to some that the World Championship title should hinge finally upon the rider's ability to adapt quickly to a strange horse—one is allowed only three minutes for familiarization, and two small jumps—especially when this form of competition hardly exists otherwise during the four-year cycle between championships. Others question whether or not it is fair to throw out all qualifying scores entirely and start the final day at "scratch" when

the best qualified rider may never have had a rail down in jumping five huge courses, and the fourth qualified rider may barely have squeaked in. In addition, the luck of the draw plays a considerable role in the final—who gets the most difficult horse last?—while there is an admitted advantage in introducing into the finals the hardest or least orthodox horse.

Be all this as it may, the finals have never failed to produce an absorbing competition and a convincing champion. From 1953 at Paris through 1956 at Aachen the World Championship title was competed for annually, the right to organize the next championship falling to the winner's nation. Spain's Francisco "Paco" Goyoaga was the first winner by the narrowest of margins: ¼ time fault over Germany's Fritz Thiedemann. Madrid in 1954 saw Hans Günter Winkler and Halla come to the fore (presaging the results in the 1956 Olympic Games), and in 1955 at Aachen Winkler triumphed again, this time with Orient. (Having watched the high-strung Halla chalk up 26 faults with Jaime García Cruz the previous year, he wisely opted not to subject Halla to the ordeal of the finals again.)

Raimondo d'Inzeo of Italy won at Aachen in 1956, and had to wait until Venice in 1960 to successfully defend his title, the decision having been made that the financial burden for most countries in trying to prepare for annual World Championships was too great. Venice seemed somehow an anticlimax after the Olympics, so a six-year gap followed in order to place the Championships in a four-year cycle following the Olympics, as they are now. Pierre Jonquères d'Oriola won the 1966 competition held in Buenos Aires in the highest-scoring finals to date, and he was the only one of the finalists to jump a clear round with his own horse, Pomone B. La Baule, France, in 1970 witnessed a fascinating group of problem horses in the final; Alwin Schockemöhle's Donald Rex was the only orthodox mount in the quartet. When it was all over, England's David Broome had given the world a lesson in "finessing" difficult horses to bring the 1974 renewal to Hickstead. There it took a rare jump-off between Hartwig Steenken of West Germany and Eddie Macken of Ireland to bring the title back to Germany, where at Aachen in 1978 the host nation's Gerd Wiltfang produced the first perfect score in all four rounds of the final to steal victory from the luckless Macken by a mere ¼ fault. This was the competition in which a team championship, won by Great Britain, was introduced for the first time. Germany declined to organize the following championship, which went to Dublin instead, but young Norbert Koof's second successive faultless performance by a West German rider brought the competition back to Aachen in 1982 for the fourth time, as France brought home the team title.

The 1986 Championship resulted in the series' greatest upset to date, when twenty-six-year-old Gail Greenough of Canada chalked up

Smooth, consistent, and always deceptively fast: Michael Matz (USA) and Jet Run, the 1979 Pan American Games champions and winners of the 1981 World Cup finals at Birmingham.

Paul Schockemöhle (brother of the 1976 Olympic Champion, Alwin) and Deister may not be the most orthodox duo stylistically, but what a record they've amassed for Germany—three successive European Championships, and countless Grands Prix!

Pages 102, 103: A good little one, and a good big one: France's brilliant giant-killer, Jappeloup with Pierre Durand, and Canada's aptly named Big Ben with the gifted Ian Millar up, both shown at the 1984 Olympic Games in Los Angeles.

four perfect rounds to prove, once and for all, that women "belonged" in an open championship instead of in the separate (and unequal) championship that existed from 1957 through 1973. Greenough, riding in her first World Championship and her first major European competition, was accorded only an outside chance by the experts, since at least two of the finalists—the U.S.'s Olympic silver medalist Conrad Homfeld and Britain's leading professional, Nick Skelton—were vastly more experienced at riding strange horses. Moreover, her mount, Mister T, was considered the most straightforward of the group, while Skelton's Apollo and Pierre Durand's Jappeloup from France, who had led all qualifiers, were expected to prove difficult. As the event unfolded, things worked out very differently, and Mister T proved deceptive, dashing Skelton's hopes and putting Durand out of the hunt almost before the event had started. Greenough's perfect score at the end of the four rounds made her a convincing winner over Homfeld with 8 faults, Skelton with 10, and Durand with 32, and one of show jumping's great Cinderella stories was history!

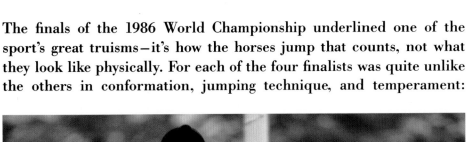

Fences rarely look very big from a seat in the stands. But just walk up to them . . .

The finals of the 1986 World Championship underlined one of the sport's great truisms—it's how the horses jump that counts, not what they look like physically. For each of the four finalists was quite unlike the others in conformation, jumping technique, and temperament:

104

One of the very best of a long string of outstanding amazones was England's Caroline Bradley, seen here with the brilliant Tigre at Hickstead in 1970.

*Real triers, both:
Melanie Smith of the United
States and the Dutch-bred
Calypso, winners of the World
Cup finals at Gothenburg in
1982 and Olympic team gold
medalists in 1984.*

Apollo a big, Dutch-bred bay gelding; Mister T a combination of Hanoverian and Thoroughbred, of medium (16.1 hands) size; Abdullah, Conrad Homfeld's mount, a striking gray Trakehner stallion, 17 hands high; and Jappeloup, a little (15.2-hand) black gelding from a combination of trotting and Thoroughbred blood. Good jumpers have come from every kind of breeding, but despite the contrast cited above, the very wide extremes of the past are tending to disappear, and some version or other of warmblood-Thoroughbred cross is beginning to predominate.

No matter what the breeding of the jumper, its training is likely to incorporate many of the same ingredients. A rail on the ground is an obstacle reduced to its very simplest form, and many jumpers start their career over fences by stepping over such a rudimentary barrier. Other horses are started loose in a pen, corral, or indoor ring, jumping very small fences from a trot and then from a canter, with complexity and size added progressively, one element at a time. It ordinarily takes at least two years to bring a horse from the rail on the ground to successfully jumping medium-sized courses, and another two to bring it to the Grand Prix level, presuming that it has the innate ability to jump those huge fences. Most jumpers' peak performances come between the ages of nine and fifteen. Before nine, they are likely to lack sufficient experience to excel on the truly big occasion (though there have been some brilliantly precocious exceptions), and from fif-

No rider in Europe has been more popular with audiences than Austria's indomitable one-man team, Hugo Simon, winner of the very first World Cup finals (1978) and the "Alternate Olympics" individual gold medal at Rotterdam in 1980. Here he rides The Freak in the 1985 European Championships at Dinard, where he placed fifth.

Conrad Homfeld of the United States, the only repeat winner of the World Cup finals (1980, 1985) with Abdullah, his silver-medal mount in both the 1984 Olympic Games and the 1986 World Championship. Few combinations have matched their perfection of style, especially over big courses and under Games pressure.

teen on, increasing age and infirmity tend to start catching up with them. Very few horses manage to maintain a high level of performance for more than eight or nine years, and the careers of horses like Idle Dice, the great American champion who was a consistent winner from the age of five until his late teens, are distinctly exceptional.

In order to bring the jumper from its first year to the highest level its basic jumping capacity will permit, there is a graduated, continuous progression of competitions in all of the principal show-jumping countries. Germany classifies its competitions as "L," "M," or "S," standing for *Leicht, Mittel,* and *Schwer* — easy, medium, and difficult. Great Britain has a lettered grading system based on prize monies earned, while the French grading system is mostly based on the young horse's age. The United States has the most comprehensive and flexible system of all. It starts with "Warm-up" or "Schooling" jumpers, which do not compete for prize money, only for the experience of jumping lots of small (3 ft 6 in/1.07 m) courses. When the young or inexperienced horse can cope with the full variety of these courses, it moves on to the Preliminary Jumper Section with 4 ft to 4 ft 6 in/1.22 to 1.37 m fences, where it stays for a full year or longer. After it wins $2,500 as a jumper it must move up to the Intermediate Section (with fences 4 ft 6 in to 5 ft/1.37 to 1.52 m, on average), and when it wins twice that, it becomes an Open Jumper, and, if it is good enough, a Grand Prix horse. There are also competitions restricted to junior riders below the age of eighteen and to amateur riders who own their own horses, so if the horse can jump at all, the rider can usually find a competition that suits it.

This system has succeeded in developing a large reservoir of jumpers in the United States, and the fruits of this have nowhere been more clearly demonstrated than in the FEI World Cup. This series of competitions around the world was inaugurated in 1978, based primarily on the winter show-jumping season indoors; competitors in the various leagues gain points that qualify them to compete (at the organizers' expense) in a final competition held at the end of April every year. Austria's Hugo Simon won the very first World Cup final at Gothenburg, Sweden — and gained a gaggle of adoring Swedish fans who have never since abandoned him.

Since then, however, North America has completely dominated the finals. Conrad Homfeld won at Baltimore in 1980 with Balbuco in the only finals held out of Europe to date; Michael Matz with the Thoroughbred Jet Run at Birmingham in 1981; Melanie Smith with the wonderful little Dutch-bred Calypso at Gothenburg in 1982; Norman Dello Joio with the French stallion I Love You at Vienna in 1983; Mario des Lauriers with the huge Hanoverian Aramis at Gothenburg in 1984; Homfeld again at Berlin in 1985, this time with his Olympic mount, the beautiful gray Trakehner stallion Abdullah; and then

The Pride of Ireland: The gifted Eddie Macken, seen above with Carroll's Foxborough at Hickstead in 1985, produced a long string of scintillating performances with Pele and Boomerang in the 1970s, and only missed winning the World Championship by the narrowest of margins in 1974 and 1978.

The 1982 World title was contested at Dublin with another popular Irish pair among the finalists: Gerry Mullins and Rockbarton, who earned the award for best horse in the final competition.

Leslie Burr-Lenehan with the Dutch-bred McLain at Gothenburg in 1986. All of these riders, except for des Lauriers, who is Canadian, are from the United States, a circumstance that has much perplexed the Europeans. Some feel that the European qualifying shows are more grueling than those elsewhere, but it may also simply be a question of the great depth in horseflesh that the North American mechanism develops, along with a commensurate depth in riders.

There are still relatively pronounced national styles in riding, and many observers consider that of the Americans—as typified, say, by Michael Matz and Conrad Homfeld—to be closest to the classic ideal at the moment, thanks in no small measure to the quarter-century tenure of Bertalan de Némethy, a former Hungarian cavalry officer, as coach of the U.S. team. The German style has tended to stress discipline, and even such an individualist as Paul Schockemöhle, their perennial European champion, seems able to put his horses on a given take-off spot virtually at will. The French and Italian riders (Frédéric Cottier and Giorgio Nuti, for example) tend to be more fluent, while British star show jumpers like Malcolm Pyrah, the Whitaker brothers, and Nick Skelton still seem to reflect something of the fox-hunting heritage in their general "look" and technique on horseback. It is important to remember that style in show jumping should never be an end in itself, since scoring (as in golf) is not a question of "how" but of "how many." Thus, a rider like Kevin Bacon of Australia, who has probably never given a moment's thought to where his toe was pointed, has probably won as much and certainly pleased more audiences than almost any paragon of equestrian refinement you can think of.

No discussion of show jumping would be complete without mention of the key contribution made by those who concoct the fences the horses jump—the course designers. Early in the history of show jumping there was not much to it, for the fences were mostly slight variations on established themes, and they were simply lined up in rows with hardly even a diagonal line to break the monotony. "Twice around the outside" was as much as the rider had to remember in many cases.

Not so today. Increasingly, the course designer has been recognized as a key ingredient in the quality of the competition, and his or her role has earned the kind of respect hitherto accorded only to the golf course architect in the world of sport. Working with such variables as an infinite variety of obstacles, their spacing in relation to the horse's average normal stride, their dimensions, and their positioning within the arena, designers can devise courses that are virtual examinations of the horse-rider combination's skills, demanding highly refined tactical and practical solutions. This is especially evident in the case of "combination" obstacles—double or treble fences with only a stride or two between them. Depending on how the skilled course

designer arranges the distances, he can readily build huge fences that anyone can jump, or small ones that nobody can. Grand Prix course designers ordinarily try to get something like 10 to 15 percent of the field into the jump-off, and that they most often succeed is a real tribute to their skill.

Most course designers are former riders themselves—and often celebrated ones at that, like Frank Chapot of the United States, a six-time Olympic rider. Some of their creations are so fascinating that one must regret the almost inviolable tradition that competitors never jump the same course twice, and never know until they walk the course, just before the competition, what kind of challenges they will face. The principal exception to this rule is found in the Derby type of competition patterned after the famous Hamburg Derby, whose course has undergone only subtle changes since its inaugural competition in 1920. Derby courses stress natural obstacles—ditches, banks, rustic materials—and are longer than most ordinary jumper courses, often running the better part of a mile. England's Hickstead, Newport in the United States, Falsterbo, Sweden, and Johannesburg, South Africa, are other fine examples of the genre.

Among the great course designers of the past have been Col. Ernst Haccius of Switzerland; Gen. Alberto Lombardi of Italy, designer of the courses for the 1960 Olympic Games; Count Greger Lewenhaupt of Sweden, creator of the scintillating course at Stockholm in 1956; Ernst

Joe Fargis (USA) had a long wait after his Pan American Games team gold medal in 1975 for another one, but the next ones proved worth waiting for when in 1984 he collaborated with a little Thoroughbred mare named Touch of Class to win both team and individual gold medals in the Los Angeles Olympics.

A tough pair to beat when the money's on the line: England's Nick Skelton and St. James, perennial leading money-winners in Europe in the 1980s. Riding Apollo, Skelton was bronze medalist in the 1986 World Championships at Aachen.

Schlikom and H. H. "Mickey" Brinckmann of Germany, master designers at Aachen for more than a quarter-century; Loic Hamon of France; Colonel Mike Ansell of England, who introduced European concepts of course design to the English-speaking world almost single-handed, and his successor, the famous rider Jack Talbot-Ponsonby; the renowned master of the light touch at Rotterdam, J.H.A. Jurgens of Holland; and the distinguished creator of the courses at the Los Angeles Olympics, Bertalan de Némethy.

Major figures from the later generations of course builders have been Pamela Carruthers, who has built all over the world, and her British colleagues Alan Oliver and Alan Ball; Philippe Gayot of France; Arno Gego, Haucke Schmidt, and Olaf Petersen of Germany; Paul Weier of Switzerland; Michel Vaillancourt of Canada; Roland Nilsson of Sweden; and Steve Stevens and Linda Allen of the United States.

Show jumping in the 1980s is a more popular, better financed, and more important factor in the horse community than ever before in its history. The number of shows has proliferated, and the number of competitors has risen to match; total premiums offered and aggregate attendance now run into many millions of pounds/dollars/marks/francs/lire, and millions, too, of people. Seventy-five different nations take part in some form of the sport, and at least twenty compete regularly at its highest levels. Germany, England, France, Canada, and the United States have shown the most consistent strength in recent years, but there are many near rivals—Holland, Italy, Spain, Switzerland, and Austria, to name only a few. (South Africa also has had some truly world-class teams, but it has been limited to national competition by political and veterinary difficulties.)

The impressive overall growth of show jumping in the past two decades has not been without its problems. The prize money in the sport is huge, but so are the expenses, and the price of good horses (which are increasingly difficult to find) can be astronomical. The standard of horse care and therapy is unquestionably higher, there is mandatory drug testing at all major events (at high cost to organizers and federations), and virtually every horse in the barn seems to be hooked up to some kind of device or other. Corporate sponsorship has assumed a significant part of the financial burden of the sport, but since sponsors are not necessarily forever, individual riders, shows, and even the FEI itself sometimes have had to scratch to find a new one on short notice or else take a big step backwards

Despite all of this, followers of show jumping—the most exciting, most glamourous, most prestigious equestrian sport of all—find their sport entering a new Golden Era. It may be a special form of madness, but it seems to gain new converts every day—quite an achievement for a sport based on taking the hard way to the other side of the fence!

The 1968 Olympic Champion in Mexico City, Bill Steinkraus, shown here with his 1964 King George Cup winner, Sinjon, was the first U.S. rider to win an individual Olympic title: ". . . I think that great riders and great horses are equally rare, though, since we breed more people than we do show-jumping horses, perhaps the great jumper is even rarer. In any case, really good horses are extremely hard to find, and in this world market, they've become almost prohibitively expensive. . . . When I started in show jumping we used to lie in bed at night, wondering how we could train our horses better and teach them to do all the complicated things the courses might require of them. Today the rider's nightmare involves a very different set of questions. 'Where can I find a sponsor? How do I come up with an angel? How can I promote all the money it takes to have a successful show-jumping string these days?' "

The 1986 World Championships produced a surprise winner and the first distaff titleholder in Canada's Gail Greenough, riding Mister T. Although she had never competed in Europe before, Greenough rode four faultless rounds in the final for a convincing victory.

Dressage

Dressage—the training of the ridden horse—cannot claim to be the oldest equestrian activity. Historians of the horse believe that primitive man probably used the horse for pulling loads or carts before he ever rode it. It is also not *quite* essential to all other equestrian activities, since the driven horse may never be asked to carry a rider, and the rodeo bronc only gets ridden for eight seconds at a time—if that! Nonetheless, this French word (which in its most general sense means simply "training") today denotes an activity that is unquestionably the most basic, the most intimate, the most subtle, and, on the Olympic and World Cup level, probably the most sophisticated and aesthetically pleasing of all equestrian activities. Some would also add, "and the most esoteric." But this is not only unfair; it is also becoming less and less true, thanks to growing public enthusiasm for the sport's newest competitive development, the freestyle ridden to music, which seems headed toward the same kind of acceptance that figure skaters' freestyle now enjoys.

The fundamental nature of dressage is reflected in the very first words of the FEI's rulebook for this discipline, which state its object to be "the harmonious development of the physique and ability of the horse" in such a way that it becomes "calm, supple, loose and flexible" as well as "confident, attentive and keen." It is hard to imagine a rider who would not wish his horse to possess all of these qualities, but it is only realistic to distinguish between those who engage in some form of what they consider "basic dressage" as preparation for some other equestrian activity, and those who work systematically toward a competitive goal within the dressage discipline itself. The numbers of the former group are legion, while those who can make the necessary total commitment to the latter (especially at the higher levels of the sport) are relatively few in number. It is something like the world of the dance: everyone can benefit from learning how to walk correctly, and everyone can enjoy recreational dancing, but relatively few enter into ballet training, and even fewer ultimately excel. Thus, national and international participation at the higher levels of dressage tends to be more restricted than in other equestrian sports, despite the fundamental nature of the basic activity.

In competitive dressage the horse and rider perform a prescribed test ride entirely from memory (except at lower levels) in an arena 22 by 66 yards/20 by 60 m in size. The arena is marked by twelve lettered points around its circumference, and there are another five imaginary lettered points down the middle line. (One of the great mysteries of dressage is how these particular letters were chosen, as no

The leading German Army rider before World War II, Maj. Friedrich Gerhard (with Fels in 1934), the silver medalist at the Berlin Olympics in 1936.

Elégance *personified: Cdt. F. Xavier Lesage of France with Taine, the Olympic champions at Los Angeles in 1932.*

Elisabeth Theurer of Austria, the 1979 European Champion, became the Olympic titlist at Moscow a year later. Here she is shown with her 1984 Olympic mount, Acapulco, in Los Angeles.

Anne-Grethe Jensen (Denmark) and Marzog, who won the World Cup and World Championship titles in 1986, are shown here at the 1984 Olympics, where they won the silver medal: ". . . The most important thing a dressage horse can have is a good temperament, a willingness to learn and to perform. You also need three very good basic gaits, because while you can improve these a bit, you can't make them if they're not there. Working with horses that lack a good temperament and good paces is mostly a waste of time. . . . For the rider, the most important qualities are patience and energy, and the combination of those two qualities is very important. You have to have a plan and stick to it, and when you get a movement where you want it, you must stop. . . . It's important to be conscious of what you're doing, and to be very correct all the time—you can't allow the horse to do something incorrect simply because you're relaxed, or don't care at that moment; you must always work correctly."

Pages 118, 119: The classical traditions of dressage are preserved by the Spanish Riding School of Vienna and the French Cadre Noir of Saumur, which still perform such "airs above the ground" as the capriole (left, performed by a Reitschule bereiter) and the croupade (right, performed by a Cadre Noir écuyer). Both movements were developed with the battlefield in mind.

logical basis for their sequence—A K V E S H C M R B P F around the outside, D L X I G down the middle—has ever been discerned.) Movements are expected to be performed *exactly* where specified by the particular test, and marks of from zero to 10 are awarded by the judges for each movement and the transitions between them. Scores for especially difficult movements may be multiplied by a coefficient of 2, as are the four "collective" marks for the horse's basic movement and the rider's position and application of aids.

What attracts those who do make the many sacrifices this very demanding discipline requires? As long ago as 1658 one of the first great writers on the subject, William Cavendish, Duke of Newcastle, described dressage as "an exercize that is very noble" and wrote of "the pleasure . . . and satisfaction that attends it." He also had a characteristically sharp answer for those who disparage dressage: "People of that character . . . are good for nothing themselves . . . [and] therefore strive to reduce everything to their own way of thinking, that it may resemble themselves." He goes on to add that if such detractors value only utility, "they must make a hollow tree their house, clothe themselves with fig-leaves, feed upon acorns and drink nothing but water, for nature needs no greater support."

Dressage was already a highly sophisticated art by Newcastle's time; there was already an elaborate, established literature on the subject. How it became so is hard to understand, because there was nothing very sophisticated about riding in the ancient world, and between then and the mid-seventeenth century, our knowledge is mostly speculative.

We know quite a bit about Greek and Roman equitation from the art and artifacts of those eras; we know that the horses were small, the bits and bridles crude (though a number of the basic "modern" forms already existed), and saddles and stirrups lacking altogether. Ancient equitation was thus entirely bareback equitation, with all its concomitant limitations. Even so, Xenophon's *Peri Hippike* from about 380 BC, the earliest work on horsemanship to have survived, can claim to have enunciated most of the fundamental principles that govern the training of the horse, following the teachings of an earlier master, Simon of Athens, whose works are lost. By the time of Xenophon, ridden horses already had raced in the Olympics for a matter of centuries, and these races—still bareback—remained a part of the Olympic agenda until the games were finally suppressed by the first Christian Emperor of Rome, Theodosius I, in AD 394.

Exactly where and when the saddle and stirrups appeared or evolved cannot be stated definitively, but most hypotheses point to the Far East and an introduction into Europe by the eighth century. The Bayeux Tapestry depicting the Norman Conquest of England in 1066 shows some distinctly larger horses and riders using saddles and stir-

rups, and we can gain quite a fair picture of medieval equitation from the paintings, sculpture, and manuscripts of the next few centuries.

By the fourteenth and fifteenth centuries a clear advance in training is noticeable, many horses showing marked collection (submission to the bit) and apparent contentment, despite the traces of cruel training practices that still remain in the first printed book on horsemanship, Federico Grisone's *Gli Ordini di Cavalcare* from 1550. Grisone's emphasis was on coercing (if necessary) a high degree of obedience and on the use of geometrical figures (just as riders still use the figure eight today); he also gave detailed instructions for the so-called airs above the ground. His work has often been compared with the earlier treatise of Xenophon and criticized for its less humane approach, though in truth the two works are hardly comparable at all; Xenophon's work, valuable though it is for the unique picture it provides of equitation in the ancient world, is hardly more than a pamphlet of twenty or thirty pages, while Grisone's is a comprehensive, illustrated work of true book length that discusses advanced equitation and offers much sage advice along with the archaic practices that are always cited by his detractors.

The enlightenment of the late Renaissance and Elizabethan Age brought further refinement and a greater humanitarianism to the precepts of Grisone and a rapid evolution in the art of riding. One of the prime embodiments of this development, the famous Spanish Riding School of Vienna, still exists today, more than four centuries after its establishment, and still uses movements and figures originally developed in the sixteenth and seventeenth centuries, including the breathtaking capriole, courbette, and other classical airs.

The rapid evolution of equitation after 1600 is reflected in a series of extraordinarily beautiful illustrated books on the subject that remain true landmarks in the literature. The first of these was Antoine de Pluvinel's *Le Maneige royale* of 1623, which deals with the equestrian training of King Louis XIII of France. It was followed thirty-five years later by Newcastle's *General System of Horsemanship*, published first in Antwerp during his Cromwellian exile in a French translation, a work still worth reading today. Then in 1733 an admirer of Newcastle's, and an even more influential teacher, François Robichon de la Guérinière, published his monumental *Ecole de Cavalerie*, a work still revered as the equestrian Bible of the Spanish Riding School.

The court, the military cavalry school, and, in the nineteenth century, the equestrian circus became in their turn important factors in the development of the equestrian arts, and the equestrian literature from 1750 to 1900 includes important works from all three sources. Principal among these are perhaps the works of the two French *écuyers*, the great circus rider François Baucher and the chief instructor from the French Cavalry School at Saumur, the Comte d'Aure, and, around

Chris Bartle (Great Britain) is a former point-to-point and event rider turned dressage and, especially, musical freestyle star. Here he rides his World Cup silver-medal partner, Wily Trout.
". . . I expect to go on doing dressage all my life. Dressage is something in which you never reach your goal—even when your horse is going well, there's always something that you want to improve. One horse will be better at some things than another horse, and so as you move from one horse to the next, what was a problem with the first horse is no longer a problem with the second, but it has another problem; so you never do reach that stage of perfection where you feel that you know it all, or your horses know it all. . . . It becomes an exercise of the mind, trying to see into horses' minds and bodies and trying to find an answer to a schooling problem by analyzing it and breaking it down into various compartments."

the turn of the century, those of the great English-born dressage rider James Fillis, the formulator of Russia's Imperial Cavalry Manual. Fillis's books are especially interesting for the numerous photographic illustrations showing such interesting feats as cantering backwards and cantering on three legs!

Today the historic roles played by the Court, the army, and the circus in preserving and developing dressage have largely been eclipsed by civilian riders training for the Olympic Games, an activity that was exclusively military when dressage was first incorporated into the 1912 Olympics at Stockholm. Since the principal cavalry schools of the world did not complete their phase-out of horses until after World War II, and were still very much in business in 1912, Olympic dressage, like the rest of Olympic equestrianism, remained almost entirely a military privilege for half a century, until the Olympic Games at Helsinki in 1952.

Winning gold medals was virtually a Swedish prerogative from 1912 through the 1924 Olympics in Paris, and it was not until the Freiherr von Langen (the only civilian rider in the competition) led his German team to victory at Amsterdam in 1928 that the Swedish monopoly was broken. Four years later, with the world racked by economic depression, the German team declined to compete at Los Angeles and in its absence Saumur's Commandant F. Xavier Lesage and the elegant Taine were the victor over only nine other competitors. Berlin in 1936 was quite a different story, with more than three times as many competitors and the German team reestablishing its supremacy, led by Oberleutnant Heinz Pollay with Kronos. Germany's Major Friedrich Gerhard was the silver medalist ahead of Major Alois Podhajsky of the Spanish Riding School (who was riding a Thoroughbred rather than a Lipizzaner on this occasion).

London's first postwar Olympic revival in 1948 was again strictly a military exercise, Capt. Hans Moser of Switzerland winning the individual title and the French the team gold. It was a different story at Helsinki in 1952, however, and the shape of things to come became clearly evident. The great Swedish officer Maj. Henri St. Cyr won the first of two successive individual titles riding Master Rufus, and led his team to the first of two successive team gold medals, reminding the dressage world of Sweden's impressive record in the sport prior to World War II. The silver medals at both Helsinki and Stockholm in 1956 were won by a lady rider, Denmark's Lis Hartel, reflecting a very significant civilian—and, especially, *female* civilian—incursion into the sport. Hartel's fine performances with Jubilee were even more noteworthy because traces of polio had left her with less than normal strength in her legs, though the handicap was completely obscured by the harmoniousness of her performances.

Helsinki in 1952 was also notable for the reappearance of a Rus-

121

Jenny Loriston-Clark, member of a famous English riding family (her brother and sister also were Olympic riders), with Dutch Courage, bronze medalists in the 1978 World Championships at Goodwood.

sian team for the first time since 1912, still riding very much in the style of that time. The team finished next to last in Helsinki, but moved up to fourth, just out of the medals, at Stockholm. There was no team medal at Rome in 1960, but if there had been, the Soviet team would have won, and there was nothing old-fashioned at all about Sergei Filatov's dazzling winning individual performance with his black stallion, Absent.

Tokyo in 1964 witnessed Germany's return to team domination, though the individual champion was the outstanding Swiss dressage rider, Henri Chammartin, with Woerman, ahead of Germany's Harry Boldt. The German team won again in Mexico in 1968, though the individual gold medal escaped as Russia's Ivan Kisimov nosed out Germany's then-reigning World Champion, Josef Neckermann, and his countryman Reiner Klimke, a former Olympic three-day event rider.

Surprisingly, a Russian team headed by then World Champion Elena Petushkova and Pepel edged past the host nation at Munich in 1972, the margin of victory being only 12 points out of more than 5,000. German pride in its national dressage prowess was restored when the Stockholm bronze medalist, Liselott Linsenhoff and her striking chestnut gelding Piaff, outperformed Petushkova for the gold medal, with Neckermann slipping down a place to the bronze.

Linsenhoff's victory was to prove the first of three successive Olympic wins for a woman rider. In Montreal it was Swiss rider Christine Stückelberger and her giant Granat who prevailed by the thinnest margin in Olympic history, a scant 6 points, over Germany's Harry Boldt and Woycek; and then in Moscow in 1980, in a competition held to only four Eastern teams by the boycott of all of the major Western powers, it was Austria's young Elisabeth Theurer and Mon Chérie who won the gold.

Germany, which had easily won the team title at Montreal and had not competed in Moscow, returned to the fore at Los Angeles in 1984, led by a sensational performance from the Montreal bronze medalist, lawyer Reiner Klimke with Ahlerich. This was the pair that had dethroned Stückelberger and Granat at the 1982 World Championships in Lausanne, and for once what seemed to be a jinx against World Champions failed to fulfill itself. "Ahli" and Klimke were in magical form and, despite a superb performance by Denmark's Anne-Grethe Jensen and Marzog, they could not be denied. (The following year the gold and silver medalists collaborated on several occasions in a beautiful pas de deux, a splendid example of sportsmanlike cooperation by two arch rivals.)

It was hard to imagine anyone taking a second successive World title away from Klimke and Ahlerich at Cedar Valley, Canada, in 1986, but a surprise injury to Ahlerich at Aachen, in the last serious competition prior to the championships, left the door wide open for Marzog

The passage, a highly cadenced, highly elevated trot, as demonstrated by the two leading dressage riders in the world today: Anne-Grethe Jensen and Marzog, shown at the 1986 Cedar Valley (Canada) World Championships, which they won; and Germany's 1984 Olympic champions, Reiner Klimke and Ahlerich, at Copenhagen in 1985.

and his tax-assessor rider, Anne-Grethe Jensen, who had already added the first-ever World Cup dressage title to their laurels earlier in the year. Riding his second horse, Pascal, Klimke managed a highly creditable fourth place behind silver medalist Christine Stückelberger and her new, young horse Gauguin de Lully, and Klimke's teammate Johann Hinnemann with Ideaal. This gave Klimke yet another team gold medal. He has not been a member of every German team, but those he has ridden on have never failed to win the gold medal!

Despite the very ancient origins and traditions of dressage, the technical conditions that govern it continue to evolve, just as with most other equestrian activities, and present-day dressage tests and judging and performance standards are unquestionably much more demanding than those that prevailed at Stockholm in 1912 when the event was first included in the Olympic Games. Today, two different tests are used in the Games and in World Championship competitions: they are the FEI Grand Prix and the Grand Prix Special. The former (which precedes and is the basis for the team competition) is a highly demanding test requiring almost seven minutes to perform, which brings out (as the FEI Rules put it) "the horse's perfect lightness, characterized by the total absence of resistance and the complete development of impulsion. The test includes all the school paces and all the fundamental airs of the Classical High School . . ." These include the collected, extended, and free walk; the collected, medium, and extended trot and canter; the passage (a highly elevated, highly cadenced trot); the piaffe (a collected trot in place); half-passes at the trot and canter (a diagonal movement); pirouettes at the walk and canter; and flying changes of lead every second stride (nine changes) and every stride (fifteen changes). There are thirty-six numbered movements in the test, three of which count double—the extended walk and the two canter pirouettes; and there are four collective marks (for paces, impulsion, submission, and the rider's seat and position) which also count double, making a test worth 430 points. The scale of marks (which is used for all dressage at every level) ranges from 0 to 10 on the following basis:

10	Excellent	4	Insufficient
9	Very good	3	Fairly bad
8	Good	2	Bad
7	Fairly good	1	Very bad
6	Satisfactory	0	Not executed
5	Sufficient		

There are five judges, and all scores count; it usually takes a score of 70 percent or better to win in top-level international competition.

The Grand Prix Special is an equally demanding, highly concentrated test of approximately seven and a half minutes which covers all of the movements and transitions required in the Grand Prix test in a

Gabriella Grillo, German team gold medalist in the 1982 World Championships and one of the leading specialists in the musical freestyle, with Ultimo, her 1976 Olympic mount: ". . . People often say, you should not think of a horse as a human being, or try to make it into a human being. They're absolutely right—a horse is a horse, and the best thing you can do is to leave him what he is and not say, 'It's not enough, I have to make you a human being.' On the other hand, we often use the same words we would use to describe human relationships, for we have nothing else in our language to describe the special kind of relationship we have with horses. . . . There is with horses something that goes from brain to brain or from heart to heart that creates a very special partnership, and for me creating that partnership is the most important thing."

Reiner Klimke and Mehmed celebrate an individual World Championship with a victory canter in front of Christiansborg Palace and the statue of King Christian IX at Copenhagen in 1974. Klimke was to claim a second World title at Lausanne eight years later.

different sequence. Only the top twelve riders from the Grand Prix compete in the Special, with no scores carried forward; the results in the Special alone are the basis for the individual medals.

Dressage judging is almost as difficult an art as dressage riding itself. The FEI has made a major effort to regularize judging—to make it more consistent and more objective—but two judges watching the same test from two different vantage points will not even *see* exactly the same thing, much less score it exactly the same. Considering the range of personal tastes, technical training, and personality traits, it must be acknowledged that great progress has been made in this area. An examination of dressage scores from some of the earlier Olympics suggests that the judges didn't even really start to score the competition until they had placed their own nation's riders at the top—and their nearest rivals at the bottom!

Below the Grand Prix, or highest level, there are also three lower international levels (Prix St. George, and Intermediate I and II, in ascending order), which are an ideal, progressive preparation for the Grand Prix tests. The Prix St. George, for example, requires only five flying changes of lead at the canter every fourth stride, and five changes every third stride; the Intermediate I asks for seven changes every third stride and seven every second; and the Intermediate II requires seven changes every third stride, and nine changes every second stride, along with canter pirouettes and two piaffe movements in which a modest amount of forward movement is permitted. (In the Grand Prix, any forward movement at all is penalized.)

Below the International, or FEI level, every nation involved with the discipline also has its "national" levels, which start at a very elementary stage of training and advance, level by level, until the horse is adequately prepared to cope with the Prix St. George. (In the United States, for example, there are five national tests, starting with Training Level and ending with Fourth Level.)

The kind of training the young dressage prospect gets is nothing if not systematic and methodical. Much depends, of course, upon the quality of the young horse, for the entire focus of Olympic dressage is the development and perfection of the natural movements of the horse. (Dressage purists condemn many of the movements that originated in the circus, such as the Spanish Walk and Spanish Trot with their exaggerated, stiff-legged movement from the shoulder, as entirely *un*-natural.) The good dressage prospect must be, first of all, sound and straight, for the innumerable hours of work that are required to bring a horse to advanced levels are all wasted if the horse ends up lame. Second, superior natural movement and good natural impulsion are a precondition if the horse is to excel competitively, though many horses of more modest attributes have been trained to high levels simply

The most demanding dressage movement for many riders is the collected trot in place, or piaffe. The lowered croup is essential, and the Grand Prix horse should not advance even a single step.

to realize their own potential, and not every horse can be a world-beater. Finally, the horse must have a good (though not necessarily placid or easy) temperament. Even a great horse like Christine Stückelberger's Granat, with his fabulous amplitude of movement, was always something of a problem to prepare for performance, and many dressage critics once questioned whether Klimke's Ahlerich would ever be reliable enough to reach the very highest class.

Dressage horses can be of any size, shape, and breed if they meet the above criteria, but horses of German breeding such as the Hanoverian, Holsteiner, Trakhener, and Rheinlander, the Swedish and Dutch warmbloods, and the French Selle Français have an advantage, having been bred more or less specifically for dressage for many generations. So, of course, have the Lipizzaner ("The Dancing White Horses") and the Andalusians, but these breeds have concentrated so much on collected movements and the airs above the ground that their extended movements tend to lack brilliance. Just the opposite may be said of the Thoroughbred, though there have been notable exceptions such as the huge, California-bred Keen, the leading U.S. dressage horse in the 1970s under Hilda Gurney. In recent years a great deal of Thoroughbred blood has been reintroduced into the Continental breeds, and this has tended to obscure the relatively clean-cut distinctions that used to prevail between different breeds—as will, no doubt, the present trend toward the "genetic engineering" of horses bred specifically for the various equestrian disciplines.

The basic training of the dressage horse is not clearly differentiated in the early stages from the training of other riding horses, except that special pains are taken to preserve the natural purity of the horses' gaits by insisting that the young horse seek the bit "from behind." Dressage emphasizes pushing the horse up to the bit through the use of the rider's legs, instead of attempting to control it primarily through the use of the hands. Pushing the young horse forward into the hands also tends to develop its straightness, which otherwise may not be so natural an inclination. Just like most people, horses are born with a clear right- or left-side preference—they turn more readily in that direction, change leads to that side more easily, and so forth. Gymnastic training for the human athlete aims at developing both sides of the body equally, and so does dressage training for the horse.

Hilda Gurney (USA) and the huge American Thoroughbred, Keen, at the extended trot. They finished fourth in the Olympic Grand Prix at Montreal in 1976 and earned a team bronze medal, a fine achievement for a nation with a relatively brief dressage tradition.

Since adjusting to the rider's weight is a considerable challenge to the young horse, much of the preliminary training is often accomplished with the horse loose, or moving on a longe line around the dismounted trainer. For dismounted work "in hand," the horse is often harnessed with side reins attached to a girth, or surcingle; these substitute for the rider's hands by providing a measure of support. Once the horse has learned to accept a rider, the rider begins very patiently and progressively to develop its natural balance, rhythm, cadence, free forward movement, straightness, and, eventually, its collection. As these qualities develop so will the horse's physical capacity, submissiveness, brilliance, and familiarity with the various required movements as it moves up the scale of competitive tests. Even with an experienced trainer and a gifted pupil, few horses arrive at the Grand Prix level before the age of eight, and it is probably unwise to ask for more than this. Many horses have unquestionably been ruined by being asked to do advanced work before the foundations for it were really firmly established. Many horses, for example, have been spoiled by having a double bridle (which is obligatory at the Grand Prix level) forced upon them before they had truly accepted the snaffle bridle; they have responded by sticking their tongue out or over the bit, or by flexing the neck at the crest instead of higher up at the poll (the point at which the vertebrae are connected to the head, which, in a properly trained horse, should always be the highest point of its neck).

Reiner Klimke (West Germany) and Ahlerich, on their way to victory in the 1984 Olympic Games:
". . . The goal of dressage is to make the horse healthier and more beautiful, just like a dancer or an athlete. If you take a young man and train him as an athlete or a dancer, training will change him completely—he will still be the same person, but he will have better muscles and balance. We try to make the horse healthier, too, and more beautiful, but you cannot bring out more than nature has provided; thus it depends on how talented the horse is. . . . The dressage horse must be intelligent enough and sensitive enough to be able to perform with joy, without pushing and without force; the whole thing must look light. . . . The horse must look happy and also show impulsion and suspension, which both the spectator and the horseman like to see, for from these come brilliance."

Few things are as beautiful as the performance of a perfectly trained dressage horse that (in the words of the FEI Rules) "gives the impression of doing of his own accord what is required of him. Confident and attentive, he submits generously to the control of his rider, remaining absolutely straight in any movement on a straight line, and bending accordingly when moving on curved lines . . . free from the paralysing effects of resistance, the horse obeys willingly and without hesitation, and responds to the various aids calmly and with precision, displaying a natural and harmonious balance both physically and mentally." Performances embodying these qualities have brought audiences to tears and to their feet for a standing ovation, belying the charge that dressage is too arcane and too subtle to develop a large following. It is true, however, that incorporating the freestyle to music has added a new dimension of enjoyment for many viewers—and for competitors too. Indeed, a growing number of those in the dressage community feel that ultimately the silent Grand Prix in dressage should occupy the same position that school figures do in figure skating, and that a freestyle to music should replace the Grand Prix Special, with an aggregate score determining the individual medals.

This thesis is being tested in a new series of FEI competitions based on the winter indoor shows. The World Cup, as it is called, brings the best qualified riders at the end of the season together for a finals, just as in the World Cup competitions in show jumping. The inaugural championship, staged at 's-Hertogenbosch, Holland, in the early spring of 1986, was won by the World Champion-to-be, Anne-Grethe Jensen of Denmark with Marzog. Though not all leading dressage riders made a major effort for the new competition, in general it was greeted enthu-

128

One of the truly great dressage combinations of recent times has been that of the petite Swiss rider Christine Stückelberger and the huge Granat, Olympic champions at Montreal in 1976 and World Champions at Goodwood two years later. Behind their afternoon brilliance and accuracy at the pirouette (facing page, top) and extended canter (bottom) lay hours of morning work in the practice arena under the watchful eye of George Wahl (above), patiently bringing Granat's very considerable enthusiasm under control.

siastically by riders and spectators alike, and it is widely expected to add a new stimulus to the growth of the sport.

Though dressage takes place today in almost fifty different countries, of which twenty-odd are capable of sending teams or individual competitors to Games-standard events, Germany remains for the moment the dominant nation in the sport. It breeds the largest number of horses that are truly suitable for dressage, has the largest cadre of trained coaches and instructors, and enjoys the greatest depth in high-level competitors. It takes only three horses and riders to win the Olympic gold medal, however, and many nations aspire to this goal and are capable of achieving it under the right circumstances. (Russia, Sweden, France, and Switzerland have all done so since World War II, and another four nations have been in medals.) Given the growth of dressage activity in North and South America, on the Continent, and in the British Isles, and the relative ease with which horses, riders, and trainers can be transported anywhere in the world, we are likely to see an international diffusion of dressage strength and influence in years to come.

In any case, one thing is sure: modern dressage has come a long way from being primarily an entertainment for royal courts, an embellishment for equestrian circuses, or a diversion for senior cavalry officers in their declining years. Indeed, dressage, far from being simply a fascinating relic from an earlier era, is today a widely popular, basic equestrian discipline that is more attractive, more challenging, and more valid than ever.

The Three-Day Event

The emergence since World War II of the three-day event as a major public sporting spectacle, participated in by thousands of competitors and literally millions of spectators around the world, is perhaps a curious phenomenon, since the origins of the sport are exclusively military and primarily Olympic. Cavalry officers in peacetime naturally also pursued the sporting activities connected with the horse; they hunted, rode races, competed in show jumping and dressage, and played polo. Of course, they also had their military training and duties to attend to, from parades and reviews to endurance marches and cross-country tactical operations. The first Olympic three-day event in 1912 was created to provide a composite event for officers and their mounts that would encompass a cross section of the challenges they should be prepared to meet, on duty and off, and incidentally to provide a basis for comparison of the breeding and training standards for the cavalries of the world. Its direct lineal antecedents were the French Championnat du Cheval d'Armes (Championship for Military Horses), started in 1902, and an international competition in Brussels under the same rules, inaugurated in 1905.

Though the military connotations have disappeared, the three-day event in its present form retains the principal elements of the original concept. It remains a multiphase test of equine endurance and versatility in which the same horse and rider perform a dressage test of moderate difficulty on the first day; an extremely demanding speed and endurance phase on the second day (including a steeplechase and cross-country jumping course); and a stadium jumping course of moderate difficulty (3 ft 11 in/1.9 m maximum height) on the final day.

The fact that show jumping is included as the final phase might seem to imply some significant similarity between the two different kinds of competition, but in practice this proves to be far from the truth. For one thing, the heart of the three-day event is the second day; the actual theoretical ratio of importance has been established by the FEI at 3 : 12 : 1. For another, eventing is a competition that starts rather sedately and then slowly builds to a climax over a sustained period of time. The typical show-jumping round takes a couple of minutes, and an entire Grand Prix may take only a couple of hours; the winning performance is likely to be measured in seconds. In contrast, it takes three days (or four, if the dressage requires two days, as it often does) for an event to build to its climax, and the aggregate performance time of a given competitor is just under two hours, all by itself!

Just as the three-day event is stretched out in time, so is it spread out in space, and this is one of its great charms. Show jumping takes

Lt. Axel Nordlander of Sweden and the seven-year-old English Thoroughbred mare Lady Artist were the very first Olympic eventing champions, at Stockholm in 1912.

Lt. Charles Pahud de Mortanges of Holland and Marcroix have the unique distinction of having successfully defended the Olympic individual title (1928 and 1932). Mortanges also won team gold medals in 1924 and 1928.

The American all-rounder Lt. Earl Thomson and Jenny Camp pulled off another remarkable double by winning the individual silver medal in both 1932 and 1936. After the war, "Tommy" earned a team gold in dressage at London in 1948.

France's Capt. Bernard Chevallier and Aiglonne won the first postwar Olympic title at Aldershot in 1948. Chevallier later became a show jumper and finally, as General, headed France's Centre Nationale des Sports Equestre.

place in a relatively small ring, often indoors in a metropolitan area; the public usually is isolated from the actual competitive surface, and rarely gets tanbark on its feet or gets to touch a fence. Eventing, on the other hand, must be staged outdoors in an area at least the size of a golf course, and both competitors and spectators share whatever elements nature has provided for the occasion. They also share the footing, for many if not most spectators walk a good part of the cross-country course themselves, often getting a very decent workout in the process. When they pause to watch a particular obstacle, they are not only close to the action, they may even become part of it by helping to catch a loose horse. Eventing is often, among other things, a picnic occasion and a real excursion in the country that is also enjoyable for small children, dogs (on leash, of course), and those who are less than addicted to either sport or horses. To attribute universal appeal to eventing is probably going too far, but the fact remains that forty or fifty thousand people on cross-country day is nothing so extraordinary, and Badminton regularly attracts more than that.

Badminton has, in fact, occupied a significant role in the evolution of eventing from an exclusively military competition to an almost exclusively civilian sport. The owner of this beautiful Gloucestershire estate, the Duke of Beaufort, was also Master of the Horse to King George VI and Master of his own pack of hounds for over half a century. When the Olympic Games of 1948 were held in England, the three-day event was staged at Aldershot, a military base. The Duke of Beaufort, as a spectator, surmised that the sport was one in which the British should excel, and that his own estate might provide a suitable venue. He invited the British Horse Society to conduct an event in 1949 and five years later saw the first European Championship run there and won by a British rider, Maj. Lawrence Rook, riding Starlight. Eventing has flourished both on the Continent and in North America since then, but it is only fair to acknowledge that England remains its spiritual home.

The competition we refer to today as the "three-day event" was originally termed, appropriately enough, The Military. At the Stockholm Olympic Games in 1912, at which it made its first Olympic appearance (as did dressage and show jumping, too), it consisted of five phases run over four days. First came a 34-mile/54.7 km endurance ride, incorporating a 3-mile/4.8 km jumping test, which had to be completed in four hours. After a rest day, there was a steeplechase over ten fences, followed the next day by a fifteen-fence show-jumping course, and then on the final day a ten-minute dressage test. All competitors were officers on active duty and the eventual winner was a Swedish lieutenant, Axel Nordlander, riding Lady Artist. (Indeed, nine successive officers were to win the Olympic individual gold medal between the victory of Nord-

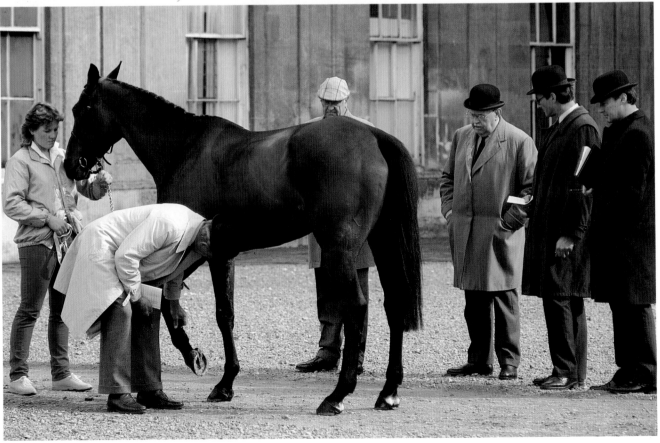

Boldness is a prerequisite in the event horse, who must perform obediently in dressage, and then simply "eat up" the steeplechase (Phase B) on the second day. Jane Starkey, often a British team rider, and Buckley attacked this Burghley fence with appropriate panache in 1986.

Veterinary inspections are fun for the spectators, who can enjoy socializing and studying the different patterns of horses, but for the competitor whose horse may be "just a bit off" they can be harrowing experiences indeed. At Badminton the Queen is not infrequently among the interested observers.

lander and the triumph of his countryman Lt. Petrus Kastenmann, at Stockholm again, in 1956.)

There have been many technical alterations to the event since 1912, but its essential character has remained. The sequence of phases arrived at its present form in 1924 at the Paris Olympics. On that occasion a Dutch officer, Lt. A.D.C. van der Voort van Zijp, ended the Swedish domination of the first two Olympics by leading his team to the gold medal and winning the individual himself. Fourth individually was a fellow officer, Lt. Charles Pahud de Mortanges, who was to achieve unique back-to-back wins at Amsterdam in 1928 and Los Angeles in 1932 riding the same horse, the German-bred gelding Marcroix. Holland also won the team gold in 1928, but in 1932 it was the host nation, led by Lt. Earl Thomson and the wonderful little mare Jenny Camp, that won its first Olympic equestrian gold medal. Thomson and Jenny Camp won the individual silver medal at Los Angeles and repeated the performance at Berlin in 1936 in another remarkable double. Germany's strong team swept the gold medals at Berlin, but were extended to do so. Capt. Ludwig Stubbendorff and Nurmi won the individual gold, and his teammate, Rittmeister Rudolf Lippert, was well placed at sixth, but it was a team of three, and all scores counted. Oberleutnant Konrad Freiherr von Wangenheim broke his collarbone in a cross-country fall, and had yet another fall in the stadium jumping, but remounted to finish the course and save the gold medal for his nation.

The post–World War II era started with another primarily military Olympic three-day event (won by France's Capt. Bernard Chevallier) in 1948. From then on, the trend was increasingly toward civilian participation and then complete domination, despite Capt. Hans von Blixen-Fineke's win with Jubal for Sweden in 1952. A parallel trend was a striking improvement in the quality of horses used in eventing, since most cavalries were limited to relatively modest maximum prices for the remounts they purchased, while civilian horsemen had no such strictures. Queen Elizabeth II of England loaned her horse Countryman III to the British team that won the gold medal at Stockholm in 1956, and all three horses on the team were outstanding individuals, and a striking contrast to the type of horse that had been able to win eventing medals in earlier Games. (The 1956 equestrian Olympics had been divorced from the rest of the summer games in Melbourne because of Australia's extremely restrictive quarantine regulations.)

The Australians had made a major effort to develop a good three-day team in time for their own Olympics, and in fact barely missed winning the bronze medal at Stockholm. Four years later at Rome this solid preparation paid off when the team from "Down Under" won a thrilling and surprising victory in the team scoring, and accounted for the individual gold and silver medals as well. Laurie Morgan and Salad

Virginia Holgate and Night Cap at Badminton in 1985, when they placed third. (She won Burghley that year with Priceless, her 1986 World Champion-to-be.) About eventing today, she says:

". . . Courses today have become much more difficult; you can no longer be twentieth after the dressage and go flat-out on the cross-country and end up first. . . . Now you have to be really good in all three phases in order to get anywhere at all. And because the sport has gone forward, the cross-country course has to go forward as well. . . . In my personal view, fences should be built with a quick route (which is obviously the big, difficult route) and a slow route, which should be very slow. Then everybody has a chance to get 'round, but it's the brave guys that are going to be in front at the end of the day, because they've saved as much as 15 to 25 seconds by taking the faster route. Nobody forces you to take the fast route—it's all your own decision."

Badminton's roads and tracks wind through the beautiful Gloucestershire countryside.

Days won handily over his teammate Neale Lavis with Mirabooka, despite a rather shaky stadium jumping course, but the real key to the team victory was the performance of forty-five-year-old Bill Roycroft and his tiny homebred, Our Solo. Four-man teams had been reintroduced at Rome, with only the best three scores to count, but the fourth Australian rider, Brian Crago, had a lame horse after the cross-country and was unable to start on the last day. Roycroft had finished but had sustained a hard fall and broken his shoulder. In the best Australian tradition he simply discharged himself from the hospital, jumped a clear round, and sealed a gold medal for his country just as von Wangenheim had done twenty-four years earlier. The civilian breakthrough in eventing was complete.

Transportation problems in getting horses to Tokyo in 1964 curtailed participation by one-third as compared with Rome, but the competition at the resort of Karuizawa was nonetheless a stirring one, fewer than forty points separating the first four teams. Mauro Checcoli of Italy with Surbean was the individual gold medalist and led his team to the team gold medal as well, in front of the United States and West Germany. One of the riders on the U.S. team was Lana duPont, the only woman rider to take advantage of the rules change permitting women to ride in the Olympic eventing. (It had taken twelve years longer than the show jumpers had required, despite the outstanding record women eventers had already established in non-Olympic competition.)

Mexico's three-day event in the 1968 Olympics also took place in a resort town away from the principal Olympic site, in this case the new golfing development at Avandaro, in the mountains a couple of hours from Mexico City. Eventers are quite accustomed to coping with the vagaries of weather and footing, but Avandaro's challenge was probably the toughest in the history of the sport: torrential rains before and during the cross-country completely changed the character of the course, turning the meandering little stream around which the course had been built into a raging torrent. By the time the last horses for each team started, rain and flooding made it impossible even to guess at the original contours of some of the obstacles, and one horse actually died by drowning. The weather cleared by the final day, but there was still some bad luck left in the air: a fall on the flat cost U.S. rider Jimmy Wofford and Kilkenny a possible silver individual medal, and taking the wrong course eliminated Pavel Deev of the Soviet Union, denying him a chance for the individual gold and eliminating his team. By the time the wettest Olympic event in history was over, a young French officer, Jean-Jacques Guyon, had won the individual laurels with Pitou, and an outstanding British team had beaten the Americans for the team award. Jane Bullen of England with the diminutive Our Nobby became the first woman eventer to share a team gold.

Great Britain's performance at Munich in 1972 was even more dominating, confirming its team's winning performances in the 1970 World Championship and the 1971 European Championship, and pushing the U.S. team back to second place for the third successive Olympics. Richard Meade of England won the individual gold with Laurieston while his teammate, individual World Champion Mary Gordon-Watson and the great Cornishman V, came fourth, the best individual performance for a woman rider up to that point.

The "bridesmaid" U.S. team finally had their chance at Montreal in 1976 as a freak injury to Lucinda Prior-Palmer's Be Fair at the very end of the cross-country led to the elimination of the British team. Young Edmund (Tad) Coffin and Bally Cor nosed out his team captain, J. Michael Plumb and Better and Better, for the individual gold, and a strong performance by the reigning World Champion, Bruce Davidson and Irish Cap (despite an unlucky fall at the water), clinched the team gold medal by a wide margin over West Germany and Australia. Fifth and sixteenth individually were Wayne Roycroft of Australia and his then sixty-one-year-old father, Bill, the hero of Australia's winning performance at Rome sixteen years earlier!

Four years later the only real winners were confusion and disappointment as only seven teams competed at Moscow in the true Olympic Games while seventeen were represented in the so-called Alternate Olympics staged at Fontainebleau. The host nation's team won as expected in Moscow, with Euro Federico Roman of Italy spiriting the individual gold away from three Soviet riders. In Fontainebleau the young European individual champion from Denmark, Nils Haagensen, who had ridden in Montreal as a dressage rider, piloted Monaco to victory in front of Jim Wofford with Carawich and Torrance Watkins with Poltroon from the United States. France won the team gold medal, thanks to the surprising elimination on the cross-country of the U.S. team captain, Mike Plumb.

Los Angeles in 1984 saw the U.S. return to its winning ways with a spine-tingling victory over Great Britain that went to the very last fence, as New Zealand's Badminton winner Mark Todd recorded the Southern Hemisphere's second individual win with his remarkable little Charisma. Karen Stives from the U.S. with Ben Arthur edged out Britain's Virginia Holgate and Priceless for the silver medal. Within the next four years the latter (now Mrs. Leng) was to win virtually everything in sight, including Badminton, Burghley, and the 1986 World Championship at Gawler, Australia.

Although all Games and major championships require full-scale three-day events, the entire sport has many different levels and many modified forms of competition that permit novice competitors to make a somewhat less taxing beginning and initial preparation in the sport.

Every eventing venue has its own distinct character, and these two, on opposite sides of the world, could hardly be more different: Susan Blane (Great Britain) and Final Edition had Burghley House as a backdrop in 1984, while Karen Stives (USA) and Flying Colors performed against a typically Australian landscape at Gawler during the 1986 World Championships.

The consistently brilliant Richard Meade (shown here on Kilcashel at Luhmühlen in 1982) was a mainstay of the British team for more than twenty years before retiring in 1986. Riding Laurieston in 1972 he won both team and individual gold medals at the Munich Olympics.

One of the soundest cross-country riders in the world, Capt. Mark Phillips of Great Britain (here riding Classic Lines at Badminton in 1983) has won a team World Championship (1970) and four Badmintons. His wife, Princess Anne, need hardly defer, however, having herself won the individual European title at Burghley in 1971.

Six times an Olympic rider and twice a team gold medalist (he was also the individual silver in 1976), Mike Plumb (USA) knows how to survive and how to excel. Here on Blue Stone at Los Angeles in 1984 he displays the perfect technique for jumping into water.

There are also one- and two-day events or horse trials that include jumping and dressage but may curtail the usual endurance aspects of the second day, and these may be set at heights, distances, and speeds appropriate to the experience level of the competitors from Training Level through Preliminary and Intermediate to Advanced (which is suitable for international competitors).

On the international level, the dressage test required on the first day is a standard one devised by the FEI, requiring roughly seven and a half minutes for performance. Though the movements required are only of moderate difficulty (working, medium, and extended gaits; half-passes at the trot; serpentines with counter-canter) and no full collection or even flying changes of lead are required, the standard of performance has become increasingly high. It was once possible to retrieve most or all of a poor dressage performance by "going like a bomb" on the second day, especially during the era in which "bonus points" were awarded for cross-country speed. Currently riders perform against optimum times on cross-country day instead, and it is only very rarely possible to make up for even an average dressage performance subsequently. Indeed, so high has the standard at the top become that major events are not infrequently decided entirely by the dressage scores, the leaders incurring no further penalties at all during the event.

The FEI three-day dressage test involves twenty separate movements worth a maximum of 10 points each, plus four collective marks (for paces, impulsion, submission, and position of the rider), making a 240-point test. As in regular dressage, perfect scores of 10 virtually do not exist, and scores that average out above 70 percent are very good indeed. Three judges mark the dressage test, their scores being added together and then averaged; following this the average mark is subtracted from 240 points in order to convert the score into penalty points and then multiplied by 0.6, to make it consistent with the basis on which the other phases are judged. After the addition of any penalty points for errors of course, the resulting score is then multiplied by a factor of between 0.5 and 1.5 "to enable the dressage scores to exert the appropriate influence on the result of the whole competition," depending on the relative difficulty of the course and conditions for the endurance phase.

The general atmosphere of the dressage day (or days) of a big event is quite consistent with that for a regular dressage competition. Silence (or hushed voices, at worst) is *de rigueur*, aside from the occasional audible collective intake of breath when a conspicuous bobble occurs. And bobbles always *will* occur, given the precondition of horses trained to a level at which they can cope with the demands of the speed and endurance phase, trying to exhibit imperturbable composure in a small ring at slow gaits in front of a lot of people, ridden by someone

who is probably quite uncomfortable in formal dressage attire and very likely somewhat nervous as well. For all of this, the best horses and riders perform very beautifully, and many former three-day riders have ended up excelling in Grand Prix dressage. (In the old days of military domination of equestrian sport, the normal progression for officers was to compete in three-day events as lieutenants and captains, thus obtaining a broad experience with the whole range of different disciplines at an age when their physical powers were at their peak; then go on to do Grand Prix jumping as field grade officers, and finally, to conclude their military and equestrian careers as general officers, performing Grand Prix dressage.)

The endurance phase of the three-day event is designed to test the "speed, endurance and jumping ability of the true cross-country horse when it is well trained and brought to the peak of condition" as well as the rider's knowledge of pace and judgment of his horse's ability and condition. It consists of four separate and independent elements:

Phase A and Phase C
Roads and Tracks, performed at a trot or slow canter (to average 220 meters per minute): from 16,060 meters to 19,800, requiring from 73 to 90 minutes, with 1 penalty point awarded for each second over the optimum time. Phase A takes competitors from the start to the start of Phase B, the steeplechase; Phase C takes competitors from the end of the steeplechase to the start of the cross-country course (Phase D).

Phase B
A steeplechase of nine or ten typical steeplechase fences to be jumped at 690 m/m, thus requiring between 4½ and 5 minutes, with a penalty point for every second over the optimum time.

Phase D
Cross-Country Jumping, a course of up to 7,980 meters performed at a speed of 570 m/m and including 28 to 32 varied obstacles (maximum height 3'11" or 1.20 m), thus requiring 13 to 14 minutes. Penalties are assessed at a rate of 0.4 penalty points for each second over the optimum time.

The roads and tracks phases are simply means of moving horses around, giving them a warm-up and a breather after the steeplechase, as well as (some argue) a certain amount of unnecessary hammering, which is nonetheless implicit in the tradition and original concept of the competition. Phase B is also relatively straightforward, and is observed primarily by grooms, officials, diehard spectators, and members of the family of competitors involved. Top horses routinely obtain the optimum score for the steeplechase and falls are relatively uncommon. Phase D, however, is what makes eventing the thrilling and fascinating sport that attracts spectators by the thousands. The character of the obstacles used has changed substantially through the years, becoming increasingly complex, fanciful, and "technical." Originally many obstacles had a typical cross-country character, though there were always some novelties to demonstrate the course designer's ingenuity.

Once eventing gets into your blood, it's hard to stop! Mauro Checcoli of Italy, the 1964 Olympic champion, was still an active competitor on Spey Cast Boy at Los Angeles in 1984.

Jumping some cross-country fences must often feel like jumping out into space! Diana Clapham (Great Britain) and Jet Set III made this spectacular leap at Badminton in 1984. (She has greased her horse's legs to minimize injury if he should get tangled up somehow.)

These often had some kind of military connotation before World War II, though the greatest prewar novelty was quite natural but very wet: Berlin's notorious pond jump in 1936 at which eighteen horses fell, the American horse Slippery Slim breaking a leg and having to be destroyed. (Some sort of water complex has been part of every serious cross-country course ever since.) Through the 1950s and 1960s the military character diminished and ingenuity increased, inspired by the example of Badminton and Burghley. Still, there were many obstacles of a sort that a brave and clever hunt-staff horse could negotiate at sight with no special training, something that is far less likely today. Modern courses tend to emphasize options—the trade-off being between speed and difficulty, enabling less confident competitors to take a longer, safer way but challenging the "hot-shots" to take the quicker but more demanding route.

Today's international event horse must be more than simply brave, clever, and a good jumper. It must have seen a lot of different varieties of certain kinds of obstacles and worked out several solutions to them, so that when its rider (who has walked the course, but has never been permitted to practice over it or even show a single one of the fences to his or her horse) indicates the chosen solution to *this* new fence, the horse can execute it unhesitatingly. The maximum height of 3 ft 11 in/

For over fifty years, water has figured prominently in most three-day cross-country courses. Burghley's Trout Hatchery is legendary, and more than a few competitors inadvertently bathe there every year, as did French rider Laurent Bousquet with Jaen de Santace during the 1985 European Championships.

144

The Trout Hatchery strikes again!

1.20 m on the cross-country course doesn't sound like much to the average show jumper, but when they see how the fences are constructed and sited, they gain a very healthy respect for them. Big drops, ditches, and banks are commonplace, and even the open water, at 13 ft 1 in/4 m, looms quite large for the tired horse. The construction of cross-country obstacles is part art, part science, part fantasy, and several parts backbreaking work, and those who have excelled at it (such as England's Bill Thomson, Frank Weldon, and Hugh Thomas, America's Neil Ayer and Roger Haller, and Germany's Wolfgang Feld) should be cherished as national treasures.

Each obstacle on the cross-country or steeplechase course is surrounded by a penalty zone 33 yards/30 m in depth, and it is only within this area that faults are scored. Fences are essentially solid in construction (though they can be disassembled in case a horse becomes "hung-up") and thus there are no knockdowns as in show jumping. Refusals or run-outs are penalized at the rate of 20 penalty points for the first occurrence, 40 for the second, and elimination for the third at the same obstacle. Falls, whether of horse, rider, or both, are penalized 60 points, but the second fall on the steeplechase and the third on the cross-country eliminate. (Some feel that this affords the possibility of too many falls in an era in which there is great sensitivity regarding cruelty to animals, but very tight veterinary control and the rising technical standard of competitors have kept serious problems to a minimum.)

The endurance phase is unquestionably stressful and demanding (just as is the primary human endurance competition, the runners' marathon) and in addition to mandatory veterinary checks during the day, there is a full-scale veterinary check of all horses that are expected to compete on the last day. This phase, a jumping test over a moderate kind of show-jumping course, is not to be considered an ordinary jumping competition, the FEI rules tell us; rather, "its sole object is to prove that, on the day after a severe test of endurance, the horses have retained the suppleness, energy and obedience necessary for them to continue in service." This is sometimes easier said than done, and though the scoring of only 5 penalties for a knockdown and 10 for the first disobedience (refusal) seems generous, standings after the second day are often so close that a single rail can make all the difference.

Selecting the three-day prospect is a difficult challenge, since the stellar performer needs so many different and somewhat contradictory qualities.

The first consideration must be soundness (and an apparent predisposition to *stay* sound), since so much work and so many miles will go into training the horse in the various disciplines it must master. Next, the temperament must be at once brave, sensible, resourceful,

145

The 1984 Olympic Champion, Mark Todd (New Zealand), flanked by the silver medalist, Karen Stives (USA), and the bronze, Virginia Holgate (Great Britain). Men and women now compete on even terms in all three Olympic equestrian events.

Mark Todd on his wonderful little Charisma at Badminton in 1984, where they almost won: ". . . Life in eventing can be a lot of fun, but there is a lot of hard work involved as well. I mean, the hours certainly aren't regular. . . . Some mornings you can be up at five and back from an event only at midnight, and usually it's a seven-day-a-week job. The advantages are that you're your own boss and, as with most things, you get out of it what you put in. . . . If you never school the horses, then you can't expect to be successful, but the harder you work at it, the more successful you become and the more enjoyment you get out of it."

and tractable, qualities that rarely come all in one package. Finally, the horse must be an above-average mover (so that avoiding penalties on the steeplechase will be easy, and just covering the distance involved will not be too taxing physically) and have an above-average jumping technique, especially with the front end. (The horse who tends to hang a knee when it gets tired or loses concentration will have far too many good opportunities to do so.) Beyond this, three-day horses come in virtually every shape and size, and may be of almost any breeding, though the courage and "nerve" associated with Thoroughbred blood is obviously very desirable.

Training the three-day horse is a time-consuming process, not only because it takes a long time to lay a solid base of fitness, but because there are so many disciplines to learn for both the mount and the rider. There are four real specialties involved: dressage, steeplechase, cross-country jumping, and show jumping, and each is distinctively different; many riders use different tack—a different saddle and/or bridle—for each one, and each one requires a different seat and length of stirrup as well as a different technical and tactical approach. (It is not unusual for a rider's stirrup length to vary as much as ten holes from the long leg used in dressage to the very short one used for the steeplechase.)

Both the more sophisticated veterinary monitoring of fitness and the adaptation of techniques used by human athletes (especially interval training) have led to a much higher average level of conditioning among three-day horses than was common in the early days of the sport, when it was not unusual, sadly, to see horses in great distress.

One of the major problems the three-day eventer faces is planning a realistic conditioning and competitive schedule for his horses, since pointing to a major full-scale event is much more like training a racehorse for the Grand National or the Derby than preparing the average dressage horse or jumper for an event of similar importance. The event really is very taxing physically, and it is virtually impossible to peak for more than two or three events per year. However, most international competitors try to have two made horses and several younger horses in their string so that they can run something in most of the major events in their sport.

Training cycles are scheduled to peak at the Olympic Games every four years. In the year following the Olympics there is a European Championship; the year after that, also in a four-year cycle, comes the World Championship; in the third year there is another European Championship (or usually, for competitors in the Americas, a Pan American Games); and then another Olympics. Other major competitions are Badminton in the spring and Burghley in the autumn in England; Punchestown in Ireland; Boekelo in Holland; Luhmühlen in Germany; and Lexington, Kentucky, and Chesterland in Unionville,

Pennsylvania, in the United States. Because events are extremely complex logistically and expensive to stage, most major competitions depend heavily upon corporate support to make ends meet, just as the leading competitors are increasingly doing also. (Provided that such subsidies are approved and administered by the appropriate National Federation, the riders' amateur status remains unimpaired.)

There has not yet been a woman victor in the Olympic three-day event (though Karen Stives of the U.S. came breathtakingly close in 1984), but the distaff record in other major championships has been outstanding. Women have won five of the last eight European Championships, including Mary Gordon-Watson's victory with Cornishman V in 1971 at Haras-du-Pin, Princess Anne's triumph with Doublet at Burghley in 1971, Lucinda Prior-Palmer's back-to-back wins at Luhmühlen and Burghley in 1975 and 1977 with Be Fair and George, and most recently, Ginny Holgate's stunning performance with Priceless at Burghley in 1985. The team record has been fully commensurate with these successes.

World Championship results have been almost as impressive. There was a rare Latin individual winner of the very first World Championship at Burghley in 1966 in the person of Argentina's Carlos Moratorio with Chalan, but Virginia Freeman-Jackson was third, behind Richard Meade, and led her Irish team to the team gold. Four years later at Punchestown, Mary Gordon-Watson and Cornishman V earned yet another individual title, sharing in the team gold as well, to bring the event back to Burghley in 1974. There the improving U.S. team nosed out Britain as Bruce Davidson won the individual title with Irish Cap, but it was a young Canadian team that prevailed in the oppressive heat and humidity at Lexington four years later, as Bruce Davidson successfully defended the individual title with Might Tango.

Since then, Britain has not missed a gold medal. At Luhmühlen in 1982 Lucinda Green (as Miss Prior-Palmer had become) led the way on Regal Realm as Britain defeated a record sixteen other nations, while at Gawler, Australia, in 1986 it was Britain's new and brilliant star Virginia Holgate Leng who continued her astonishing run of major titles. Riding Priceless again, Leng finished strongly, with one of the scarce clear rounds in the final phase, to lead her country to the team gold as well. (It might have been quite a different result had not Tinks Pottinger's mount Volunteer, competing for New Zealand, failed the final soundness test, dropping the team to fourth and costing Pottinger a clear run at the individual title; but such is the nature of sport in general, and of eventing in particular.)

With the focus of attention now turning toward the Seoul Olympics in 1988 and the 1990 Stockholm World Championships (where all of the principal FEI championships will be staged together), it is clear

148

Bruce Davidson (USA) and Might Tango press their attack on "Fort Lexington" during Bruce's quest for an unprecedented second successive World Championship at Lexington, Kentucky, in 1978. They prevailed in one of the most grueling contests on record. Davidson earned his second Olympic team gold medal at Los Angeles in 1984.

". . . I don't consider eventing dangerous, any more than I think timber racing or riding in the Grand National is dangerous. If you are a schooled rider and you understand what you're asking yourself to do, and your horse is schooled and understands what you're asking him to do, then the danger element is so greatly diminished that it would probably be much more dangerous to drive into London on any given day. . . . Danger doesn't interest me or intrigue me now, and it certainly never did initially; the level of agreement and understanding the horse and rider achieve is much more interesting to me. If I'd been equally interested in people, I would have been a doctor or done something else, but it's the relationship with horses that captivates me, and so I give my life to them."

Geronimo! Cathy Wedge (Canada) and Abracadabra needed more than magic to retrieve this overly bold jump at Lexington's Head of the Lake in 1978. More conservative tactics elsewhere earned Canada its first World team title.

Perfect stadium-jumping form: Karen Stives (USA) with Ben Arthur, the 1984 Olympic silver medalists. The fences may not look like much after the cross-country, but they do come down, and final-day scores often profoundly affect the final standings. Ben Arthur gave this Los Angeles fence a lot to spare, but an unlucky rap in the triple cost his rider the individual gold medal.

Most riders sit back and "slip" their reins somewhat when jumping into water and then reorganize during the landing stride as Bruce Davidson is doing at Lexington in 1983.

Page 150: Nobody has ever looked more comfortable "going like a bomb" across country than Lucinda Green (formerly Prior-Palmer), seen here at Aldor in 1986. European Champion in 1975 and 1977, World Champion in 1982, and winner of an even half-dozen Badmintons (a record), Green has been less lucky in the Olympics, but this will surely change.

Page 151: Britain's Virginia Holgate Leng, here riding Murphy Himself at Chatsworth in 1985, has an elegant, seemingly effortless style, doing anything on horseback—but just try to keep up with her! The 1984 Olympic bronze medalist, she has since added the European and World titles to her credits and is a serious threat every time she starts.

that the old military sport of eventing was never healthier than it is today. Nor has it ever enjoyed a broader base of support internationally (second only to show jumping), a higher standard of training and of horseflesh, or more enthusiastic support from the general public. No longer a practical test for the military, or even an off-season recreation for the fox hunter, eventing has made it as an important sport in its own right, and its future seems bright.

153

Polo

If there were protocol among the equestrian sports, polo would have to outrank all others. It has been a sport not only of kings and queens, princes and princesses, but also of rajahs and maharajahs, Oriental potentates, the rich and powerful on every continent. Moreover, it is by far the most ancient stick-and-ball game in the world. Although primarily a ball game rather than a contest of equestrian skill, polo would be impossible without well-trained ponies. It is the horse that sets polo apart from all other games, generates its breathtaking speed and spectacular beauty.

An ancestral version of the game is recorded in Chinese and Persian manuscripts and paintings as early as 600 BC as a pastime of royal courts in Asia and Asia Minor. (The word *polo* is of Tibetan origin, *pu-lu* meaning "willow root," which is what the ball is made of.) It was then sport mingled with pageantry, involving numerous richly garbed players (women also had their teams) and hundreds of ponies; but the principle was the same: two mounted teams dispute the possession of a ball and attempt to strike it with a flexible, long-handled mallet through enemy goalposts at the end of a long, grassy playing field.

Completely unknown in the Western world, the game declined in the Orient with the fall of the Moghul Empire, remaining most active in remote regions of the Himalayas. There it was discovered by English planters and cavalry officers of the British Raj during the 1850s. It was an ideal sport for the place and time: there was suitable terrain, plenty of well-trained riders and small, handy Indian ponies, and ample leisure. A modified version was devised to become the pet pastime of British and Indian officers alike, as well as of the Indian nobility, proud to revive their sporting heritage.

The first polo club was founded in 1859 by Indian Army officers in the Kashmir: the Silchar Club. By the end of the century there were 175 clubs throughout the subcontinent.

The first game played on British soil was a match between the 10th Hussars and the 9th Lancer regiment on Hounslow Heath in 1869. Fascinated spectators called it "hockey on horseback"—which, in a way, it was.

In 1875 the Hurlington Club was founded to organize the game and establish standard rules (which have changed considerably since). It was the forerunner of the present governing body, the Hurlingham Polo Association. The Indian Polo Association followed, with rules of its own. Then came others in Argentina (where the game had been introduced by Irish and English settlers), in Australia and New Zealand, South Africa, and various British Empire outposts where cavalry

154

The winning English team of the first Westchester Challenge Cup in 1886: Capt. T. Hone, Capt. John Watson, Capt. Malcolm Little, Capt. R. T. Lawley, and umpire the Hon. C. Lampton.

The American 40-goal "dream team" that successfully defended the Westchester Cup in 1939: Stewart Iglehart, Thomas Hitchcock, Jr., Cecil Smith, and Mike Phipps.

The throw-in. After the teams have lined up in the middle of the field, the umpire bowls the ball down the line and the game begins.

and naval officers were stationed. For many years polo was primarily the recreation of a military elite.

It was a civilian, however, who brought it to the United States: James Gordon Bennett (1841–1918), a wealthy New York newspaper owner and prominent sportsman who lived mostly in France. Already active in racing and yachting, the financier of such adventures as an Arctic expedition and Stanley's search for Livingstone in Africa, he discovered polo in England and was enthralled by it. On one of his returns to New York, in 1876, he brought with him trunkloads of polo mallets and balls for his equestrian friends, to whom he taught the game. They too became instant addicts—a not uncommon reaction. Before long, Bennett and his friends formed the Westchester Polo Club in Newport, Rhode Island, its charter membership drawn from a coterie of sportsminded American aristocrats. Soon there were ten fields on Long Island, and others all along the Eastern seaboard. Harvard College started playing polo in 1885.

In 1886, the Americans felt ready to challenge the British at their own game. The Meadow Brook Team of Westbury, Long Island (whose founders included Thomas Hitchcock, Sr.), represented the United States against the best that Hurlingham could muster for the Westchester Challenge Cup. The first match was played in Newport, thereafter in the country of the winning team, under that country's rules.

England won the first and second. Not until 1909 were the Americans able to wrest the Cup away from them, and it took one of the most famous polo teams in history to do it: the never-beaten "Big Four" composed of the Waterbury brothers (Lawrence and "Monty"), Capt. Harry Payne Whitney, and Devereux Milburn. Meadow Brook's 1921 lineup was awesome: Louis E. Stoddard, twenty-one-year-old Tommy Hitchcock (already a top player, eventually to become a legend), left-handed J. Watson Webb, and Devereux Milburn. The Hurlingham teams also enlisted memorable players: Lt. Col. Tomkinson, Maj. Barrett, Lord Wodehouse (the patron), Maj. Lockett, Lewis L. Lacey (a masterful Canadian-born Argentinian who often played for Britain), the Irishman Capt. Roark. As early as 1900, the game was flourishing in England, with two thousand registered players. Many of the best were killed in World War I, including Capt. Leslie Cheape, perhaps the best of all.

By that time polo was being played in every region of the United States, principally on Long Island, and in Texas and California. Leading West Coast players included several of international class: Eric Pedley, son of a polo-playing English officer; Elmer Boeseke, Jr., a giant of a man and a formidable back. The Texans played a polo all their own, in cowboy attire and Western saddles; it became a popular weekend pastime, almost as popular as rodeo.

The evolution of polo in Argentina was quite different. Though not born there, polo found an ideal homeland in Argentina, with its vast cattle ranches, a breeding industry able to produce an inexhaustible supply of suitable ponies, enormous fortunes, and a population that learned to ride at the same time it learned to walk, if not before, and was temperamentally attracted by speed and danger. Today polo is a leading spectator sport, surpassed only by soccer; it is played by children on backyard lots throughout the land, as well as by the best polo players in the world. The only 40-goal match in history took place at the famed Palermo Stadium, with the Buenos Aires skyline in the background, in 1975; only in Argentina could two teams composed entirely of 10-goal players have been mustered.

In 1922, the Americans founded the United States Polo Association to establish rules (slightly different from the English ones) and players' ratings. This is a system of handicapping that sets a value on individual players in terms of "goals," on a scale ranging from minus 1 (minus 2 in England) to 10. By matching aggregate team totals, or by crediting a lesser-rated team with a goal advantage corresponding to the difference, even matches are ensured. Polo matches also are rated: there are nonrated games; low-goal play between teams rated from 0 to 6; medium-goal from 9 to 16; high-goal from 16 to 20—and up, characterized by expert play, high-quality ponies, excellent grounds, and dazzling speed.

Polo practice on wooden "horses" is part of every polo player's training.

Action after the throw-in is instant and intense. At this point, each player has assumed his assigned position, but there will be much role-switching during the course of the game.

Pages 158–159: Two exceptional polo players vie for the ball during a match at Cirencester Park: Claire Tomlinson, the highest-rated woman player in history and in the world (6 goals); and HRH Prince Charles (4 goals), who may be her sovereign one day but at the moment is simply a sporting adversary.

Among the details that exemplify polo: 1) A polo mallet and ball, and the red flag used to signal goals. 2) The polo pony's braided tail, tied up to avoid becoming entangled with a mallet. 3) In the player's gloved left hand, reins and a whip; in his right, the mallet (even if the player is left-handed).

Players' ratings are adjusted every year by a special committee. High-goal ratings (5 or over) are not awarded lightly; there have been only twenty-seven 10-goal American players in history, fewer than fifty in the world. (Some players say there should be an honorary 12-goal rating for superplayers Tommy Hitchcock and Juan Carlos Harriott, Jr., captain of the Coronel Suarez team of Argentina.)

The 1920s and 1930s were the Golden Age of polo. International matches attracted enormous crowds of socialites, royalty, elegant beauties, and ordinary polo fans. Some wonderful players were active then, many bearing names of famous sporting dynasties: Devereux Milburn (a top player since 1909, captain of many U.S. teams), Philadelphia department-store heir Robert E. Strawbridge (who often managed the team horses), Louis Stoddard, J. Watson Webb, Roddy Wanamaker, Laddy Sanford of carpet millions, Raymond Belmont, Averell Harriman, J. Cheever Cowdin, "Sonny" Whitney.

In 1928, a challenge cup between North and South American teams was inaugurated: the Cup of the Americas. By then the Argentinians had achieved a supremacy in players and ponies that they have maintained ever since. When polo was first featured in the Olympic Games in Paris, 1924, the Argentine team won—as it did again in Berlin in 1936. Unaffected by World War II, Argentine polo increased in depth and strength, while the game was totally suspended elsewhere.

It might have disappeared forever from Great Britain without the magnanimous efforts of Lord Cowdray, who revived the Hurlingham Association, imported Argentine ponies, and provided fields on his splendid estate at Cowdray Park in the early 1950s. A fine player before the war, he'd lost an arm at Dunkirk, but had a wooden one made that permitted him to play (and play well) into his seventies. He was a great friend of another ardent polo player, Lord Mountbatten (who wrote the classic polo textbook under the name of "Marco"). Uncle and mentor of Prince Philip, Mountbatten indoctrinated his nephew in the game and the Prince did the same for his son Prince Charles. The royal interest undoubtedly did much to spur the postwar development of polo not only in England, but also abroad.

Its revival in America was spearheaded by the polo-playing scions of aristocratic sporting families: the Guests, Phippses, Whitneys, Gerrys, Harrimans, Igleharts, and Bostwicks—who were soon joined by the growing group of postwar millionaires: real estate developers, movie moguls, movie stars, and financial speculators.

Paul Butler, a Chicago paper manufacturer with a passion for equestrian sports, offered a new home to the U.S. Polo Association at a model polo establishment in Oak Brook, Illinois, which thus became the polo capital of the United States for several decades. (Since 1986, it has been located in the Kentucky Horse Park, Lexington.) Robert Uihlein created another polo complex in Milwaukee, Wisconsin.

Polo was reestablished in California, especially in Santa Barbara, thanks to enthusiasts like Aiden Roark and Australian-born Bob Skene (a 10-goal player for nine years). New clubs were founded in Texas, where top teams were formed as well as top players, including ex-cowboy Cecil Smith, a cool-headed strategist with classic strokes and perfect understanding of his ponies; his record of twenty-five years as a 10-goaler is unlikely ever to be equaled.

Under the leadership of Bill Ylvisaker, an all-round horseman and top player (7 goals), Chairman of the USPA from 1970 to 1975, many projects were undertaken to promote polo on every level. The U.S. Polo Training Foundation, for example, was set up to develop young players in clubs and colleges throughout the country, now that the mechanized cavalry no longer filled that role. In 1976, already seeing the way the wind was blowing in the world of sport, Ylvisaker offered the first money prize at Oak Brook. Always an innovator (he made a fortune in electronics), he built an extraordinary complex in the late 1970s in Florida: the Palm Beach Polo and Country Club, with a schedule of polo and other equestrian events all year round. Along with similar establishments at Lake Worth (the Gulfstream, sponsored by Philip Iglehart and polo-playing associates) and in Boca Raton (founded by John Oxley), it consecrated Florida as the polo Mecca during the winter.

The Texans, never to be outdone, also built new clubs capable of fielding and attracting high-goal teams: Retama in San Antonio and Willow Bend in Dallas. On the East Coast, Peter Brant, a young publishing tycoon and polo addict, created a polo club complete with residential development in Greenwich, Connecticut, and another in partnership with Thoroughbred owner-breeder Will Farish in Saratoga, New York.

In 1983—at last!—an International Polo Federation was founded, with headquarters in Buenos Aires. Because of the political situation after the Falklands War, the British Hurlingham Association is not yet represented, nor is South Africa for other political reasons, so it may be some time before it achieves its goals of standardizing polo rules and regulations throughout the world and integrating ratings. But scheduled for April 1987 is the first Polo World Cup, similar in concept to that of football: a year-long series of worldwide elimination matches, culminating in a final playoff. Also on the agenda is a project to reintegrate polo as an Olympic feature.

Twice revived, the game of polo is more widely supported than ever before. Since 1980, membership in the USPA has increased by 40 percent, with similar expansion elsewhere. There are over seven hundred active polo clubs in sixty-seven different countries. The official number of registered players (600 in England, 100 in France, 2,500 in the United States, 6,000 in Argentina, more or less) does not take into account the many others who regularly enjoy informal games

Gonzalo Pieres, 10-goal Argentinian player:
". . . To be 10 goals is a lot of pressure. But you need the pressure to keep you there. . . . The secret of maintaining your handicap is to maintain the level of your horses, and it's very difficult to make a living from polo if you don't sell them. That means you spend most of your time looking for horses to replace the ones you've sold. . . . It's different every time you play a different horse, you know. You've got to adjust to the horse in the first minute of the chukker. Even the same horse moves differently on different grounds. I think the best ability I have is that I can play on any horse."

Alfonso Pieres, Gonzalo's younger brother, also a 10-goaler:

". . . The main reason I play polo is because I love horses. The horse is more important than the sport itself. I think it's more or less the same in other horse sports. The love for the horse, the way you feel in touch, is a big part of it. . . . I'd be lying if I said I don't forget about the horse at some point of the game. When you compete as seriously as we're doing now, all over the world, I think that to be a good polo player you have to forget about the horse for the seven minutes you are on it, otherwise you do not have a chance. But you stay along with the sport probably more because of the horses than because of the sport."

on weekends, after work, or after school. Polo's aura of elitism persists, although an increasing number of men, women, and children have discovered that one doesn't have to be a millionaire to enjoy this wonderful game. Polo is far more democratic than is generally believed.

While private patronage is still indispensable, polo, like many other sporting activities, relies increasingly on commercial sponsorship of teams and events—without, however, tarnishing its exclusive image. Its sponsors—champagne makers, international jewelers, automobile manufacturers—wish to share the image of luxury that has always been associated with polo.

While the game of polo is not difficult to describe, it is rather more complicated to follow, if only because of the speed of play on such a vast terrain and the many rules concerning fouls and penalties.

A polo field is 300 yards/274 m long and 200 yards/183 m wide. At midpoint of each end of the field there are goalposts 24 ft/7.3 m apart. Two teams, composed of four players each, confront each other in the middle of the field. (Arena polo, or indoor polo, is similar but played on a smaller surface with a leather-covered inflated ball and three players to a team.) The referee bowls (underhand) a 4-ounce/113 g white willow root or plastic ball 3¼ inches/18.2 cm in diameter onto the line between the teams, and the game begins. And what a thrilling, spectacular game!

It is divided into periods, called "chukkers," of seven and a half minutes, with three-minute intervals between them and a five-minute interval at halftime, during which the spectators take over the field to stamp down the divots. High-goal matches generally consist of six chukkers (eight in Argentina), others four or less. A goal is scored when the ball passes through the enemy goalposts or between their vertical extension, as judged by a "flag man" posted behind each goal. The game is also supervised by one or two striped-shirted, mounted umpires on the field and a referee in the stands. After a goal is scored, the teams line up again in the middle of the field, changing ends (as they also do at halftime). A new ball is thrown in and play resumes. If the score is tied at the end of the last period, there is a five-minute rest period and then a "sudden death" chukker, the first team to score winning the match.

The players carry mallets of varying length (usually 49 to 53 inches/124 to 134 cm), weight, and flexibility, made from bamboo cane with a wrist loop and a cigar-shaped hardwood head, often custom-built to suit their owners' needs and taste. The mallet is carried in the player's right hand, even if he is left-handed. The head is always set on at an angle of 77.5 degrees, to lie flat on the ground when the ball is struck. It is struck, incidentally, not by the point, as in croquet, but by the side of the head. An extraordinarily good striker can drive the ball

163

There's no time out when a polo pony is tired or injured. During the President's Cup, 8-goaler Armando Gonzales switches to another from his string as quickly as possible in order to resume his position on the field.

150 yards/137 m. A player may own twenty different mallets, selecting one or another according to the size of his pony and to the position he is playing. Each player wears white breeches, brown boots with dull spurs, kneeguards, a protective helmet with a chin strap (and sometimes a mask), and a team jersey bearing the number of his position.

Numbers 1 and 2 are primarily offensive, 1 being the goal-hitter and 2 the set-up man. Number 3 is the strategist (often the captain and best player) who supports and feeds the ball to 1 and 2. Number 4 is the back, primarily defensive, often the biggest, strongest player with the biggest, strongest pony and the longest reach. (Two famous American backs, powerful Winston Guest and intrepid Elmer Boeseke, Jr., measured a towering 6 ft 4 in/1.93 m.) In actual practice, there is much exchanging of roles as play proceeds. The captain calls the shots. "Leave it!" is an inviolable command. But experienced teammates seem to coordinate their moves by intuition. The great Meadow Brook team of the 1930s was renowned for its uncanny teamwork.

Each player "marks" or guards an opponent. Number 1 marks the opposing back, number 2 the opposing 3, number 3 the opposing 2, the back the opposing 1. But during play there are lightning-fast shifts between offensive and defensive moves, as the ball is advanced by drives and passes—often intercepted, blocked, or deflected.

If the ball is struck over the sideline or boards, the teams line up as at the start, 5 yards/4.6 m from the point where the ball went out of play. If the ball is hit over the backline, the defending side hits it in from the point where the ball crossed the line, with the attacking side at least 30 yards/27 m away, the defenders wherever they like. Many rules concern the players' right of way in every situation. Infringement of these and the committing of other fouls incur immediate sanctions ranging from a free shot from midfield to a free goal for the opponents.

There are eight basic polo shots: near shots (from the pony's left side) forward, backward, and diagonally; off shots (the same on the pony's right side); under the pony's neck at right angles to its body; under its tail. One of the most beautiful sights is the penalty shot, when the player gallops to the ball and with a mighty swing hits it (ideally) through the goalposts in a high, soaring arc.

Defensive tactics include hooking an opponent's mallet with one's own—but only from the same side as the ball, directly in front or behind; "cross-hooking" over or under an opponent's pony is a serious foul. Tommy Hitchcock was a master of the "hook and hit" play, turning a defensive move into an offensive one in a fraction of a second. Bumping and riding-off, when two ponies gallop side by side at breakneck speed to gain or block a shot, are also spectacular, reaching speeds of 40 miles an hour/64 kph. Need it be added that polo is a perilous sport? Concussions, broken bones, and falls are commonplace. Ponies, protected only by leg bandages or boots, are also some-

165

The pony lines during a match at the Guards Polo Club in Windsor. Each player needs several reserve ponies in order to change his mount after every chukker, and may play as many as six or seven ponies in an important high-goal match.

times injured by mallets, in falls and ride-offs, and they are prone to tendon trouble because of the strain imposed by so many quick stops and turns.

As in most sophisticated games, there is quite a difference between elementary club play and polo at the international level. While the first kind may indeed seem like "hockey on horseback" to the novice spectator, high-goal polo is more like highly accelerated "chess on horseback," cerebral as well as athletic.

The polo player has frequently been pictured as a prototype of the handsome, rich playboy, a carefree devil surrounded by beautiful women, leading a luxurious life. Postwar polo personalities like Prince Aly Khan, Porfirio Rubirosa, Claude Terrail (owner of the Tour d'Argent restaurant in Paris), Elie de Rothschild (of the banking clan), and theatrical producer Michael Butler did nothing to dispel the myth. But the fact is that no idle playboy would survive for long or get very far in so demanding and sometimes ruthless a game.

A good polo player has to be a fine athlete and very fit. Mastering even the rudiments of the game requires hours of practice and expert training, starting out on a wooden horse in a "polo pit" or on a bicycle, continuing with stick-and-ball work, gradually progressing to actual play in practice chukkers, attending player schools and clinics. It takes at least five years and lots of money to become proficient. Even the best players continue to strive to improve their strokes as long as they play (which may be into their seventies, as with Dr. William Linfoot). The more experienced also train their own ponies, a job that takes about five hundred hours. Hardly a life of idleness!

Are there special aptitudes and qualities that make a good polo player? Yes, indeed, and there are many of them, mental and moral as well as physical. Money, as always, helps. But it is by no means the most vital. He (or she) must be disdainful of pain and brave to the point of fearlessness without becoming reckless. Rapid mental and physical reflexes and concentration are essential, as is "ball sense." Good polo players are often also good at other ball games like tennis, squash, and golf. Endurance may be more important than sheer strength, though both are desirable. As in all ball games, timing rather than force is the key to those long drives. Balance, anticipation, hand-eye coordination, suppleness, a sense of team play and strategy are among the attributes of a good player. One should perhaps add a good dose of aggressiveness, as polo is an intensely competitive game. Will Rogers, the beloved American humorist, a polo player himself, once remarked, "Polo is called a gentleman's sport for the same reason that a tall man is called Shorty."

What about equestrian skill? Of course, a certain degree of riding

Tommy Wayman, leading American polo pony breeder and 9-goal (formerly 10) player:
". . . Whenever you're going to play against a team, you hopefully get to watch it play. First of all, you concentrate on their horses so you'll pick your strong horses against their strong ones and your weak ones against their weak ones. If they have a weak player, you create plays involving that player. If you see a player having problems getting a horse to the right, you put all the balls to the right because he can't get there as quickly. When you play against Gonzalo Pieres, he's mounted so well that you try to keep the ball away from him. You've got to watch the competition all the time. . . . But there's no room for feuds, because one week you may be playing against someone, and the next week playing with him."

Is this player whispering endearments in his pony's ear, or thanking him for a fine chukker? Polo players attribute 75 percent of their success to the quality of their mounts.

Page 168: The basic polo shot, the offside forehand drive, is executed in masterful style by Jesús "Chuy" Baez during a Gold Cup match at Cowdray Park. A really big hitter can send the ball from one end to the other of the 300-yard-long field in two hard drives!

Page 169: Polo on the frozen lake in St. Moritz is a novel attraction of the chic Swiss resort. But the serious polo season moves south during the winter to Florida, South America, the Caribbean, and other warm climes.

ability is necessary, but it could not be more different from that of a dressage rider, for example. During a match, the polo player's seat is out of the saddle as often as in it; he stands in the stirrups to drive the ball. His upper body must be able to act independently of the lower part. While he communicates with the horse through his legs, his hands must remain light in the horse's mouth, or his pony will suffer. A "soft mouth" is one of the most desirable characteristics of a polo pony—and Argentinian trainers are famous for developing this. There is, in fact, greater equestrian skill involved in training than in playing. A polo player on a well-trained, experienced pony is more concerned with strategy and mallet technique than with equestrian arts.

Today it is a full-time job to achieve a player rating of 6 or 7 goals and over. Consequently, many of the world's leading players are professionals, many of them Mexicans and Argentinians, members of cattle- and horse-raising, polo-playing families. The best of all, according to his peers, is Gonzalo Pieres, whose huge Argentine clan includes some sixty polo players. The family owns its own polo club, La Espadana, winner of the 1984 and 1985 Argentine Open Championship. His compatriot Ernesto Trotz, an aggressive, intrepid player famous for long, powerful drives, is another of the world's best and has played on many leading teams. Guillermo "Memo" Gracida, a cool-headed master with classic style, and his younger brother Carlos are recent American citizens, sons of the legendary Mexican polo master "Memo," Sr., who ships well-trained ponies all over the world from his ranch. These four are the only players accorded a 10-goal rating by the USPA in 1985 (although there are others in Argentina).

Close on their heels with a rating of 9 are six more Argentinians, including Gonzalo Pieres's brother Alfonso and ex-10-goaler Gonzalo Tanoira, the top English player Howard Hipwood (a hard-hitting back whose brother Julian is rated 8), and a lone American, Tommy Wayman (once a 10-goaler, also a leading breeder and trainer at his ranches in Kansas and Texas and at his father-in-law's Argentine *estancia*).

The best players in France are the Macaire brothers, Lionel (7 goals) and Stéphane (6), whose grandfather is generally credited with launching postwar polo in Paris, Deauville, and Vichy. After a dazzling decade or two, the French political and economic climate became less suitable for so plutocratic a sport, and the Macaires play more often for foreign team patrons in England and America than in their native land.

Since the 1982 Falklands War barred Argentine players from Great Britain, the best English stars are in great demand to form high-goal teams: following the Hipwood brothers there are Alan Kent (7 goals), Paul Withers (mainstay of the Cowdray Park team), Patrick Churchward, Charles Beresford, John Horswell, and Robert Graham. They are often joined by Commonwealth nationals, such as New Zealander

167

Stuart MacKenzie (8 goals) and Podger el Effendi (8) and his brother Wicki (7), Pakistanis of Afghan origin whose later father was a polo-playing officer in the Pakistan army, their mother Australian.

While the present generation of the Argentine dynasties that brought such verve and panache to British polo is for the moment absent, it is prominent on the American scene: Carlos "Charlie" Menditeguy (another legend, who often used to play on British teams); the young twin brothers Gonzalo and Horatio Heguy (sons of the all-time great 10-goaler Alberto, who was a member of the famous 40-goal Coronel Suarez team); and, until he died in 1986, Edouardo Moore (a great player-trainer too)—in addition to the super 10-goalers.

The United States could boast of none in that supreme category in the mid-1980s, although there were several on the brink: Owen Rinehart (already rated 9 in England, an excellent, orthodox player with an amazingly accurate eye), "Red" Armour III (high-rated for many years, a great team player with uncanny ball sense); Harold "Joe" Barry (long, hard-hitting member of an illustrious Texas polo clan); Bart Evans (who also breeds and trains top ponies on his Texas ranch); and Californian professionals Rob and Bill Walton.

Polo talent exists in every land where the game is played, with non-rated and low-goal players constituting the broad base of the sport, and women increasingly active. Ratings are, incidentally, variable from year to year, from country to country, from indoor to outdoor polo. For example, Winston Guest was rated 10 goals indoors when he was 9 goals outdoors; Lord Mountbatten, whose naval career led him to polo fields as well as ports around the globe, used to have a 5-goal rating in England, 8 in Malta, 9 in Jamaica.

Immutable, however, are the records of great players of the past revered by succeeding generations. Among them: Foxhall Keene (America's top player from 1891 to 1920); the incomparable Tommy Hitchcock; Stewart Iglehart (a marvelous athlete who also excelled in ice hockey); Cecil Smith (a 10-goal player for a record twenty-five consecutive years); Harry Payne Whitney (one of modern polo's pioneers, a splendid organizer); Louis Stoddard (who could play any position, but most often number 1); Malcolm Stevenson (a leading 10-goaler of the 1930s); Devereux Milburn (when asked to select an ideal polo team, Tommy Hitchcock replied, "Milburn, Milburn, Milburn, Milburn"); Alfredo and Juan Carlos Harriott (the latter considered the finest stylist of all time, playing with power but also infinite finesse); his Argentine compatriots Manuel Andrada and Roberto Cavanagh; and Rao Rajah Hanut Singh (clever, small, and lithe, the son of an Indian officer, he held a 9-goal rating from 1910 to 1939 and was the immensely popular star number 1 of the Jodhpur team of that memorable era).

At Sotogrande on the southern coast of Spain, Ignacio "Nacho" Domecq, scion of an eminent Spanish yachting and equestrian dynasty, currently the highest ranking polo player in Spain, can sail in the morning and play polo in the afternoon.

Preceding pages: During the finals of the World Cup at Palm Beach in 1986, Gonzalo Pieres (in black) seems set for an easy tap-in, but somehow Memo Gracida has contrived to put a goalpost in his way. Luckily, goalpost construction is planned with this kind of spirited action in mind.

Polo teams of all levels are organized by polo and hunt clubs, schools and colleges, by army regiments where mounted cavalry still exists. But international high-goal polo is supported chiefly by a few well-established or richly endowed clubs, increasingly the enterprise of commercial sponsors and private patrons.

The latter is often an addicted amateur player. He underwrites and organizes a team, which can vary in composition from one season to another, even from match to match, but it usually includes himself along with several contracted professionals. His motivation and reward? The ineffable thrill of playing high-goal polo. He pays all of the expenses (which can amount to $1 million a year), provides equipment, stabling, staff, transportation, and ponies—as many as sixty (although many professional players prefer to use their own).

The prestige and thrill of "owning" a polo team has attracted an international coterie of wealthy sportsmen: the Maharajah of Jaipur, a 9-goal player who died on the polo field in 1970; Brazilian shipping and mining magnate Renaldo de Lima; Guy Wildenstein, a French art dealer and racing man, for whose Diables Bleus team Prince Charles (4 goals) often played as back before joining Geoffrey Kent's Windsor Park team in 1987; and Anthony Embiricos, heir to a Greek shipping fortune. Egyptian Alex Ebeid is patron of and a player on the Falcon

During the 1986 World Cup, Bill Ylvisaker is making a heroic effort to interfere with Memo Gracida's offside backhand shot.

team, which has won the Gold Cup at Bagatelle in Paris five times; Usman Dantata, a Nigerian entrepreneur, is patron of the Chasqui team; Canadian Galen Weston plays and pays for the Maple Leaf team, of which Julian Hipwood is a regular member.

Henry de Kwiatkowski, a refugee Polish aristocrat and war hero, made a fortune in the aviation business and enviable success as a racehorse owner (Horse of the Year Conquistador Cielo was his, as well as 1986 Belmont Cup winner Danzig Connection), before succumbing to the spell of polo. His Kennelot team (named after his first racing filly), based in Florida, soon became one of America's best. Peter Brant is another newcomer to make a maximum impression in minimum time. A 5-goal player and an astute entrepreneur, already successful in racing as owner of Kentucky Derby winner Swale, his White Birch team, based in Greenwich, Connecticut, starring Gonzalo Pieres, almost at once became "the team to beat" in major American polo events.

Norman Brinker, a philanthropic restaurant chain owner and former Olympic rider, founded the Willow Bend polo complex and team in 1972 near Dallas, Texas. Texas oilman Steve Gose (a 3-goal player with a 4-goal son, Tom) established the Retama Polo Center and team in San Antonio, the largest polo facility in the world, scene of the 1985 U.S. Open Championship. Bill Ylvisaker, whose role in developing American polo is inestimable, is also patron of the Piaget team, to which he lends his expertise and sometimes his presence. John Oxley's Boca Raton team has won ten out of twenty-three America Cup championships, with father and son in the lineup.

A very special patron is the Sultan of Brunei, who has a passion for polo and an immense fortune. On the grounds of his sumptuous palace in northeast Borneo, he organizes private polo matches with his superb ponies and leading players, for his own enjoyment. Who could refuse an invitation from such a lavish host?

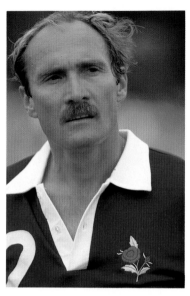

Julian Hipwood, the top-rated (9-goal) polo player in England: ". . . The important thing in polo or in any other ball game is that the ball does the work. You can't move as fast as the ball, so one player hits it to another. The horses are very important, and the higher the polo, the more important they are. Because we all hit the ball equally well, it's whoever gets to it, gets away with it, and can do something with it that counts. If you don't get to the ball, you can't hit it, so you need a good horse. But there are very few of them around. I'm always looking for horses."

Players and patrons are, of course, essential. But according to Tommy Hitchcock and most other experts the contribution of the polo pony is 75 percent of the game. In fact, a top player with a mediocre string soon sees his rating drop, while a lesser player finds his game miraculously improved when he acquires a superior pony.

High-goal matches need a lot of ponies, as many as six per player. A year-round professional has at least twelve from which to choose, and it is not unusual for top teams to keep twenty-six on the string during the season. Since they gallop at up to 40 miles per hour/64 kph practically nonstop during each chukker, one pony can play no more than two chukkers during a high-goal match, with a rest period of at least two chukkers in between, and they play no more than three times a week.

An important part of polo strategy is knowing the qualities of the opponents' ponies as well as of one's own, saving the best for the "fatal fourth" and "crucial sixth" chukkers. Different positions also require slightly different qualities: speed is all-important for the offensive number 1 position; handiness and boldness for strategic 2 and 3; substance as well as speed for number 4. Those who know them best maintain that good polo ponies are without a doubt the finest equine athletes of all.

During the early years of polo, all sorts of ponies were used: small native breeds of England, Ireland, New Zealand, and Australia; Arabians, Indian ponies, American Quarter Horses, and the Argentine Criollo pony. Then the Americans began to use small Thoroughbreds. In 1912, they abolished the 14.2-hand height limit. Now polo ponies are not ponies at all but small horses, generally 15.2 hands and under, most of them Thoroughbred or Thoroughbred cross. Even the Criollo, descended from seventeenth-century Spanish imports, has become seven-eighths Thoroughbred due to Thoroughbred crosses and subsequent selective breeding.

Many breeds and crossbreeds make useful mounts for club play, but in high-goal circles the Thoroughbred or near-Thoroughbred Argentine pony reigns supreme. Outside Argentina, high-quality polo ponies are bred also at important farms in Mexico, North and South America, Australia, and New Zealand.

An experienced professional may ride a pony as young as three or four years during a single chukker, because of its speed. But most ponies are five or six years old in high-goal play; the average in club play is closer to twelve, their prime being from seven to twelve.

Do ponies understand the game? Do they enjoy it? Many seem to, despite the effort and stress involved. A curious incident occurred during a polo game in Hong Kong in 1922, when Lord Mountbatten was playing number 1 position. His number 3 hit a long, low ball that struck his borrowed Chinese pony underneath the tail. The pony clamped his tail down and galloped through the goalposts, where he stopped, raised his tail, and dropped the ball to the ground. Was it an instinctive response? Was it a goal? Many players claim that an experienced pony will try to place the player in striking position without rider guidance; most of them learn that the purpose of an all-out gallop down the field is to be the first to reach the ball. What a pity that they cannot, however game-wise, be expected to appreciate the award to the Most Valuable Pony that is made after the match!

Perennial 10-goal Argentinian star Juan Carlos Harriott, renowned for his power, style, and finesse, and long considered by his peers to be the finest polo player in the world.

The polo season now lasts all year 'round. Florida, Texas, and California in the winter, England in the spring, Deauville in August, Argentina in the autumn and early winter, Australia and New Zealand in between. This is the high-goal circuit. Club play, intercollegiate and interregimental matches are an uninterrupted activity, moving indoors for arena polo when outdoor play is impossible. Polo matches at all levels are played regularly in most Central and South American countries, throughout Asia, Africa, and the Caribbean. Wherever British cavalry and naval forces have been stationed, a polo tradition survives.

There are polo clubs in most European nations, principally in France, Spain, Italy, and Germany. In England, the Queen's Cup launches the season in the spring at the Guards Polo Club in the park of Windsor Castle, where later the Coronation Cup (founded in 1911 to commemorate King George V's accession to the throne) and the Silver Jubilee Cup (a tribute to his granddaughter, the present Queen) are held. The Warwickshire Cup match is played at Lord Bathurst's Cirencester Park estate near London; the Cowdray Park Gold Cup (the British Open), on the field in front of Lord Cowdray's magnificent ruined feudal castle.

The United States Open Championship changes venue each year on a rotation basis. The pinnacle event is the World Cup at the Palm Beach Polo and Country Club. The most recent four-star match is America's Polo Championship, inaugurated at the Greenwich Polo Club in the summer of 1986, with the highest rated match seen in many years, between a 39-goal Argentinian team and a 38-goal American foursome. But polo has expanded so much in America in recent years and so many new events have been created, that it is impossible to enumerate them all.

The same can be said of Argentina, where the polo calendar is more crowded than any other. The Argentine Open, played on the hallowed grounds of Palermo in Buenos Aires, is the virtual world championship, attended by crowds of forty or fifty thousand knowledgeable spectators, televised throughout the country.

In Australia and New Zealand, too, polo players lead busy lives, with numerous matches at every level, including a number of important high-goal events.

The most picturesque polo rendezvous is certainly St. Moritz in Switzerland for the Polo World Cup between Europe and South America, played on the frozen lake with a smaller field, an inflated orange ball, and studded shoes to prevent the ponies from slipping.

Largely due to the excellence of the Argentinians, most high-goal teams today are international formations. Nationalism, which was once the rule, survives only theoretically in three historic challenge cups: the Westchester Cup between Great Britain and the United States, contested eleven times between 1886 and 1939, was the occasion of polo at its finest, it is said. The Cup of the Americas, between the United States and Argentina, founded in 1928, was revived in 1980 but has not been challenged since. An attempt to revive the General Manuel Avila Camacho Cup, a traditional contest between the United States and

During the 1986 World Cup, Hector "Juni" Crotto, a 9-goal Argentinian player, displays the style that has made the high-goal Argentinian polo player a most desirable teammate.

Two high-goal players,
"Chuy" Baez and
Carlos Gracida, in action
during the Warwickshire Cup
match at Cirencester, England.

Mexico, named after a former Mexican president and ardent polo sup-porter, came to naught in 1986.

The dazzling play of international high-goal polo may bear only slight resemblance to Saturday afternoon matches at the local hunt club, or "country polo" on ranches, pampas, and open fields. But the same passion is evident at every level. Moreover, those who attend a polo match for the first time should beware: for spectators as well as players, it can become addictive.

Rodeo

Is any folklore hero so widely known, admired, and imitated as the American cowboy? He may be big and strong or short and wiry, more or less handsome, more or less intelligent; but he is invariably brave, wryly humorous, extraordinarily impervious to pain, ready to defend his ideals of right and justice. Instantly recognizable from his attire (leather chaps worn over blue jeans, silver-buckled belt—gold, if he is a Rodeo World Champion—high-heeled boots with pointed toes and spurs, a wide-brimmed, more or less high-crowned hat), he walks with a relaxed, hip-swiveling gait, and he rides like a centaur. His relationship with his horse is, in fact, more intimate than with the women in his life, whom he reveres. His devotion to his friends is unconditional. Could he be an Americanized version of the medieval knight?

The cowboy reality is perhaps somewhat less pure, more mercenary, than the myth. Nevertheless, a disarming aspiration for achievement, courage, and integrity, solidarity with one's comrades, a sense of being a special breed of humanity, are nowhere more evident than in the world of rodeo. Behind the outer aspects of an exciting (mostly) equestrian sport, there lies an almost mystical nostalgia for a pioneer society and the ideals on which it was founded.

Neither American cowboys nor rodeo sports would have existed if Spanish expeditions during the fifteenth and sixteenth centuries had not brought cattle and horses to North America, where indigenous wild horses had become extinct. Columbus took thirty-four Andalusian steeds with him on his second voyage to Hispaniola in 1494; Cortez brought cattle as well as horses to Mexico in 1519. Many terms still used in Western riding derive from the Spanish. The word *rodeo* itself is Spanish for "round-up," generally pronounced ROE-dee-oh in much of North America, but roe-DAY-oh where Spanish traditions still prevail, as in California.

As the Spanish conquest spread through what is now the American Southwest, Catholic missionaries established not only churches, but also ranches where they bred horses and cattle. Other settlers followed. At first the horses were intended for their breeders' own use, the cattle for their own consumption. Then, with the development of a nationwide railway system, the ranchers began supplying the needs of fast-expanding cities. Immense stockyards and a flourishing meat-packing industry in Chicago, Denver, and Kansas City shipped their products all over the country. Cowboys drove herds from ranches over cattle trails to rail junctions, where the animals were loaded onto box-

This bucking horse being saddled in the chute as the cowboy prepares to ride him seems deceptively quiet. In a few seconds, he'll behave very differently.

Lewis Feild on Whispering Wind at the 1986 Prescott Rodeo shows how to ride a bareback bronc in champion style.

178

cars and shipped to the stockyards; but they sometimes had to camp for days or weeks before they heard the long-awaited train whistle. In order to relieve their boredom and fill their time, they held informal contests in the skills they used daily: roping calves, riding unbroken horses, handling cattle.

These same skills were useful after the Civil War in the late 1860s, when former Confederate soldiers rounded up longhorn cattle and escaped cavalry horses that had gone feral and migrated westward. They tracked them down, appropriated and branded them, drove them to ranches in Louisiana, Kansas, Texas, and as far as California.

Cattle raising remained a rather nomadic occupation until barbed wire was invented in the 1870s, whereupon the cowboy found a more permanent home on the range. He was no longer a knight errant.

"Go West, young man!" was the magic slogan of the late nineteenth century in America. There were fortunes to be made! One might also encounter hostile Indians, but that only added excitement to the adventure. In 1883, William Cody, an Iowa-born buffalo hunter, scout, plainsman, ex–Pony Express rider (though never a working cowboy), perhaps inspired by the example of P. T. Barnum who was making millions with his "Greatest Show on Earth," organized a sort of traveling circus. Buffalo Bill's Wild West Show was an extravaganza featuring trick roping (by Buffalo Bill himself and Buck Taylor, "King of the Cowboys"), trick shooting (starring sharpshooters Annie Oakley and Calamity Jane), mock combats between cowboys and Indians. It toured America and Europe and was widely imitated.

Saddle bronc riding at the Cheyenne Frontier Days Rodeo of 1907 had quite a different look from the modern event. Bucking horses still buck the way Old Steamboat did, but today's rodeo professionals would find this cowboy's riding style, angora chaps, and Texas Ranger-style hat rather quaint, to say the least.

The cowboy image was enhanced and propagated by Western magazines and "dime novels" which flourished from the mid and late nineteenth century. A novel of considerable influence and literary quality appeared in 1902: Owen Wister's *The Virginian*, the bestselling "Western" in history. Even Zane Grey's famous *Riders of the Purple Sage* (1912) has not surpassed its sales. At the same time, the budding cinema industry shrewdly exploited the charisma of the cowboy: the first feature film made in the United States was *The Great Train Robbery* (1906), and some of the most adulated early movie stars—Ken Maynard, Tom Mix, Tex Ritter—were cowboy heroes. The President of the United States himself, Theodore Roosevelt (a fine horseman, sportsman, and wildlife lover), was often photographed in cowboy attire.

Cowboy skills were featured as exhibitions, then as contests in Wild West shows. The shows gradually disappeared, but the contests survived. Rodeo cowboys became athletes rather than performers. The first genuine rodeo took place on July 4, 1886, at Prescott, Arizona, marking the death of a spectacle and the birth of a sport.

In the early 1900s, rodeo competitions moved to town to become a stadium sport, often a feature of horse shows and agricultural fairs. At the same time, informal local rodeos, organized by itinerant impre-

In the early 1900s, the Pendleton Roundup in Oregon was already one of the most important rodeos in America.

sarios, proliferated throughout the West. Sometimes the impresario absconded with the receipts. But if he didn't, a cowboy could earn as much during a few seconds' ride on a bucking bronc as he could during weeks of toil as a ranch hand. The professional cowboy was born.

The early sport was disorganized and not always honest. During the first professional rodeo held in Boston in 1936, contestants formed the Cowboys' Turtle Association (so called because it took so long to form) in order to defend their interests and bring order to the sport. In 1945 its name was changed to Rodeo Cowboys' Association, the reins placed in the able hands of Bill Linderman, a World Champion Saddle Bronc rider (whose record winnings earned him the nickname "The King") as well as an effective organizer. Under his leadership rodeo rules were drawn up, safety regulations (physical and financial) made and enforced. Rodeo became a genuine professional sport which grew in popularity, attendance, and participation. In 1985 there were 617 Professional Rodeo Cowboys' Association (PRCA) rodeos in forty-one states (and thousands of unsanctioned ones) and 8,000 registered professional cowboys (and countless amateurs).

During the 1950s and 1960s, some exceptionally expert, charismatic performers attracted attention and inspired vocations, among them: Jim Shoulders (five times All-Around Cowboy Champion between

1949 and 1960, four bareback championships, and seven bull riding titles); Harry Tomkins (holder of sixteen world titles, four of them consecutive All-Around Cowboy championships); Casey Tibbs (the model of a Western hero, nine times World Champion and still the idol of saddle bronc and bareback riders); and Larry Mahan (the biggest star of the 1960s, All-Around Champion from 1967 to 1970 and again in 1973). These impressive world championship titles were (and still are) awarded at the National Finals Rodeo, first held in Dallas in 1959, then in Oklahoma City in 1965, and since 1986 in Las Vegas, where the fifteen top winners in each rodeo event in terms of money won compete for the supreme title.

While roping and riding skills continued to be useful on the ranch, many traditional cowboy activities were gradually supplanted after World War II by modern methods of herding (Jeeps and helicopters) and by the use of electric prods for penning cattle. An increasing number of cowboys, addicted to the traditional arts, became professional sportsmen. Rodeo schools, rodeo college scholarships, high school and collegiate leagues, even "Little Britches" competitions for youngsters, fostered future champions.

Many rodeo contestants are now college students or graduates, like Dave Appleton, an Australian-born bareback and saddle bronc star, who even made the dean's list for his high academic grades while competing in collegiate rodeos. Jim Bailey, an Oklahoma steer roper who made the 1985 National Finals, is a qualified equine veterinarian with a diploma from the University of Minnesota. Jimmie Cooper, 1981 All-Around Champion, earned a degree in agricultural economics at New Mexico State University, as well as that gold buckle. Dee Pickett, 1984 All-Around and Team Roping Champion, was a football star at Boise State University in Idaho who finally chose rodeo because "You're your own boss." Most of them are also from ranching backgrounds, with relatives in rodeo, and most have started young. Joe Beaver, 1985 Champion Calf Roper, is the son of two rodeo competitor parents who had him chasing after goats on a Shetland pony at the age of five.

In 1975, the RCA added "Professional" to its name and became the PRCA, with headquarters in Colorado Springs, complete with a Hall of Fame and Rodeo Museum and computerized systems for entries and results. The new generation of champions gained greater fame and more money than ever before: Joe Alexander (perhaps the best bareback bronc rider in history, World Champion from 1971 to 1977, now a California rancher); Don Gay (a fearless bull rider); and Roy Cooper (one of the fastest calf ropers ever).

Already a major sport in certain parts of America, rodeo too began to seek commercial sponsorship in the 1980s, culminating in 1986 with the inauguration of the Winston Tour. In this series of ten super-rodeos, the leading fifteen competitors of the various events form

Typical scenes behind the rodeo arena: a Western hat seller; a cowboy awaiting his turn to ride, seated in his saddle on the ground, rehearsing the action he'll perform in the arena on a bucking horse.

With all four feet in the air, Alley Strip sheds Ted Hughes at Evanston in 1984 — making it six feet in the air.

Pages 184–185: The bare essentials of a rodeo arena: a bronc, a cowboy, and a lot of sky.

Ted "T-Bone" Clark, retired saddle bronc and bareback rider:

". . . Saddle bronc riding is more technical than bareback. The critical part is measuring the rein, because some horses buck with their head down, some with their head up, and you have to lift on that rein to keep your butt in the saddle. Bareback riding is the most physically demanding of all rodeo events, which is why bareback riders are generally younger. They're sort of weird-looking when they bring their biceps together and one arm's three inches bigger and even slightly longer. Some guys even carry weights when they're driving from one rodeo to another, to build up that arm. If your arm isn't prepared for it, things are gonna pop when you get on a strong bareback horse."

Bareback riding and saddle bronc events have little to do with breaking wild horses. On the contrary, the rider encourages the horse to buck wildly and continually in order to get a good score. Lewis Feild (top) is likely to do just that in his bareback go-round; but the bronc rider below seems to be in serious trouble.

eighteen teams, or "outfits" (as they used to be called in the old ranching days), to vie for prize money in an annual tournament, on a basis of elimination rounds. The idea, of course, is to increase rodeo's appeal as a stadium sport and television event, since only the very best contestants are seen.

Will this innovation enable rodeo to compete with such telegenic attractions as football, baseball, show jumping, and tennis? Why not? No sport is more spectacular. Certainly none more epitomizes American traditions and ideals.

There are five standard rodeo events. Contestants compete in a varying number of "go-rounds," sometimes as many as ten, depending on the rodeo and the amount of stock available; most often it is one or two with a finals. Prize money is awarded to the winner of each go-round as well as to the top overall scorer in each event.

Saddle Bronc Riding, which evolved from the need to tame wild horses for ranch work, is virtually synonymous with rodeo to many people. The cowboy tries to ride a saddled bucking horse with the aid of a plain halter and a single, braided rope rein. He lowers himself gingerly into the saddle while the horse is in a chute, and a bucking strap is tightened around the horse's loins. As the gate opens, the rider must have his spurs over the horse's shoulder and touching the horse when its front feet hit the ground as it jumps out of the chute; failure to do so incurs elimination. His major preoccupation is then to stay in the saddle until the bell rings, marking the end of an 8-second period. But that is not enough to win. Bronc riding is a "judged" event; quality also counts. The more the rider uses his spurs, the more he swings his legs from front to back, the higher the two judges will score his round, on a scale of zero to 100. He'll get zero if he touches the saddle, rein, or horse with his free hand, loses a stirrup, or changes hands on the rein.

Rodeo cowboys consider this the most beautiful event to watch; some compare it to ballet dancing! They also consider it the most difficult to master. Saddle bronc champions, like the legendary Casey Tibbs and present title-holder Brad Gjermundson, are often slender and relatively small, since the technique is based on timing, rhythm, balance, and rapid reflexes, rather than on sheer strength.

Bareback Riding became an official rodeo event only thirty years ago. It is similar to saddle bronc riding in that the cowboy has to remain on the back of a bucking horse for 8 wild seconds, aided only by his "rigging": a leather surcingle 10 in/25 cm wide with a stiff "handle" into which he wedges his gloved hand; the other hand must remain in the air. His feet must be in constant motion, spurring ("marking") the horse in the shoulder from the moment it leaps out of the chute. This is also a judged event, criteria being spurring technique and control of the horse. Strength as well as balance and timing are essential. The

187

judges give top points (100 being the unattainable perfect score, 89 the highest in history) to the cowboy who performs the most daring ride in the most skillful manner. The present World Champion, Lewis Feild, excels in bronc riding and participates in team roping as well, thus winning points in two or more events, sufficient to earn him the supreme title of All-Around Champion in 1985 and again in 1986.

What about the bucking horses who also star in these two typically Western riding events? They are much admired by the cowboys, who particularly respect the most "ornery" ones that give them the opportunity to produce winning rides. Bronc riders (bull riders, too) often file entries for different rodeos on the same day, check after the draw (the animals used to be drawn by lot, but are now assigned by computer), then select the rodeo that offers them the best bucker. Top bucking horses become as famous—even as beloved, one might say—as top roping and steer-wrestling mounts.

Bucking stock is provided by contractors, many of them retired cowboys like Jim Shoulders. Gene Autry and Roy Rogers, popular singing stars of Western films, both went into the rodeo livestock business. A top bucking horse is as hard to breed or find as a top hunter or jumper. Some are spoiled saddle and ranch horses; others are range-bred or specially bred from bucking strains. Their natural disposition to buck is encouraged by the bucking strap; without it, they'd be apt to try more devious means of unseating their rider, like biting him or crushing him against a wall or post. Animal lovers need not weep for them. They enjoy their work (so say the cowboys, who know them well), and their working conditions are enviable: fifty or sixty appearances of 8 seconds or less per year! Between which they are well treated, though never "gentled," by their owners. A good bucking horse is too valuable to spoil.

Calf Roping is a contest to determine which cowboy can rope and tie a calf in the shortest time. The cowboy and his horse are teammates. The horse has to adjust his speed to that of a fast-moving calf as it is given a head start out of the chute, stop short as soon as the calf is roped, then back up to keep the rope taut as the cowboy dismounts and sprints to the calf to throw it to the ground and tie any three legs. The instant this is done, the roper throws his hands in the air, then remounts and rides forward to slacken the rope, after which the calf must remain tied for 6 seconds.

It is a contest directly derived from practical ranch work, when calves are roped for branding, vaccination, or shipping to market. It requires speed, agility, and superior horsemanship in addition to roping skill. Should the cowboy miss the calf with the first throw, he has a second chance. Of course, he loses time (champions do it all in less than 8 seconds) as well as any chance of winning the go-round. But if he's under the 35-second time limit, it keeps him in the running for the overall average.

188

A calf roper waiting in the chute with his loop ready in his hand, the piggin' string between his teeth, and his horse keyed for action. Clayton Cooper, a successful calf roper and 1985 Team Roping Champion with partner Jake Barnes, explains the vital role played by the roping horse:

". . . In calf roping, you need a horse that can break out of the box and catch a calf real quick to give you the quick throw. The horse feels my shift in weight in the stirrup and he sees me spill the rope and that cues him to stop. But it takes three or four years of pretty good training, just doing that every day, with a guy roping and galloping him around, throwing the rope out and stopping him, making him back up. After a while they get like machines. Well, some do, some don't."

A good calf roper throws his loop at the running calf, calculating the throw so that the animal practically runs into it.

189

192

Rodeo cowboys spend a lot of time fussing with their gear. This rider is strapping his boots for added security in riding events.

Steer wrestling is an exciting contest, so fast that it might take longer to read these lines than to perform the action shown here! Lane Johnson (top) leans out of the saddle to hook the steer's horn inside the elbow of his right arm; former World Champion Ote Berry shows what happens a fraction of a second later, as he grasps the left horn with his left hand; then he'll twist the animal's neck to throw it on its side.

Pages 190–191: The moment the calf has been roped, the horse stops short and backs to keep the rope taut as the cowboy dismounts and runs to the calf to tie three legs together. Performed by an expert roper and a fast, clever horse, the entire scenario takes no more than 8 or 10 seconds.

Calf ropers form such a close partnership with their horses that they seldom loan or lease them to other contestants, as is customary among the steer wrestlers.

Steer Wrestling used to be called "bulldogging." A wild longhorn steer is released into the arena from a chute. The contestant, aided by a mounted "hazer," sprints alongside the running steer, while the hazing horse on the other side keeps the animal straight. The "bulldogger" leans out of his saddle to grasp the bull by the horns, jumps down, twists the bull's head, and throws it on its side. And he must do it faster than his rivals, since this is a timed event. Champions do it in less than 4 seconds! They've got to be agile, have a fine sense of balance, timing, a knowledge of leverage—and a smart, fast-sprinting horse. Although they say that strength is less important, size and weight must help: Ote Berry, the present World Champion, measures 6 ft 3 in/1.91 m and weighs 215 pounds/97.5 kg; his closest rival and previous Champion, Marty Melvin, is 6 ft 2 in/1.88 m and 210 pounds/95.3 kg.

Like bareback riding, this event developed in the rodeo arena and was never part of ranch work. Close coordination between the hazer and the wrestler is vital to the success of their efforts; but it is the wrestler, not the hazer, who competes. A cowboy with a good hazing horse often teams up with several different cowboys during the same contest.

Bull Riding is the final feature of many rodeos, the most dangerous by far. The cowboy has to try to ride a 2,000-pound/908-kg bull during 8 seconds, hanging onto a flat, braided rope snugly wrapped behind the bull's withers. A heavy bell (sometimes two) attached to the rope underneath the bull's belly pulls it free at the end of the 8-second round when the rider releases his hold. Brahma bulls are the most vicious, even more than those raised for bullfighting, although their horns are blunted. Santa Gertrudis are more common.

The bull rider wears a leather glove on his reining hand, dull spurs on his boots. He lowers himself onto the bull's back as the chute opens, one hand grasping the rope, the other in the air. Spurring can win extra points in this judged event, as can an upright position—easier said than done. The "spinners" are terrible to ride; others will charge a fallen cowboy with murder in their eyes. This is why there are always mounted pick-up men and rodeo clowns in the arena, intrepid bullfighters who distract the angry animal from unfortunate contestants.

Team Roping is a relatively recent rodeo contest, increasingly popular, and a standard event in eleven Western states. Two cowboys work as a team. The "header" throws a loop around the horns of a released steer, then wraps ("dallies") the rope around his saddle horn. He slows down and turns the roped steer to one side. His partner, the "heeler," immediately moves in from behind and ropes the steer's two hind feet, then dallies his own rope. The clock is stopped (it is a timed event) when both horses are facing each other with the steer between

them and both ropes taut. It is a display of teamwork not only between the two ropers, but also between each cowboy and his horse. Top teams work with incredible speed and accuracy: champions have been timed in under 5 seconds.

Steer Roping requires a single cowboy to do the work of a roping team of two, against the clock. An older event than team roping, it is increasingly rare. The steer roper first has to rope the horns of a hard-running steer. He then lays the slack of the rope over the steer's right hip, angles his horse to the left to tighten the rope and spin the steer to the ground. As the horse leans into the rope to keep the steer prone, the cowboy dismounts, runs to the steer, and ties any three legs. A good steer roper must thus be expert in all of the traditional cowboy arts, including that of training his horse and developing a perfect working partnership with it. Roy Cooper, one of the best, with eight World Championships to his credit, can perform the entire procedure in less than 10 seconds.

Barrel Racing is quite different from other rodeo events: it is a timed race over a cloverleaf course marked by three barrels forming a triangle. Each contestant individually sprints through the starting line, makes a 360-degree turn to the right around the first barrel, a full turn to the left around the next two, then races back across the finish line, ideally without having knocked over a barrel or made a wrong

Though horses play only a minor role in bull riding, it is one of the most thrilling, dangerous, and difficult rodeo events. At the Calgary Stampede, this young 'dogger seems headed for trouble, but the rodeo clown will come to his aid if necessary.

turn. It is a test of agility as well as speed, and Quarter Horses excel. So do girl riders. One of the best, Charmayne James, was World Champion at sixteen with her extraordinary Scamper.

Simpler versions of barrel racing are also popular, but this is the professional event, the only one in which cowgirls compete (and which is restricted to them) during PRCA rodeos. The Women's Professional Rodeo Association sanctions cowgirl rodeos that include roping and other riding events; but only in barrel racing contests at horse shows and in barrel futurities for four- and five-year-old horses do the girls compete on equal terms with men—and very often beat them.

Thousands of rodeos are held throughout the year, from the most informal dude ranch kind to important international events like the Cheyenne Frontier Days, Prescott's Frontier Days, the Calgary Stampede, the Pendleton Roundup, and those that are highlights of stock shows in Denver, Houston, Fort Worth, San Antonio, and San Francisco. Regional circuits organize their own finals and crown their own champions. And there are college and high school rodeo tournaments too.

At the beginning of December, National PRCA Finals are held in which the fifteen leading cowboys in each event vie for the World Champion title and the award of a coveted gold belt buckle. Even more coveted is the title of All-Around Cowboy Champion, won by the cowboy with the greatest total annual earnings in two or more events. The list of former All-Around Champions is a *Who's Who* of rodeo, among them Everett Bowman, Bill Linderman, Larry Mahan, Jim Shoulders, and Casey Tibbs. They generally specialize in either riding or timed events.

Title aspirants have to chase around the country to accumulate their winnings. It can mean two or even three different rodeos during a single weekend, exhausting nights of driving along interstate highways, expensive chartered planes. They often form a partnership to share the driving chores with other cowboys competing in the same specialties. Knights of the road, knights of the air, knights of the arena, they live in a world apart. And they are attached to their lifestyle, hard as it is, tinged with nostalgia, devoted to values that may seem naive or old-fashioned to many. Their "World Championship" titles themselves are rather naive, since rodeo as a professional sport hardly exists outside North America.

Rodeo cowboys are great believers in positive thinking, self-achievement, fair play, friendship, loyalty. There is a striking absence of envy and cheating in the rodeo world. How can one cheat with a bucking horse or a streaking calf? How can one betray one's friend? Although the dollar is the measure of success (as in other professional sports), unique to rodeo is the underlying dream of self-realization in a fabled image.

CUTTING CONTESTS

Cutting contests, while not a professional rodeo event, are featured in many rodeos as well as in competitions sanctioned by the National Cutting Horse Asssociation (NCHA), the American Horse Shows Association, and the American Quarter Horse and other breed associations.

A normal activity on the ranch in order to separate (cut) animals from a herd for branding, veterinary care, and shipping to market, calf cutting became an arena contest at the turn of the century and has been increasingly popular as a sporting activity since the NCHA was founded in 1946. Its practice is by no means restricted to cowboys and ranchers. Many of the fifteen thousand members (concentrated in the United States, but also in Canada, Australia, New Zealand, Europe, and South America) own a cutting horse for the sheer pleasure of competition. Some employ trainers and professional riders as racehorse owners do, but many more own, train, and ride their own horse. The NCHA sponsors six of the world's richest horse events, with million-dollar purse money: the Futurity for three-year-olds, the National Cutting Horse Derby and Super Stakes for four-year-olds, the NCHA Classic for five-year-olds, and the NCHA Challenge for six-year-olds. But there are many more throughout the year for horses of every level and for amateur and professional riders.

While horse and rider work together as a team to demonstrate their cattle-handling skill, the horseman's art is exercised more in the training corral than in the arena. In fact, the rider must give the horse complete freedom on a loose rein during the cutting contest.

It is a fascinating, highly entertaining event. A herd of twenty or more yearling or two-year-old calves, weighing 500 to 600 pounds/227 to 272 kg, is driven into one side of the arena. The team of horse and rider quietly approaches the herd so as not to disperse it, and the timekeeper presses the button. The rider selects a calf that seems likely to provide his horse with a good opportunity to prove its ability, and indicates it to the horse which then attempts to nudge the animal gently out of the herd and into the center of the arena. At this point, the horse has to use its own judgment and devices to prevent the calf from rejoining the herd, blocking its instinctive efforts with equal rapidity and agility; it has to demonstrate "cow sense" by anticipating the calf's moves, never losing control of it. Good cutting horses have uncanny anticipation, astounding athletic ability in making sizzling short stops, 180-degree turns on the haunches, lightning-fast sprints. The allotted time of 2½ minutes is sufficient for cutting two or three calves, and one of the rider's principal responsibilities is to judge the right moment for dropping one calf and returning to the herd to cut another.

There are usually two eliminating go-rounds and a final third one. In important events, five judges (fewer in smaller contests) score each horse's performance on the basis of the challenges made by the calves cut, the horse's instinctive reactions, and errors in judgment made by horse or rider. The highest and lowest scores (ranging from 60 to 80) are discarded, the others totaled to obtain the final number of points. Penalties are incurred for cueing the horse in any way, scattering the herd, or using the back fence for turn-back purposes. If the cutting horse turns his tail toward the calf that he is working, an automatic low score of 60 points is given. Two mounted herd handlers and two turn-back men are in the arena to control the herd and drive back the calves that are dropped.

In short, cutting contests are designed to judge the horse's natural ability and training; the rider's role is to display them without interfering (visibly, at least) with its work. Still, many subtleties are involved, as in all keen competitions, and most cutting horse champions are ridden by professional experts.

The most successful cutting horses are Quarter Horses, Appaloosas, and Palominos—breeds with a long heritage of cow work and the physical conformation able to produce short stops, sudden spurts of speed,

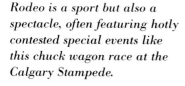

Rodeo is a sport but also a spectacle, often featuring hotly contested special events like this chuck wagon race at the Calgary Stampede.

and turns so sharp that they are really pivots on the hindquarters. They obviously love their work. Without belittling the vital role of a good trainer, cutting seems to offer these horses an outlet for some deep instinct, like that of an English setter pointing game, or a sheepdog herding a flock. How intensely they concentrate on the calf they have been asked to cut from the herd! How determinedly, how cleverly, they block the calf's moves to rejoin it! And how many spectators of a cutting contest must have had the same thought: could generations of zoologists have been greatly underestimating the intelligence of the horse?

REINING CONTESTS

Reining contests are different from cutting contests in that they test the skill of the rider in displaying his horse's perfect obedience to his signals, rather than the skill of the horse in working calves unaided.

Always an important feature of Western horse shows, they became more widely popular when the National Reining Horse Association (NRHA) was founded in 1966, with members and sanctioned competitions throughout the United States, offering money prizes (in all but youth events), sometimes a coveted bronze trophy, and year-end championship awards.

Reining horses, like cutting horses, are ridden Western-style: deep-seated in a Western saddle, holding the reins in one hand, guiding the horse by neck-reining, which places pressure on its neck in the direction *toward* which the horse is asked to move (right-rein pressure for leftward movement, and vice versa). They perform one of nine official patterns outlined in the rulebook, as designated by the Show Committee for each class, including all of the movements useful in actual ranch work: backing, circles, figure eights, changes of lead, sliding stops as long as 30 ft/9 m, rollbacks and pivots, spins, sudden sprints as fast as 45 miles an hour/72 kph. In a Non-Pro (amateur rider) event, a single pattern may be required; in important contests, there are two preliminary rounds—in Finals, three—with different patterns. Quality as well as precision is judged on a scale of 60 to 80 points (60 amounting to elimination, 70 an average score, 80 virtually unattainable perfection, as in cutting competitions).

Reining shows offer events in eleven divisions for horses and riders at every level of expertise, for professionals and amateurs, youths and ladies. The most important are the Futurity for three-year-old horses, the Derby and Super Stakes for four-year-olds, and the Open. These are generally dominated by professional trainers and riders like Dick Pieper, President of the NRHA and 1985 Open Championship winner; Bob Loomis, who has won more Futurities than any other rider-trainer; Bill Horn, one of the busiest competitors; Canadian Roger Brazeau, noted for his articulate reining technique; Craig Johnson, rider of the

199

Barrel racing is the only event in which girl contestants compete at PRCA rodeos. Some of the best are in their early teens. Their success is due to their speed and skill, of course, but perhaps also to the special rapport these young cowgirls have with their horses.

1985 Futurity Champion, Sparkles Rosanna; and Rocky Dare, a leading trainer no longer active as a "showman." Some expert trainers, in fact, never show the horses they prepare for competition; some top professional riders have neither the time nor the patience to train.

Some horses are, by conformation and breeding, more suitable for this sport than others. Quarter Horses excel, but there are also some Appaloosas and Paints and the occasional Mustang. However, even for the Quarter Horse, with its heritage of ranch work, the movements he is asked to perform on command in the show arena are not instinctive; they demand hours of work with a patient, knowledgeable trainer, then with a rider. Perfect teamwork is vital to success, and each horse, each rider, has his own style.

Competition has become extremely keen, and no less so in the Non-Pro division where classes are huge and there may be as many as fifty or seventy potential winners despite the daunting requirements. An example of these? The prescribed movements for Pattern 7 give an idea:

1. Run at speed to the far end of the arena past end marker and do a left rollback—no hesitation.
2. Run to the opposite end of the arena past end marker and do a right rollback—no hesitation.
3. Run past center of the arena, do a sliding stop, back straight to the center of the arena. Hesitate.

4. Complete four spins to the right.

5. Complete four and a quarter spins to the left. Hesitate.

6. Beginning on the right lead, complete 4 circles to the right, the first two large and fast, the second two small and slow.

7. At the center of the arena change leads.

8. Complete 4 circles to the left, the first 2 large and fast, the second 2 small and slow.

9. At the center of the arena, change leads.

10. Begin a large fast circle to the right. Do not close this circle but run straight down the side of the arena past the center marker and do a sliding stop approximately 20 feet from the wall or fence.

11. Rider must drop bridle to the judge. [All of the patterns end with this instruction to permit the judges to examine the bit.]

In important contests, five judges score each go-round according to its precision and quality. A good reining horse should be "willfully guided or controlled with little or no apparent resistance, dictated to completely." Any movement on its own, any deviation from the pattern, is considered a temporary loss of control and must be penalized. After deducting penalties, credit is given for smoothness, finesse, attitude, quickness, and authority in performing the various movements at controlled speed. The slightest delay in changing leads, a variation of as little as an eighth of a turn when a certain number of turns is required by the pattern, incurs a penalty.

In its Western way, reining might be compared to classical dressage. Adherents (fanatics, some would say) of each discipline profess great admiration for the other. But when a reining exhibition was held during the World Dressage Championship at Toronto in 1986, it was the dressage contingent that could hardly believe its eyes!

Combined Driving

It is really quite astonishing that the driving of horses in harness, which as chariot racing is the most ancient of all equestrian sports and for that matter of *all* sports, should also encompass today one of the newest, fastest-growing horse activities as well as one of the biggest, richest ones. The newer activity, a test of driving versatility patterned roughly after the three-day event, is called *combined driving*, while the "rich uncle" is of course harness racing, a major spectator sport (and gambling medium) all the way from Scandinavia to the South Pacific.

The actual origins of driving are prehistoric, but archaeologists reckon that man's first domesticated animal, the dog, was harnessed to some sort of drag or skid and used for pulling loads, and that a larger version of the same vehicle was developed for the first domesticated horses long before man thought about getting on their backs. (Certain nomadic tribes still use an arrangement of poles similar to the American Indians' *travois* to transport their belongings even today.) Thus, driving—or at least, something that can be considered a form of it—constituted the first expression of man's working relationship with the horse.

Skids or drags evolved into sleds, but the truly profound technological breakthrough came with the invention of the wheel in the Bronze Age. Putting wheels under the load made the horse so functional a source of motive power that the role of the driven horse would survive for five millennia more as man's most efficient and most convenient mode of transport, until gradually replaced first by steam and then by the internal combustion engine in the nineteenth and twentieth centuries.

It is not surprising, therefore, that the driven horse appears so often and so conspicuously in the art and artifacts of the ancient world. The chariots found in the tomb of Tutankhamen and those depicted in the heroic reliefs of Ramses II and III at Karnak and Abu Simbel are already highly refined vehicles. Equally remarkable are the Assyrian reliefs of kings Ashurbanipal and Tiglath-pileser, which show them variously hunting, fighting, or parading ceremonially in their chariots, while the reliefs and artifacts from Angkor in Cambodia and the funerary statuary of the Han Dynasty in China offer eloquent testimony to the importance of the driven horse in the Far East.

Chariot racing was a part of the oral history of the Olympic Games even before the first recorded competitions of 776 BC, although no equestrian competitions were included in those particular Games. However, racing with four-horse chariots was introduced into the twenty-fifth recorded Olympics in 680 BC and remained a prominent

The father of four-in-hand driving in Germany, Benno von Achenbach, driving at Berlin in 1899.

Tibor Pettkó Szandtner (Hungary), pioneer exponent of the Hungarian style, driving a five-in-hand at Aachen, Germany, the cradle of international driving, in 1928.

Down the road at Szilvásvárad: a traditional Hungarian five-in-hand, as viewed from the driver's seat.

Perfect turn-out for the Presentation applies to grooms and drivers, too!

The combined driving groom has a lot of responsibility to bear—especially if you're young, and you might have a tandem to untangle!

Left: Alone in the Kelso countryside, this pony is competing in the Marathon phase of the 1982 Scottish Horse Driving Trials.

feature of the Olympics almost continuously thereafter until the Games were abandoned as pagan rituals over a thousand years later. In the interim, races for everything from pairs to ten-horse hitches (an innovation of Nero's) were contested, along with ridden races for mares, two-year-olds, and stallions.

What we know of the ancient Greek and Roman horses suggests that the main reason why they were so much more often driven in teams than ridden is that they simply were not very big. (Consider the horses shown in the beautiful Parthenon friezes, for example.) This problem was obviously largely overcome during the Dark Ages, for the Norman horses that are depicted in the Bayeux Tapestry are clearly able to support the weight of a knight in chain mail. Oxen were used for the heaviest loads (as they have continued to be almost up to the present time), but obviously there had been some selective breeding of horses for size, strength, and speed.

Thus, while it had been the driven horse that was dominant in the ancient world, it was the ridden horse that became more important during the Middle Ages, a shift that also owed much to the development of stirrups and saddles, which came to Europe from the East well before the end of the first millennium. Even so, the driven horse continued to be used extensively for agriculture, for the transport of people and goods, and in warfare for the transport of supplies throughout the Middle Ages. The importance of the driven horse in warfare was significantly increased by the development of the longbow and then gunpowder, for these tended to minimize the importance of the mounted knight. After about 1650 highly mobile horse-drawn field artillery became almost as important as cavalry, and by World War I it had become the decisive force on the battlefield. (Despite the mechanization of much of the world's cavalry prior to World War II, both mounted cavalry and horse- or mule-drawn field artillery were still employed on a limited scale in that most "modern" conflict.)

Better roads and the need for greater speed in transport and communications produced continuous improvement in and refinement of the art and science of coaching over a period of hundreds of years. This long evolution may be said to have climaxed during England's Golden Age of coaching in the first half of the nineteenth century, when it was abruptly terminated by the growth of the railways. The speed and comfort of nineteenth-century coach travel are hardly dazzling by today's supersonic standards, but for the time, both the distances and the speeds were very impressive. London to Liverpool—a distance of 203 miles/327 km—could be traveled in twenty-one scheduled hours in the 1830s, a vast improvement over what could be done on foot or on horseback. Yet such travel may only rarely have been predictable or uneventful, if we can believe the extensive pictorial documentation of the coaching era by such painters as Henry Alken,

Lavish amounts of spit, polish, and elbow grease go into a high score on Presentation, where even specks of dust can cost precious points.

The FEI President as whip. Prince Philip, whose initiative it was to develop combined driving as an international sport, submits to the judge's scrutiny during Presentation at Windsor. His is the traditional English turn-out.

A traditional Hungarian turn-out, with breastplates instead of collars. György Bárdos (Hungary), the 1978 and 1980 World Champion, trying for the "hat trick" at Apeldoorn, Holland, in 1982. Despite good Dressage, he was ultimately nosed out by a native son, Tjerd Velstra.

C. B. Newhouse, and James Pollard. Even aside from vicissitudes of weather that ranged from blizzard to flood, there were sometimes highwaymen to contend with, and, in the western United States, Indians. Railways were not immune to such incidents either, but nineteenth-century travelers must still have been most grateful for the advent of the steam engine, which easily replaced the horse as a source of motive power for long-distance transport in a matter of only a decade or two.

The driven horse by no means disappeared, however, for as commercial coaching phased out, private driving phased in. The Industrial Revolution had tended to broaden the base of horse ownership (which earlier had been primarily a royal, aristocratic, or military privilege) and bring it within reach of most business and professional people, not to mention farmers and ordinary citizens. By the second half of the nineteenth century, a large segment of society was tooling around in its own vehicles behind a single horse or a pair, and London, Paris, and New York became cities of mews, of harness makers, and of horse auctions. Hansom cabs, public or private, were the way to get around the city, and there was even an instructional literature featuring tactics for negotiating especially tricky intersections with a coach-and-four. The Victorian era also witnessed an astonishing proliferation of sporting activities for the driven horse—horse shows, trotting races, coaching marathons—all flourished along with the more than faintly competitive Sunday afternoon excursions in the park or on the concourse.

In the last seventy-five years the driven horse has been completely replaced in most of its utilitarian roles by cars and trucks, and the vast amount of knowledge and skill relating to horses that existed prior to World War I has very nearly disappeared. (There are people still alive who vividly remember the old fire horses and horse-drawn street railways, and how upsetting horses found the first automobiles, but such personal reminiscences will, sadly, soon be a thing of the past.) Although the driven horse's practical utility is now severely restricted, except on small farms and in isolated pockets like the Amish country of Pennsylvania, the sporting uses of the driven horse continue to flourish. Harness racing, the oldest horse sport, is a big, modern spectator sport in many countries, while national driving championships, horse show harness classes, driving derbies, and coaching marathons not only hold their own, but grow.

Individual competitions and countries have long developed their own rules for judging such competitions, but it was not until 1969 that the FEI took official cognizance of driving as a competitive discipline and, at the instigation of its then President, Prince Philip, drew up its own international rules. The form of competition it sanctioned—combined driving—is a test of versatility, driving skill, and conditioning that distinctly resembles the three-day event, on which it was patterned. (Interestingly, the man charged with the task of creating a

practicable competitive format was neither a driving expert nor an eventer; he was Col. Sir Michael Ansell, who is revered as the principal architect of Britain's postwar renascence in show jumping.) Prince Philip's interest resulted from his exposure to the driving competitions held in Germany at Hamburg and Aachen. (At the time of his first exposure to driving his personal equestrian interest was in polo, but when injuries curtailed his polo career, he turned to carriage driving, with considerable success.)

The Aachen competition dated from the mid-1920s and was for combined driving, unlike most competitions of the time, which tested only turnout or only long-distance driving. Aachen regularly attracted teams from Switzerland and Hungary in addition to the host nation, in which the considerable historical driving interest had been greatly stimulated and focused by the celebrated whip Benno von Achenbach (1861–1936). In this respect Aachen can be credited with a key role in the conception of the new FEI driving competition.

Official driving rules having been codified and published, they were put to the test in an international competition at Windsor in 1971, and later the same year in an official European Championship staged at Budapest. (This was won by a frequent and successful competitor in Aachen, the great Hungarian whip Imre Abonyi, ahead of his team-mates Sándor Fülöp and Josef Papp.)

Hamburg's Fahr-Derby (and Aachen's Fahrturnier) *featured international driving competition in Germany long before the promulgation of combined driving rules by the FEI.*

The rules for championship competition have been refined and amplified since then, but the basic structure remains unchanged. The competition consists of three contrasting types of competition and takes place over three or four days. (As in the three-day event, the first element may require two days for completion.) Competition A consists of two sections: Presentation, in which the turnout, cleanliness, condition, and general impression of the horses, harness, and vehicle are judged, along with the driver and his two grooms; and Dressage, which is held in an arena 44 by 110 yards/40 by 100 meters in area and marked just like the arena for ridden dressage. The test, which must be driven from memory, is about ten minutes long and tests the driver's accuracy, horsemanship, and control as well as the horses' paces and movement. The paces required are the walk and the working, collected, and extended trots; figures performed include circles and serpentines, and the horses also must halt and rein back. Scoring is identical to that for ridden dressage.

Competition B, the Marathon or middle competition, is also divided into sections, in this case, five. Sections A and C are done at the trot (9 miles at 9 mph/15 km at 15 kph) and fast trot (3 miles at 11 mph/5 km at 18 kph), respectively; Sections B and D at the walk (both up to 1,300 yards at 4 mph/1,200 m at 7 kph). There is a ten-minute halt

Dressage at Kelso, 1982, with Prince Philip driving the Queen's pony team on the lawn in front of Floors Castle.

after Sections B and D, to give the horses a blow and the veterinarians time to check them, and then comes the real heart of Competition B, a trot of 6 miles at 9 mph/10 km at 15 kph, including seven or eight extremely ingenious, testing obstacles or hazards, each of which must be negotiated against the clock, with penalties for putting a groom down and a time limit of five minutes. (Though grooms are essential to all FEI disciplines, they ordinarily work behind the scenes, unheralded. Not so the two driving grooms, who must attend to and ride on their vehicle in all three competitions, and are almost as important a part of the competitive team as the driver.)

The final competition, Competition C, is an obstacle course of 547 to 875 yards/500 to 800 m in length, the obstacles consisting of up to twenty cones spaced only slightly wider than the vehicle's wheel track, which must be negotiated at a minimum speed of 13 mph/21 kph. Each displacement of an obstacle is penalized by 5 points, and competitors start in the reverse order of their standings, which makes for an extremely exciting and nerve-wracking conclusion. The overall ratio between the four phases of a combined driving championship is stipulated as: 0.5 Presentation : 3 Dressage : 10 Marathon : 1 Obstacle Course. This is a trifle misleading, as is the ratio for the regular three-day event, for the final phase often exerts the critical influence on the final result.

210

Pages 211, 212–213: As in the three-day event, water is frequently a complicating factor for Marathon competitors, and the same twin dangers apply: too much reluctance, or too much speed. Royal Windsor, 1983.

It is hard to imagine a more beautiful Marathon venue than Windsor Great Park, site of the first combined driving competition under FEI rules (in 1971) and always a major fixture in the driving schedule.

215

Dierdre Pirie is one of the leading U.S. whips, and the only woman consistently competing on the World Championship level. Here she negotiates Windsor's Water Crossing in 1982.
". . . I don't think an enormous amount of strength is involved if the horses are trained properly. It's when horses are not trained properly, or are unresponsive for some reason, or scared; then, the more strength you have, the better."

György Bárdos (Hungary), the most successful competitor in combined driving history (twice World Champion, twice silver medalist), negotiates a hazard at Szilvásvárad in 1984.

A full national team consists of three four-in-hands, though only the two best scores in each phase count. This makes the training, maintenance, and transportation of a full team a very expensive proposition, especially since the drivers use an entirely different set of harness and vehicle for Presentation and Dressage than for the Marathon (for which they often use the training vehicle), and there must of course also be spare horses, adding even further to the obvious costs. For this reason, there has been some recent shifting of emphasis from four-in-hands toward pairs and single horses, and the pairs now have their own world championships in the alternate years between four-in-hand championships.

The 1971 European Championships in Budapest were considered so successful that the following year the first World Driving Championship was staged at Münster, West Germany, contested by eighteen drivers from seven nations, with six full national teams. The Hungarian team led into the final day, but an unforeseen technical problem—the protruding hubs on their vehicles' wheels—caused many obstacle penalties and pushed them out of the medals. A British team led by the Queen's Crown Equerry, Sir John Miller, defeated Switzerland and West Germany in the team standings, but the Swiss whip Auguste Dubey nosed out Miller for the individual title, with Britain's Douglas Nicholson placing third.

Two years later the British won again at Frauenfeld, Switzerland, from a field of competitors almost twice as large as that in the first Championship (thirty-five drivers participated). Two Hungarian drivers were eliminated after the Marathon for a technical violation, but the third team member, Sándor Fülöp, ended up the individual gold medalist over Christian Iseli of Switzerland and Britain's George Bowman, a scrap-metal dealer from Cumbria who had once ridden in rodeos! (The two-year spacing between championships, instead of the four-year cycle of the other major FEI championships, is due to the fact that driving is not an Olympic sport, a condition that driving enthusiasts hope to see altered eventually. Considering the special role of driven horses in the ancient Olympic Games, it would certainly seem appropriate.)

Fülöp's win at Frauenfeld was prophetic, for he was to prove the first of four successive Hungarian drivers to win the individual title. In 1976 at Apeldoorn, Holland, it was the turn of the great Imre Abonyi, complete with handlebar moustache, to lead his Hungarian team to its first World Championship and win the individual gold medal from West Germany's Emil-Bernhard Jung (who has since become an American citizen) and Zygmunt Wasiszewski from Poland. The 1978 Championships at Kecskemét, Hungary, saw the host nation in even more dominant form, winning all three individual medals as well as the team crown. The individual title went to a seventh-generation horseman and former show jumper, György Bárdos, with Fülöp second; the silver and bronze team medals went to West Germany and Great Britain, Prince Philip himself being a member of the latter team.

Forty-two drivers from eleven nations took part at Windsor in 1980, the largest entry to that date, as Bárdos successfully defended his title. The competition was hardly a Hungarian cakewalk this time, however, for Bowman of Britain and Tjerd Velstra were hot on Bárdos's heels, and the host nation (with Prince Philip again a member) pushed Hungary back to second place in the team standings. The Marathon proved one of the most difficult yet, nine teams failing to complete the course, and many of the finishers sustained some damage to their vehicles.

Apeldoorn in Holland was awarded its second World Championship in 1982 and had the pleasure of seeing its team prevail and a native son, Tjerd Velstra (another former show jumper), win the individual gold medal, depriving Bárdos of a third successive title. Third was another Hungarian whip, Abonyi pupil László Juhász, an aggressive and daring driver.

The Championships returned to Hungary for the first time in six years in 1984, and the host nation again rose to the occasion by producing an overwhelming victory. Juhász nosed out teammates Bárdos and Mihály Bálint, another Abonyi pupil, in a sweep of the individual medals, and clearly outdistanced the Swedish and British teams in the team standings. Two years later Hungary's dominance was challenged again, however, as the Championship came to Britain for the second time, this time to Ascot. In one of the closest competitions of all, the Dutch former World Champion Velstra bested his teammate Isbrand Chardon and the defending title-holder Juhász to win his second individual crown; the margin between first and second was a scant 4 points (less than a single obstacle penalty) and that between third and fourth, only 3 points. Holland could, of course, not be denied the team title as well, with defending champion Hungary second and West Germany third. The fourth-place finish of the United States equaled the best result yet for a nation in which the interest in combined driving is growing very rapidly.

One of the most fascinating things about driving is the fact that even the individual competitor's score involves a true team effort, a complex collaboration between three individual human personalities and four individual equine personalities at the very least! And if this were not enough complexity in itself, it is probably true that the acceptable range of temperament and physique for both the horses and the humans is wider than in any other equestrian discipline. Horsemen like to say that anyone can ride, or that a good jumper, for example, can be of any size, shape, breed, or coat. This is only really true within certain parameters, however; there are human and equine body types that are utterly unsuitable for the three Olympic equestrian disciplines, but that might yet aspire to achieving a highly competitive standard in driving. This is not to say that the physical and temperamental qualities demanded by the sport are any easier—they are simply somewhat different.

In his excellent book, *Competition Carriage Driving*, Prince Philip discusses eighteen different breeds of horses and ponies that make suitable harness horses, without by any means exhausting the subject. Among the best, judging from results obtained in the World Championships, are the Hungarian Lipizzaner and Magyar Félvér, the German Holsteiner, Hanoverian, and Oldenburger, the French Selle Français, and the Welsh Cob, but there have been outstanding teams of many other breeds, not to mention mixed breeds and mixed teams.

The early stages of breaking a horse to drive are exactly the same as those for breaking the horse to ride, and many horses are far advanced under saddle before they are ever hitched to a vehicle. (The Swiss Army has been known to compete at Aachen with a Grand Prix dressage horse as the near leader of the four-in-hand, and many driving horses are sometimes exercised under saddle as a change of pace for their entire careers.) A typical progression is to start on a longe line, and then go on to driving in long reins, with the "driver" simply walking behind the horse. Harness is introduced very gradually, a piece at a time, for there is a lot of it and some things—such as the crupper that goes over the tail, and the breeching that touches the hind legs—can be

László Juhász, the 1984 World Champion, snakes his way through Ascot's Obstacle Course in the 1986 World Championships, in which he was bronze medalist. Juhász now manages the stud farm on which he started as a herdsman twenty years ago.

". . . I have seen some accidents in driving, and have already had an accident myself, but it was nothing serious—I didn't even break an arm or a leg, nothing. . . . However, some people think that this is quite a passive sport, that you only sit in the carriage and do nothing. I suggest that the one who thinks it's a lazy sport, then he should try it. . . . A driver doesn't necessarily have to be very strong. He has to have very good reflexes, and he has to have brains, of course, because with four horses it's not the same as going for a walk. For example, if I want to go in one direction, it's not always sure that the horses want the same thing; so if you want to win, you surely can use a little 'Hungarian virtue.' There must be a very close relationship between the horses and the driver; they must become accustomed to each other, so that the horses listen to what the driver says."

very upsetting to the green horse. The idea of pulling something is also introduced gradually, starting with a light object, such as a log or a car wheel.

When all the preliminary lessons have been learned, the horse is finally hitched to a simple, long-shafted, two-wheeled vehicle, and when it goes well in that, to a larger, four-wheeled vehicle as one of a pair of horses. From there it is a relatively easy step to move on to two pairs—a proper four-in-hand—or to one of the more exotic hitches, such as the tandem (with one horse in front of the other) or unicorn (with two wheelers and one leader). The real key to the whole process lies in patience and progressiveness, and having enough capable people on the ground to help before things go seriously amiss. Bad experiences can be very difficult or impossible to erase from the horse's mind, and it is always better to take the extra time and avoid them whenever possible.

There are two basic ways of harnessing and bitting the competition team. In "Hungarian" harness, the horse wears a breastplate and some form of snaffle bit, often with double rings. The customary "English" harness consists of a regular horse collar and a regular driving bit with a curb chain and a choice of positions for the rein, depending on the amount of severity required.

There are also different basic driving techniques. The classic English and German style involves holding all four reins in the left hand and using the right hand to lengthen and shorten them by making "loops" which are caught under the right thumb and released gradually as required. This method facilitates the very sharp, slow turns that driving in the city requires. Quite different (and probably more functional for competitive driving) is the old American stagecoach driver's technique of holding two reins in each hand, and this is the method with which the Hungarian drivers have achieved such notable success. Whichever method is used, a great deal of training and practice are required to produce the kind of pinpoint accuracy, at speed, that is needed if one is to succeed in negotiating the hazards and obstacles without penalty, and to perform the dressage with the complete control and beautifully smooth transitions the judges are looking for.

There is also a wide latitude for individual taste in the matter of vehicles. In the earlier days of the sport the same vehicle was sometimes used both for Presentation and in the Marathon, but this is a thing of the past, now that the FEI has standardized the vehicles' weight and width of tread. The Marathon/training vehicle is now a lightweight super-tough vehicle made especially for the purpose, and the Presentation vehicle, too, will now be something especially designed for the purpose. (Owners of cherished antique vehicles need no longer subject them to the risks involved in transporting and competing with their vehicles; the last to do so was France's lone competitor at Ascot, Franck Deplanch, who used a 1908 dog cart as his Presentation carriage.)

Overall view of Competition C, the Obstacle Course, more commonly called "The Cones." This was the scene at Szilvásvárad during the 1984 World Championships.

220

The current World Four-in-Hand Champion, Tjerd Velstra of Holland, negotiating The Cones at Ascot in 1986.

Whatever the origin of the carriage used in the Presentation competition, it must be immaculately turned out and fully and appropriately "appointed" with obligatory spares, candle-lit lamps, and a first-aid box. Horses, driver, and grooms must be equally spotless and just as correctly and appropriately harnessed or dressed. (Lavish displays are, however, frowned upon, for the dominant standard of taste is an understated one.)

Of course, all of this changes on the Marathon day, when both the vehicle and the competitors' clothing involve no display at all, and are chosen entirely with functionality in mind. Since the entire Marathon is run like a rally with minimum speeds and maximum times, good time-keeping and navigation are essential, and the most important "appointments" are now stopwatches. Crash helmets are not obligatory, although they would be quite appropriate, for real risks can be encountered, and even though vehicles are constructed to be as tough and stable as possible, accidents and overturns are by no means uncommon. Indeed, the obstacle phase of the Marathon is very much characterized by the same scent of risk and potential danger that permeates the air during the cross-country phase of a three-day event. Whatever else, combined driving is no sport for the timid, as anyone who has ever attempted to drive four 1,200-pound/545 kg horses at speed can attest. Four horse-power doesn't sound like much to the modern motorist, but carriages don't have hydraulic brakes, and if one gets into trouble, it's not possible simply to turn a key and switch the motor off!

Driving enthusiasts maintain that their sport is the fastest-growing of the major equestrian disciplines, and that may well be true, even though it must be acknowledged that the sport started from a relatively narrow base. More than thirty nations now participate in combined driving on some level, and there is a very solid base of competitors in Western Europe, the British Isles, North America, and in the state-supported Eastern European teams. With further growth likely as pair competitions establish themselves more firmly, it certainly appears that driving—either the oldest or the newest of the principal equestrian disciplines, depending on how you look at it—has earned an important role in the modern equestrian world.

Harness Racing

Harness racing is the most widespread, popular form of competition for horses that are driven rather than ridden. Derived from ancient chariot racing, it is also the oldest of all equestrian sports.

In its modern version, drivers ("reinsmen") seated in a lightweight two-wheeled vehicle (a racing sulky) guide their horses around an enclosed oval track in a trot or pace, the winner being the horse that finishes first without having broken gait. (The trot is a two-beat gait in which each diagonal pair of legs moves alternately; in the pace, also a two-beat gait, each lateral pair of legs moves alternately.)

Why not the gallop, the gait of Greek and Roman chariot races? It is the horse's fastest: Dr. Fager's mile/1,600 m record for a Thoroughbred galloper is 1:32⅕, while the American trotting mile record set by Prakas in 1985 is 1:53⅖, and Niatross's 1980 pacing record is 1:49⅕. But the gallop is also far more tiring for the horse over a distance, and far more dangerous for a driver exercising rather remote control. Moreover, trotting, pacing, and related gaits like the running walk and rack were the fast gaits of working horses on farms and plantations, where modern harness racing originated in the early nineteenth century as a rural, plebeian sport.

All-purpose trotting breeds existed in Holland, Denmark, and France long before the English Thoroughbred came into existence. Trotters are believed to have been introduced to Great Britain in 1015 by the Danish invader King Canute. Medieval war chargers went to battle at a trot, not a gallop. Trotters were used for fox hunting in England before the Enclosures Act produced the conditions that brought the galloping Thoroughbred into being.

One of the most successful breeders of a superior trotter was a Russian nobleman, Count Alexis Orlov. Brother of Empress Catherine II's famous lover, he conspired to put her on the throne in 1762 and was rewarded with the appointment of Commander of the Imperial Navy during the Russo-Turkish wars. One of the tributes to the victor offered by the defeated Turks was a magnificent Arab stallion, Smetanka. Presented to the mares of the Orlov stud near Moscow, which included Dutch and Danish imports as well as native Russian mares, Smetanka founded the Orlov Trotter line that contributed its blood to many other trotting breeds in Europe and America.

The pride of the British was the Norfolk Trotter and its lighter version, the Hackney Horse (a mixture of Norfolk Trotter, Arab, and Thoroughbred), still an elegant coaching breed. The French had developed their famous Norman Trotter. Americans discovered the amazing

At the turn of the century, harness racing was a popular feature of county fairs and small tracks (like this one at Booneville, New York), and in the 1930s Goshen, New York, was the harness racing capital of America. Its Hall of Fame of the Trotter pays tribute to the men and horses who helped to make the sport what it is today. How astonished they would be by the changes since those early days!

prepotency of a versatile, indefatigable little horse foaled in 1793 called Justin Morgan, founder of the breed that bears his name. But the supreme achievement of American breeders was the Standardbred. Its name refers to the "standard" of speed per mile required for inclusion in the first stud book: 2 minutes 30 seconds for a trotter, 2 minutes 25 seconds for a pacer (fairly modest by modern standards). Designated as foundation sire was an English Thoroughbred, Messenger, imported to Philadelphia in 1788.

He was a mildly successful gray Thoroughbred racehorse who traced back to the Darley Arabian through his sire and to both the Godolphin Arabian and the Byerly Turk through his dam. His descendants include trotters and pacers, as well as flat racers—among them Whirlaway and Equipoise. One of Messenger's great-grandsons, Hambletonian (1849), has perhaps an even stronger claim to the title of Standardbred foundation sire, since most living American trotters and pacers descend from him. Although he never raced, he fathered no less than 1,335 foals between 1851 and 1875, many of them superior racers who transmitted the ability to succeeding generations.

One of the most famous was George Wilkes, an ill-starred animal whose dam died after foaling him in an open field. Nursed on cow milk, the orphan grew up to be a formidable champion trotter, whose victory

Modern harness racing presents quite a different picture from that depicted in this pre-1850 painting by an anonymous artist. Wheels as high as the horse's back, the driver sitting upright and bent-kneed in a high-seated sulky . . . all this has changed radically. Only the trotting gait remains the same, and even that is faster due to improved equipment, faster track surfaces, better training methods, and selective breeding.

By the time Dan Patch made harness racing history in the early 1900s, setting a pacing record that remained unbroken for fifty-seven years, the racing sulky and driving style had already undergone great changes—with more to come.

Greyhound (1932) was a great horse by any standard. His trotting achievements are unsurpassed: twenty-five long-standing world records over all distances, under all conditions! He so annihilated his competition that most of his racing exploits were against the clock.

Bret Hanover (1962) was another phenomenal American harness racing star, a veritable pacing machine who also broke and set many records, and who, like Greyhound, captivated the public by his personality as well as by his achievements.

in a historic match race against Ethan Allen presaged the decline of the Morgan as a racing trotter and the rise of the Hambletonian. Although he ended up an alcoholic, corrupted by greedy management, George Wilkes founded the illustrious lines of Axworthy and The Great McKinney, who contributed to the excellence of the modern French trotter through his son Kairos.

One of Hambletonian's outstanding grandchildren was Goldsmith Maid, a fabulous trotting mare, winner of 350 races between 1864 and 1877, and a geriatric wonder: she set her fastest time at the age of nineteen (when she was already holder of four world records), gave birth to her first foal at the age of twenty-two and produced two others later.

The earliest trotting races were mostly match races based on private wagers, and many early participants, like Commodore Cornelius Vanderbilt, were gentlemen owner-drivers. But as urban aristocrats took up flat racing in emulation of the British, harness racing became primarily a rural sport, an attraction of county fairs, a pastime for farmers and ranchers. It has never really developed beyond that stage in the British Isles.

On the Continent, however, organized trotting races, under saddle as well as in harness, were popular in Holland, Belgium, Scandinavia, Germany, Italy, Spain, and eastern European nations, but especially in France, since the early nineteenth century.

The first recorded French trotting event was organized by a young officer of the National Stud, Ephrem Houel, at Cherbourg in 1832. The *Société d'encouragement à l'élevage du cheval français*, the governing body of the French trotting world, dates back to 1864. The Trotting Stud Book was established only in 1906, but the five foundation sires it designates were all born around 1870: Normand, Lavater, Niger, Conquérant (the most influential), and Phaéton (son of a Thoroughbred sire and a Norfolk Trotter mare who was also the dam of Conquérant; the esteemed Quo Vadis and James Watt families descend from him). Their names figure in the pedigree of most modern French trotters, many of which also have ties to two twentieth-century American imports: The Great McKinney and Sam Williams.

At first a provincial activity, French trotting races moved to Paris in 1879, when the flat track at Vincennes was arranged to accommodate harness racing. Tracks were built at Le Tremblay (once the principal trotting training and racing establishment), at Enghien outside Paris, at Toulouse and Bordeaux, and at Cagnes on the Côte d'Azur. Caen and Saint-Malo in Normandy remained among the most important.

In 1920 the Prix d'Amérique, an international event, was run for the first time at Vincennes. Named in tribute to the American Expeditionary Force of World War I, its winner is recognized as Champion European Trotter of the Year. The first was Pro Patria. The next two

228

runnings were won by Passeport, driven by Paul Viel, founder of a harness racing dynasty: his son, Albert Viel, leading owner in 1978 and from 1981 through 1984, was President of the French trotting association for many years; his grandsons now are trotting trainers.

After the outbreak of World War II, trotting races, like flat racing, continued on a reduced scale during the German Occupation. The horses had feed ration cards. Many of the best were exported to Germany. Some were repatriated after the war; others disappeared forever.

Due to the postwar passion for distraction and to a succession of brilliant trotters, the sport soared to new heights of popularity. Gélinotte was a national celebrity. She won fifty-four out of eighty-seven races (compare that figure to the twenty or so races of the average Thoroughbred), including the three most important international events at Vincennes in 1956: the Prix d'Amérique, the Prix de France, and the Prix de Paris, run on successive Sundays. And she repeated the sweep in 1957.

Her Irish-born trainer-driver Charley Mills was also a celebrity. He had owned a successful trotting establishment in Berlin before the war and was persuaded to emigrate to France during a chance meeting on a train with Marcel Boussac's secretary. Mills took Gélinotte in hand after several other trainers had abandoned her, despite the promise of her pedigree: her sire was Kairos, her grandmother the legendary racing mare Uranie, three-time winner of the Prix d'Amérique (1926–

After the race the groom takes over. This one displays a "Hambletonian" emblem on his jacket, a superior label indeed. Hambletonian, the horse, was the "great father" from whom 99 percent of modern American harness horses descend, and the race for three-year-old trotters that bears his name, now run at the Meadowlands in New Jersey, is one of the most prestigious on the American harness racing calendar.

Preceding pages: Idéal du Gazeau, a superstar French trotter, enjoys a relaxing stroll on the sandy shores of Mont-St.-Michel in Normandy, the region where the vast majority of French trotters are bred, trained, and introduced to racing on the many regional trotting tracks.

1928). Mills was undiscouraged by her previous record. "The perfect horse does not exist," he said. "If you insist on perfection, you'll never have a horse in your barn or a woman in your bed." Mills's training genius was not limited to horses; many leading drivers learned their skills from him.

Jamin (1953) brought the excellence of the modern French trotter to the attention of the American harness world. Driven by Jean Riaud, he won everywhere, over all distances, setting many speed records: forty out of seventy-one races, including the Prix de Paris and Prix d'Amérique twice, and a triumphant American campaign in 1959 during which he won the Roosevelt International over the mighty Italian trotter Tornese (perhaps the best Italy has ever produced) and the reigning American champion Trader Horn. He then proceeded to break track records at Springfield and du Quoin, Illinois. American Standardbred breeders were stunned, American racegoers captivated by the dark brown horse. When the press reported that Riaud fed Jamin a daily ration of fresh artichokes (a luxury vegetable then), his stable was inundated with truckloads of them.

Jamin's reign inevitably came to an end in 1960, when he failed in his attempt to win the Prix d'Amérique for a third time, faced with an insurmountable handicap of 55 yards/50 m against top competition. His third place was 2 seconds faster than that of the winner, Hairos II,

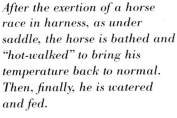

After the exertion of a horse race in harness, as under saddle, the horse is bathed and "hot-walked" to bring his temperature back to normal. Then, finally, he is watered and fed.

but such were the rules of the game in France. Nor did Hairos II lack speed: his 1959 time-trial record of 1:13.4 per kilometer remained unbroken until 1986, and he followed his Prix d'Amérique victory with another in the Roosevelt International.

Prosperous at home, admired abroad, the French trotter was given a residence worthy of its standing in 1964: the Domaine du Grosbois, a magnificent national training complex on the outskirts of Paris, with a lovely château in the background, over fifty English-style training "yards," 200 acres/81 hectares of training terrain, and the most modern equine hospital in Europe. Harness racing is a nationalized industry in France; no private enterprise could provide such sumptuous installations.

During the 1960s the Domaine became a matriarchy, ruled by a succession of trotting mares. The first was Masina, owned and driven by Henri Levesque, a leading figure in French harness racing until his death in 1984, when his widow took over the operations if not the reins. Masina sent more money to the bank than any French horse in history. Ozo, a precocious filly owned by a lucky farmer, won the Prix d'Amérique in 1963 and 1965. From 1966 through 1968 Roquépine, another Levesque discovery, assumed monopoly of the race. He drove her to victory in the 1967 and 1968 Roosevelt International, dethroning the American champion, Su Mac Lad, as the world's richest trotter.

On major American harness racetracks, like Roosevelt Raceway in New York, pacing events far outnumber trotting races. The pace, clearly demonstrated here, is a two-beat gait in which the lateral legs move forward simultaneously. It is slightly faster than the racing trot.

Last of the matriarchs was Une de Mai, who won everything, everywhere—except for the Prix d'Amérique. She rather belied her name. The first of May is a national holiday throughout Europe, and the most important festival in the Communist calendar; whereas Une de Mai was the Queen of Vincennes, a capitalist at the bank, and her owner was Count de Montesson.

Bellino II, a big athletic horse driven by expert reinsman Jean-René Gougeon, was the French champion from 1975 to 1977. Then appeared Idéal du Gazeau, a genuine superstar. What was so special about him? Nothing in his outward appearance. Although his pedigree traced back on both sides to Quo Vadis and Sam Williams, he was an ordinary-looking little black horse with a blaze and an eye that showed a lot of white (not a reassuring sign to horsemen, as a rule). But he proved his superiority in almost every nation where trotting races exist, often breaking speed records in the process. He won the European Championship twice (in 1981 and 1983); he equaled the record set by Une de Mai by winning the Grand Circuit Trophy, awarded to the winner of the major European trotting events, three times (1980–1982). Three times he won the Roosevelt International (1981–1983). Leading money-winner at the track, he set another record in 1983 when, having retired from racing at the age of nine (ten is the legal maximum in France), he was sold to a Swedish breeding syndicate for $1.5 million. French fans lamented the fact that he would not reap full rewards for his glorious achievements: in the interest of safety and maximum production, his breeding activities would take place entirely by artificial insemination.

Lurabo, Lutin d'Isigny, Minou du Donjon, Mon Tourbillon, Ourasi, and Pontcaral were leaders of succeeding generations. (In France, each year is given a certain letter of the alphabet, and all foals born that year must bear a name starting with that letter.) The most exceptional may well be Ourasi, who won the Prix d'Amérique in 1986, as well as fifteen out of fifteen major races, with an uncanny racing instinct that amazed his trainer-driver Jean-René Gougeon. His owner, Raoul Ostheimer, a dedicated elderly Normandy breeder, had been selling the family furniture in order to maintain his modest farm when Ourasi's success made him a millionaire and the most envied trotter owner in Europe.

Harness racing in America developed parallel to the European sport at first, as was quite natural since they share the same history and breed origins. But in the latter half of the nineteenth century their paths deviated in slightly different directions, as indicated by the terms they use to designate the sport: "le trot" in France comprises mounted as well as harness races, exclusively in the trotting gait; "harness racing" in America is exclusively in harness, but in pacing as well as trotting gaits (with pacing races predominating four to one).

Pages 232–233: Harness racing in America as elsewhere is an all-weather sport. Drivers and horses soon learn to take all kinds of track conditions in their stride—in this case the trot.

In America, too, the important early races were for trotters. Pacing had a serious drawback: once broken, the gait was difficult to resume. Then pacing hobbles (also "hopples") were invented around 1885, a device linking each lateral pair of legs with leather straps, making a break of stride practically impossible, and the drawback became an advantage. Pacing races are unaffected by breaks of gait, often imperceptible from the stands; bettors consider pacing results less influenced by luck. Pacers also are race-trained more quickly and easily than trotters, and they earn a return on their investment sooner. Dominant in America, popular in Australia and New Zealand, pacing races are, however, virtually nonexistent elsewhere.

American and European governing bodies have adopted different methods of equalizing the chances of all the horses in a race. Successful European trotters are penalized by distance—as much as 110 yards/100 m in the case of Uranie (although this tradition is gradually disappearing). The automobile-mounted starting gate, or "autostart," is thus precluded from handicap events and from races where there are more than twenty starters, as is often the case in France, where the elastic starting tape is still used at times. European horses warm up for three minutes on a track adjacent to the course (misleadingly called a "canter") before they cross the starting line. American trotters and pacers—averaging eight to a race—warm up on the track itself and start the race by coming into line behind the moving autostart. When the horses cross the starting line, the autostart speeds ahead out of their way and the race is on.

In America, the most common distance is one mile/1.6 km, which would be a sprinting distance in Europe, where major events are trotted over 2,600 to 3,100 meters (1.6 to 2 miles), sometimes more. In Europe distances are measured in meters, and the horse's speed is "reduced," or translated into the time it would have taken the horse to cover one kilometer. European tracks are wider and longer, with more open turns than those of typical American ½-, ⅝-, and 1-mile ovals, which are banked around the curves but otherwise flat. At Vincennes, there are uphill and downhill stretches.

Slightly different methods penalize a trotter for breaking gait, which is a constant risk since the horse's instinct beyond a certain speed is to gallop. Motorized gaiting judges supervise the race. In Europe, when an irregular stride occurs, the horse is "distanced" or placed last. In America, if a horse that has broken gait finishes among the winners, less than 1 length ahead of the legitimate second-place horse, he is said to be "lapped on" and is automatically set behind the latter. But both rules require the driver to pull over to the side of the track at once and resume a proper gait; he is not permitted to gain ground in a gallop (nor may he cut in front of another unless he is 2 lengths ahead).

235

Trotting races on small tracks in rural settings are typical of the harness racing sport in France, as here at Mont-St.-Michel in Normandy.

Trotters break gait for many reasons: fatigue, overexcitement, unbalance, interference (in which case the interfering horse could be disqualified after a justified protest). A break of gait most often destroys all hope of winning a race; but it can be a boon to a rival boxed in behind the breaker, who then has a clear way ahead as the breaker pulls aside.

Finally, trotters race under saddle as well as in harness in Europe, an almost forgotten tradition in America, perhaps because they are very difficult to ride. Nor do many trotters excel in both disciplines. Some who have were Masina, Bellino II, and Kaiser Trot. But the most spectacular was Tidalium Pelo, who won the French championship for mounted as well as harness trotting (the Prix du Cornulier and the Prix d'Amérique) in 1971 and again in 1972. Remarkably game and resilient, he was the victim of a series of accidents that would have finished off most horses: a bruised hip, cut ankle, tendon trouble requiring six months in a plaster cast, and a harrowing experience in 1969 when the boxcar in which he was returning to France from a successful Italian campaign was abandoned on a sidetrack in the middle of winter. He was rescued at last, half dead from cold, thirst, and hunger, standing guard over the body of his companion Roc Williams, who had frozen to death.

236

Mounted trotting races still exist in Europe but have disappeared from the American scene.

At urban American harness racetracks such as Roosevelt Raceway in New York, night races, held in a glamorous atmosphere, are on the increase.

At Vincennes, outside Paris, where some of the most important European trotting races are run (including the virtual European Championship, the Prix d'Amérique), night racing in a luxurious environment has transformed an informal rural sport into a sophisticated evening entertainment.

The United States and France, the leading harness racing nations, have produced slightly different horses with the qualities geared to the two nations' different racing conditions: stamina and speed during relatively long careers for the French trotter; speed over shorter distances, briefer but more precocious careers for the American Standardbred. Consider the eight-year, hundred-race career of Idéal du Gazeau, and the mere two racing seasons of the American pacer Niatross, Harness Horse of the Year as a two-year-old in 1979 (who could vote against him?—he'd won thirteen of thirteen races), and again in 1980 (winning twenty-four of twenty-six), whereupon he was retired to stud.

The first official American trotting event took place on Long Island in 1826. By the middle of the nineteenth century, trotting races were so popular in the Northeast and Middle West (Southerners tended to snub the sport at first), that it spread from the country to the cities. In 1870 an association was formed to establish rules and supervise the sport, the predecessor of the present ruling body, the United States Trotting Association.

Toward the turn of the century, the invention of the automobile led to a drastic decline in the horse population and a decline in harness racing, which survived as a rather quaint sport, seen mostly at county fairs and on provincial tracks.

But harness horsemen were inventive too. Pacing hobbles, as mentioned, came into use around 1885. In 1893, a racing sulky with pneumatic bicycle tires replaced the high-wheeled, heavier vehicle previously used. It was adopted throughout the harness-racing world, remaining basically unchanged until the 1970s, when the wooden frame was replaced by one of steel or aluminum, with shorter, straighter shafts. A little later, the wheel spokes were covered with plastic discs in the interest of safety and aerodynamics.

During the first half of the twentieth century, American harness racing flourished, perhaps because of a succession of wonderful horses, some of whom became as rich and famous as Thoroughbred racing stars:

Dan Patch, for example, toured from coast to coast in his private railroad car, greeted by cheering crowds at every way station. He was a dark bay pacer, 17 hands tall (huge for a Standardbred), who so annihilated his competition during the early 1900s that his career was devoted mostly to time trials and exhibitions. He paced miles of 1:57 and 1:56 with incredible regularity, and set the record of 1:55¼ that stood for thirty-three years until Billy Direct bettered it by a quarter-second in 1938. During ten years of racing (without hobbles), he paced a two-minute (or less) mile thirty times—another record that seemed unbeatable until Bret Hanover scored his thirty-first two-minute mile

237

in 1966 during his sixty-second race—and with that final triumph, retired. The present holder is Rambling Willie, who performed the feat seventy-nine times between 1972 and 1983.

During the 1930s, harness racing attracted nationwide attention thanks to the charisma of a big gray gelding named Greyhound, perhaps the greatest trotter ever born. His dam was a daughter of Peter the Great, his sire Guy Abbey of the McKinney line. Trained and driven by Sep Palin, he had a naturally high head carriage (ideal for a trotter, since it tends to keep the horse from breaking trotting gait) and an unusually long stride that covered 21 feet/6.4 m. From his racing debut in 1934 until his retirement in 1940, he set twenty-five world records, some of which still stand, ranging from distances of ¼ to 2 miles/400 m to 3.2 km, over half-mile and mile tracks, in harness, in double harness, during races and in time trials, even under saddle (ridden by the late Frances Dodge, co-owner with her husband, Frederick Van Lennep, of Castleton Farm in Kentucky, where many champions are bred and trained). He failed to win only four races during his career, three of the losses as a novice two-year-old. By the time he was five, he had practically run out of competition and raced mostly against the clock. The image of that handsome horse, forging ahead like a majestic ship under full sail, was an unforgettable sight to all who saw him—and most Americans did, if only in newsreels and newspaper photos.

After World War II, American harness racing enjoyed a boom due to the surge of interest in all sports, but also to energetic promotion and controls by the U.S. Trotting Association to dispel the slightly shady reputation that had always haunted it; the introduction of night racing, pari-mutuel betting, and the mobile starting gate gave further impetus to the sport. Entrepreneurs built luxurious new hippodromes like Roosevelt Raceway in New York; historic ovals were expanded and renovated. Four hundred fairground tracks and fifty harness tracks are now active from New York to California, though still concentrated in the eastern United States and Canada, and in the Middle West. The most modern of them, like the Meadowlands in New Jersey, are equipped for all kinds of racing and equestrian sports. Richly endowed harness races were founded to supplement the Classic events. The Breeders' Crown, created by the Hambletonian Society in 1984, consists of a series of six-figure races throughout the country.

The most famous harness racing Classics are the 1 mile/1.6 km, two- or three-heat three-year-old events that constitute the Triple Crowns:

For trotters these are: the Yonkers Trot (at Yonkers Raceway), the Hambletonian (now run at the Meadowlands), and the Kentucky Futurity (at Lexington's historic Red Mile since 1893). Only five horses have won all three: Scott Frost (1955), Speedy Scot (1963), Ayres (1964), Nevele Pride (1968), Lindy's Pride (1969), and Super Bowl (1983)—the

Undefeated pacer Forrest Skipper, who was voted 1986 Harness Horse of the Year in a close finish with undefeated two-year-old Jate Lobell, has given his trainer-driver, Lucien Fontaine, every reason to smile: ". . . I may never again get a horse like Forrest Skipper. That doesn't bother me, because I see myself as a lucky man—there are so many horsemen out there who are talented enough to handle a great horse, but never lucky enough to get one. I can't believe we debated who should be Horse of the Year! There was no free-for-aller like Forrest Skipper in the years that Bret Hanover and Niatross won the title as two-year-olds. . . . I think my best chance to have another Forrest Skipper is to breed to Forrest Skipper."

238

last four sired by Castleton Farm's phenomenal stallion Star's Pride, the last two trained and driven by masterful Stanley Dancer.

For pacers these are: the Messenger Stakes (at Roosevelt Raceway), the Cane Futurity (at Yonkers Raceway), and the Little Brown Jug (highlight of the Delaware, Ohio, County Fair). The pacing Triple Crown has been won by Adios Butler (1959), Bret Hanover (1965), Romeo Hanover (1966), Rum Customer (1968, also driven to world-record winnings by the late Billy Haughton, a top trainer-driver for over forty years), Most Happy Fella (1970, a Stanley Dancer protégé and now the leading money-winning sire), Niatross (1980, son of the eminent sire Albatross, and now a star stallion in his own right), and Ralph Hanover (1983).

Among the other major events in the U.S. harness racing calendar are international races to which foreign trotters are invited, such as the Yonkers Challenge Cup and the Roosevelt International, which is the unofficial world championship. French trotters have won it ten times during the past nineteen years. In pacing, however, the American Standardbred reigns supreme.

Two of the best pacers in history were Adios Butler and Bret Hanover, both of them sons of Adios, a successful racer for five years and a sensational sire for eighteen, during nine of which he was the leading pacer sire of America. His crowning achievement was Bret

Taking a turn on an American harness track. The driver sits with widespread legs braced in fixed "stirrups." His seat is low to ensure the balance of the lightweight racing sulky in such circumstances.

239

Hanover, who dominated pacing during the 1960s, winning sixty-two of sixty-eight races, setting nine world records and breaking two more, in addition to countless track and event records. He performed even more two-minute miles than Dan Patch, whose record had stood for fifty-seven years, and was voted Harness Horse of the Year for an unprecedented three times (1964–1966) while his trainer-driver Frank Ervin was Harness Horseman of the Year for the third time in 1966.

Could Nihilator, a son of Niatross, grandson of Albatross, voted 1985 Harness Horse of the Year, be, as some maintain, the greatest pacer ever? He is certainly the most precocious. At the age of three, trained by Billy Haughton and driven by Bill O'Donnell, he'd already won the most money and paced the fastest racing mile. Or will it be Jate Lobell, undefeated in fifteen races as a two-year-old pacer, setting records everywhere he's raced?

The most important trotting record defied generations of harness racers: Greyhound's trotting time for a mile in 1:55¼, set in 1938. But that, too, finally fell before the assault of a chunky, high-strung little horse called Nevele Pride, who set a new mile record in 1969 of 1:54⅕ that stood for eleven years before it was equaled by Lindy's Crown in 1980 (driven by Howard Beissinger), and bettered by Arndon in 1982 (driven by Del Miller, a leading harness racing figure since 1929). Fancy Crown (driven by Bill O'Donnell in 1984) and Cornstalk (driven by Howard Beissinger the same year) both shaved off another quarter-

Trotting races are run rain or shine, but not so often in the snow, as here at St. Moritz.

Niatross (1977), a pacer driven by Clint Galbraith, made harness racing history not only by winning races, but also by setting new speed records. His time of 1:49⅕ for the mile—set at Lexington, Kentucky, in 1980 —is still the world record for all-age as well as three-year-old pacers.

Nevele Pride (1965), driven by Stanley Dancer, was an American superstar trotter who broke Greyhound's longstanding mile record and whose own time of 1:56⅕ for the mile on a half-mile track still stands.

second. The present record holder is Prakas, driven by Bill O'Donnell in 1985 at 1:53⅖ in 1985.

America's trotting hero of the early 1970s was Super Bowl, followed by Classical Way, the unofficial world champion after her victory over Idéal du Gazeau in the 1980 Roosevelt International. Sent to France to face the best European trotters on their toughest track, Vincennes, she was an unlucky third in the Prix d'Amérique, but reaped revenge the following week by setting a new track record when she won the Prix de France.

What does it take to make a champion harness racer, a top driver? The same basic essentials as in any sport: innate talent and acquired technique.

Harness-horse trainers spend more time in training each horse than do their Thoroughbred colleagues, as much as several hours a day. It is a step-by-step procedure, starting with driving in long reins with the trainer on foot, then with harness shanks alone, next hitched to a training sulky (slightly heavier, less fragile than the racing kind), then to the racing sulky itself, finally in timed sprints (or "hits") over measured distances. The racing trot is far more extended than the "working" variety. Much of the trainer's art and the driver's skill lies in knowing how to stretch his trotter to the limit without exceeding the breaking point and without becoming unbalanced. Pacers are simpler and quicker to train. While pacing is considered an acquired gait for horses (though natural to the camel and giraffe), a tendency to produce it has been inbred in certain lines, and hobbles reinforce it.

Aside from hobbles, pacers and trotters wear the same basic harness and tack: a rather elaborate affair at first sight, consisting of a breast collar, saddle pad and girth, split reins with looped handholds leading to the bit and bridle, check rein, martingale and crupper strap, and most often leather leg and joint protection. Both types are hitched to the same racing sulky with standard wheel dimensions; but rein length and the length and separation of the shafts are adjusted to each horse's individual conformation. Bitting is also a matter of individual preference. A head pole and check rein oblige the horse to hold its head high, which tends to keep a trotter trotting; a shadow roll across the nose, to block the horse's view of the track underfoot, may help to keep it from "spooking." An expert farrier can cut seconds from a harness racer's time; judiciously calculated weights in toes or heels can increase extension and improve balance.

Harness drivers possess limited means of control over their horses compared to mounted jockeys. Their principal communication is through the reins. Their legs and feet, placed in fixed stirrups, secure their position and that is all. Nor are voice aids of use in harness racing, for the horses' ears are usually stuffed with cotton and covered with an ear hood to stifle the noise. When his horse crosses the starting line, the driver has to rely a lot on his familiarity with the horse's aptitudes and idiosyncrasies, as well as those of his competitors. Some are by nature "front-runners"; others prefer to come from behind. Some drivers use a stopwatch to pace their horses during a long race, but most of them develop a built-in chronometer. Top drivers wield their long whip with great discretion—like John Campbell, Bill O'Donnell, Norwegian Ulf Thoresen, Hervé Filion (nine times American Driver of the Year between 1969 and 1981), whose record number of 637 wins in a single year is approached only by that of his fellow French Canadian, Michel Lachance, top winning U.S. driver of 1984 and 1985. Do not be misled by wild gesticulations. The best drivers are also the least spectacular.

Since the 1970s, harness racing, like most other equestrian sports, has become increasingly international. World-renowned stars include Germany's Hans Fromming and Belgium's Pierre Vercruysse. The Swedish presence is particularly striking for so small a nation. Haakon Wallner runs important establishments in Sweden and the United States with Berndt Lindstedt. Sören Nordin, preeminent in Sweden for almost half a century, has established headquarters in Florida with his son Jan, while his son Ulf runs a trotting stable in France—where his compatriot Stig Engbers is a leading trotting trainer.

A wet day at Vincennes, but spirits are undampened. Merely to qualify for a major race here is an achievement.

242

From its origins as a rural activity for the pleasure of farmers on Saturday afternoon, harness racing has thus become a sophisticated, multinational business. As in flat racing, there is increased emphasis on two-year-old events and on shorter racing careers in order to allow early stallion syndication for sums undreamed of a decade ago. Nevertheless, the tradition of breeder-owner-trainer-driver is still very much alive. In France, for example, the Levesques, Viels, Marys, Riauds, Dreux, Hallais, and others perpetuate family vocations, while many individuals fill multiple roles: Léopold Verrokken (leading trainer-driver since the late 1970s), the Gougeons, René Baudron, Daniel de Ballaigue, Alain Laurent, Gérard Mascle among them. Ninety percent of the four thousand trotting owners in France are also breeders, trainers, drivers, or all three.

Owning and racing a harness horse is less onerous and less intimidating than owning a Thoroughbred racehorse. Alec Weisweiller, John Gaines, and Nelson Bunker Hunt are among the few Thoroughbred owners to race trotters as well. Flat racing trainers François Boutin and Olivier Douïeb and champion jockey Yves Saint-Martin also "moonlight" as trotting owners in France. But in America harness racing is a world apart. And in Great Britain, its modest existence attracts little attention, while its aristocratic relative, combined driving, thrives.

Other Equestrian Sports

From the Sahara desert to the Himalayan plateaux, from the steppes of Asia to the Argentine pampas, wherever there have been men and horses there have been equestrian sports and games, often derived from the activities essential to the survival of isolated communities: warfare, hunting, and agriculture. It would be impossible to include them all in a single volume, along with those more important horse sports that enjoy the official sanction of major national and international governing bodies. But it would be unfair to ignore completely the amazing variety of mounted games and sports that exists throughout the world.

Their number is virtually infinite. Some survive as part of folklore, revived only on special occasions, and are perhaps more pageantry than sport, like the spectacular Moroccan *Fantasia*, the annual *Palio* horse race in Siena, and the yearly jousting tournament, *Alka Singska*, in Yugoslavia. Some are too cruel for other societies to have adopted, like pigsticking in India, bullfighting in Spain (or even in Portugal, where the bull is not killed), or *buzkashi* in Afghanistan, a game in which the players fight over the possession of a slaughtered sheep or goat. Other horse games are immensely popular, but only in a certain country or region. *Pato*, for example, a gaucho game resembling rugby on horseback, is an official national sport of Argentina; tilting-the-rings, evocative of medieval jousting, is much practiced in Maryland. Many ancient versions of polo are still played: *chaugan* in Persia, *korak* or *okrah* in Arabian lands, *tskhen-burfi* in Russian Georgia, *da-kyu* ("spoon polo") in Japan, China, and Tibet. Various kinds of mounted ball-and-racket games include polocrosse and the Netherlands' popular pushball.

With a regretfully brief salute to all of these riding activities and to the horses that make them possible, let's take a somewhat closer look at a few of the most important "other equestrian sports."

FOX HUNTING

No equestrian sport can boast of more noble origins, none is more picturesque, more thrilling to the rider, than fox hunting. And yet it is one of the few that has not expanded during the latter part of the twentieth century. Some people view it as an anachronism, others as an elitist activity that is beyond their means. To the anti-blood-sports activists it is an abhorrence. To those who follow it assiduously, however, it is more than a sport, it is practically a way of life. That their numbers

The Duke of Beaufort, MFH of the Duke of Beaufort's Hunt for over sixty years:
". . . That spring day I shared a wonderful hunt with the Huntsman. A spark was lit in me that soon grew into a flame destined to last the whole of my life—a true and dedicated love of fox hunting in the deepest sense. I am sure that everyone who has had the good fortune to feel the exhilaration, the excitement, and—what is more—the sense of achievement that is experienced when a successful hunt is concluded, will know what I mean. It is by no means a feeling of personal achievement, but comes from a subtle combination of being at one with both horse and hounds."

are limited is due far more to the disappearance of suburban farm-land, to urbanization, road-building, modern methods of farming and predator destruction, than to a lack of devotion and enthusiasm on their part.

Alexander the Great hunted fox in Asia, as did Persian potentates as early as the fourth century BC and Roman nobles at the dawn of the Christian era. Edward I of England (1272–1307) appointed a Royal Huntsman—aptly named William de Foxhunte. By 1700, the sport was well established among landowners in Great Britain, where Reynard the Fox, the incarnation of wile and stealth, was the bane of farmers, poultrymen, and shepherds. By the end of the eighteenth century, fox hunting was a widespread, established country pursuit in England and Ireland and increasingly democratic. Within the next half-century, the sport consisted of a few large packs owned by aristocratic landowners, and many more smaller ones maintained by country squires or groups of farmers—forerunners of the modern hunt clubs.

On the Continent, it has remained restricted to the more privileged sectors of society and provincial landowners. But almost everywhere, the tradition of privately owned packs hunting over privately owned land is vanishing. The modern hunt is likely to be organized by a hunt club which hires a Huntsman and staff to maintain its pack of hounds, while members provide their own mounts and elect a Master of Foxhounds (MFH).

Fox hunting was brought to America by the British colonists. In 1650, Robert Brooke landed in Maryland with his family, twenty-eight servants, and his pack of hounds. George Washington hunted regularly with his friend Lord Fairfax. The sport remains concentrated in the original colonial states of Virginia, Maryland, Pennsylvania, the Carolinas, New York, and New Jersey, although there are hunts in other states as well. But nowhere is fox hunting as widespread as it is in England and Ireland.

The American Hunt and Pony Racing Association was founded in 1893, but fox hunting in America was governed by the National Steeplechase and Hunt Association until 1934, when the registration and recognition of hunts came under the exclusive authority of the Masters of Foxhounds Association.

Owing to the different kinds of fox and other quarry hunted, different hunts have developed different lines of foxhounds with aptitudes suited to their particular hunting country and prey. They may be distinctive in appearance, but all of them must be purebred English or American foxhounds. Many of the most famous breeds of hunting hounds were created during the early eighteenth century in England: the packs of the Duke of Beaufort and of the Quorn, Pytchley, Belvoir, Cottesmore, Badminton, and Berkeley hunts. In America the Warren-

245

ton, Blue Ridge, Old Dominion, Rosetree, Radnor, Millbrook, and Elkridge and Harford hounds are renowned.

A pack of hunting hounds consists of at least twelve couples; for drag hunting, only six. Some hunts set forth with as many as thirty or forty; some maintain a bitch pack and a dog pack. (To fox hunters, a "dog" is a male hound; all other canine breeds are curs.)

The field of horsemen is also extremely variable, ranging from perhaps a dozen die-hards on a rainy day to twenty-five or thirty in America and three or four times that number in England and Ireland on a sunny holiday weekend—plus a handful or a throng of motorized, pedestrian, and mounted enthusiasts (the latter called "hill-toppers," because they observe the hunt from various vantage points without actually following the hounds).

In fact, fox hunting is really more of a canine sport than an equestrian one. A pack of well-trained, well-disciplined hounds is essential; the horses and riders merely follow them.

Almost any breed of horse that is well behaved in company and can jump is suitable for fox hunting somewhere, but generally speaking, the best are Thoroughbreds. Irish Hunters are famous for their speed, courage, and jumping ability over the banks and streams frequently encountered on Irish hunting grounds. Over the sandy, rocky terrain of the western United States, Quarter Horses or Quarter Horse–Thoroughbred crosses are preferred.

Fox hunting country also varies enormously: from 100 acres to 250 square miles/40 hectares to 650 km² of farmland and woods where foxes build their lairs, studded with fences, ditches, stone walls, hedges, banks (especially in Ireland), and streams to be jumped, gates to be opened. Because of the widespread use of barbed-wire fencing, many hunts install jumping panels made of split rails or chicken coops in order to reduce the danger. But danger is ever present, with so much jumping for hours on end over varied obstacles on uncertain footing, often at breakneck speed. Few individuals or clubs own sufficient land, so it is often leased. Friendly arrangements also are made with farmers and landowners to permit the hunt to cross their territory in return for an indemnity if fields or crops are damaged. The fox hunting season is scheduled to reduce the risk, starting after the autumn crops have been harvested and ending before spring seeds are sown. Cub hunting (or cubbing), to train young hounds and give experience to green horses, takes place earlier.

The object of such elaborate preparations? In England and the eastern United States, it is the red or gray fox; in the West, coyote and hare, all of them fast and cunning. In France and Eastern Europe, deer, stag, and wild boar are the traditional prey and larger hounds are used to hunt them. In order to offer sport where no such quarry exists, "drag hunts" are organized. The Huntsman and his staff set

The wily fox is a killer of sheep and poultry, and hunting him has—perhaps ironically— given birth to one of the most scenic of all the equestrian sports.

A Huntsman with his hounds in Virginia, a state with a long tradition of fox hunting. George Washington himself hunted there!

246

a cross-country course by dragging a bag containing scent for the hounds to follow.

The Master of Foxhounds is in charge of all proceedings. The Huntsman (usually a professional, when it is not the Master who fills both roles or, as they say, "carries the horn") manages the pack, aided by his liveried whippers-in who keep the pack together and "whip in" stray or lagging hounds. He instructs the hounds with a variety of sounds on his hunting horn as well as by voice signals; he interprets the yips and yelps that are euphemistically called "the music" of the pack. A Field Master is in charge of the riders.

The hunt assembles at the appointed venue with a certain amount of traditional ceremony. Even the riders' appointments are rigorously prescribed. The brass-buttoned scarlet coat (called "hunting pinks" supposedly after a famous nineteenth-century London tailor whose name was Pink) is reserved for gentlemen riders of experience, while the black hunting cap is a distinguishing mark of the Master, of hunt officials and servants, and of children. The others wear black bowlers or, on formal occasions, top hats. Hunt colors worn on the collars of ladies' black coats and gentlemen's black or pink ones, like the hunt insignia on the buttons, must be earned and granted by the Master. To "receive the button" is a mark of distinction.

When the Master gives the word, the Huntsman moves the pack to the first cover where he expects to find a fox. The hounds begin "casting," seeking the scent. Once roused, the fox usually takes off for open country. A series of sounds on the Huntsman's horn and a shout of "Tally Ho!" indicate that the fox has "gone away," and the chase is on. Some foxes run straight, some circle, some head for home if they are outside of their own territory. All are fast and exceedingly wily in trying to elude their pursuers. A "run" can last from half an hour to all day long.

The hounds lead the hunt, accompanied by the Huntsman and the whippers-in. The Master leads the field, staying far enough behind the pack to avoid interfering with its work. Protocol governs places in the field: senior members and distinguished guests up near the Master; junior and elderly members and inexperienced horses toward the rear.

If the hounds lose the scent, there is a "check" and the Huntsman gathers and recasts the pack. If it seems irretrievable, he "lifts" the pack to another spot where he hopes to pick up the line. Runs and checks continue until the fox is either caught and killed, or has "gone to earth" (found refuge in his den or in a hole where the hounds cannot follow). In fact, actual kills and the subsequent traditional ceremonies are rare in most countries now.

The Huntsman then leads the pack to another cover where a new

A fox hunt setting forth: The Huntsman and hounds accompanied by the whippers-in in front, followed by the Master and the field.

Pages 250–251: Once hounds are running and there are fences to be jumped, every field (like the Quorn, seen here) soon sorts itself out.

249

fox is raised, and it is again "Gone away!" And the hunt continues until the Master has decided it is time to turn for home.

How can one convey the fascination of fox hunting in words? One has to experience personally the thrill of the chase with its speed and risks, the natural beauty of the countryside viewed from horseback in these unique circumstances, the incredible efficiency and enthusiasm of a good pack of hounds, the unforgettable panorama of it all. Only then can one understand why so much of our finest sporting art and sculpture has depicted fox hunting, why much of the wisest and wittiest equestrian literature is concerned with it, why so many famous horsemen throughout history have been obsessed by this exhilarating, spectacular sport, so glorified and so maligned.

Fox hunting in Ireland is renowned for its great variety of banks, walls, and ditches. Here, a follower of the County Limerick Hunt makes a bold attack at a difficult ditch.

HORSE SHOWS

Horse shows are the modern version of an old country tradition: the horse fair, where working farm horses, heavy harness breeds as well as driving and riding horses, were judged by experts, bought, and sold.

Some horse shows are still a feature of agricultural and livestock fairs, but to many people a horse show is synonymous with show jumping. Although this is indeed the most exciting part—the easiest to follow, the most telegenic—jumping is merely one division of twenty that are recognized and governed by the American Horse Shows Association (AHSA); even more divisions are recognized by the British Horse Society. Hardly a single weekend passes in America, England, and Ireland without a number of horse shows taking place somewhere, outdoors or indoors. On the Continent there is no exact equivalent on a similar scale, except perhaps the annual Salon du Cheval in Paris.

In its vast computerized headquarters in New York City, the AHSA records show results, establishes, revises, and enforces regulations, registers members, authorizes judges, tabulates Horse of the Year points, hears protests, manages drug testing, publishes rules and regulations for authorized events in various divisions. The list ranges from A (for Arabian) to W (for Western), and there are more than two thousand of them. Even so, the majority of horse shows are informal events, unsanctioned by the AHSA.

What sets a horse show apart from most other equestrian contests is that horses of various breeds, ages, and training are judged not only on their performance, but also sometimes on their quality, beauty, and style. Take as an example the AHSA Hunter Division, the most popular in the eastern United States, where horse shows have existed for over a century.

Three divisions are devoted to Hunters: Hunter, Hunter Breeding, and Hunter and Jumper Pony for riders under eighteen years of age.

In order to reach the venue of most American fox hunts, the horses have to be transported by vehicle. But in Virginia (as here) and in Maryland, too, hunt members often hack to the meet and home again at the end of the day.

The first is further subdivided into Breeding classes (shown in hand rather than ridden) and Conformation (in which performance over a course of typical hunting obstacles determines the winners). There are over thirty possible different classes for Working Hunters alone. The most popular section, whose entry list is first to fill, is that reserved for Amateur Owners.

It takes two hundred pages of small print in the rulebook to enumerate the events of every division. Needless to add, no show offers all. Each Show Committee prepares its list of classes, taking into account the facilities and time available and the particular equestrian interests of the area in which the show is held. Hunter and Jumper events thus predominate in England and in most shows in the eastern U.S., which may consist of nothing else. Western riding contests predominate in the West. Classes for Saddle Horses and Hackney and Harness ponies are extremely popular in the Middle West but are less often scheduled elsewhere.

Moreover, many horse shows are organized by breed associations, reserved for that breed and with competitions specific to it. The Morgan Horse, for example, an appealing, strictly American breed that originated in the Northeast, competes as a park horse, parade horse, pleasure horse, trail horse, driving horse, road hack, stock horse, cutting horse, roadster, working hunter, and jumper. In the "Justin Morgan class" (named after the foundation sire) he is required to trot a half-mile/.8 km in harness, then run a half-mile under saddle, next show in the ring at a trot, walk, and canter, and finally pull a 500-pound/ 225 kg stone boat a distance of 6 feet/180 cm in work harness.

Arabian Horse show events are no less varied: there are Western specialties such as pole bending and barrel racing, cutting and reining contests, as well as riding, driving, sidesaddle, jumping, dressage—and an event in which the riders wear gorgeous Arabian costume. Arabian versatility extends beyond the show ring, onto the racetrack: Arab racing is a growing sport in England and America, and has long been popular in certain regions of France, Africa, and the Middle East.

The Appaloosa is so distinctive and versatile a breed that it too has its own events and its own shows, governed by the Appaloosa Horse Club. Instantly recognizable from its striking coat and markings (a white or roan base with black or brown spots scattered mostly on the hindquarters), the Appaloosa is a native American breed developed by the Nez Percé Indians in Idaho, originally as a war pony and hunter. They can now be found around the world on ranches, on endurance trails, in the hunting field, on the racetrack, in the jumping arena, in the show ring. There, in addition to the classic Western events, they may be ridden Eastern-style as well, and also compete in various Appaloosa games like the stump race (similar to barrel racing, with

Many American Saddlebred horses are bred and trained especially for the show ring. The Three-Gaited type appears with a clipped mane and tail. The Five-Gaited type (above) wears its mane and tail long and flowing, and in addition to the walk, trot, and canter, it is trained to perform a slow gait (the stepping pace) and a fast one (the rack).

254

two contestants racing against each other in opposite directions) and the rope race (a variation of Musical Chairs).

The American Quarter Horse can be trained to do so many different things that they also have shows all to themselves in addition to the AHSA Western Division: 2,400 of them every year are recognized by the Texas-based American Quarter Horse Association, one of the most dynamic and fast-growing of all breed organizations, with an elaborate, diversified range of activities and functions.

The breed began in Colonial Virginia, where the Arab, Barb, and Turk stallions accompanying Spanish explorers were bred to imported English mares. The result was a compact, heavily muscled horse that was a phenomenal sprinter; its name comes from the quarter-mile/ 0.4 km distance that was its specialty. With the opening of the West, the Quarter Horse turned from sport to work and proved to possess superior ability in handling cattle and as a trail-driving horse. Later, as the use of horses for ranch work gave way to mechanization, the breed seemed in danger of extinction. The AQHA was founded in 1940, dedicated to the protection and promotion of Quarter Horses—a goal achieved with such success that there are now over 2 million listed in its registry, and over 700,000 Quarter Horse owners throughout the world, both figures far exceeding those of any other breed.

A sizable class of Five-Gaited Saddlebreds vies for the judges' approval at the Devon Horse Show, one of the oldest and most prestigious outdoor shows in the United States.

255

Quarter Horses compete in an incredible variety of events at more than 2,500 breed shows every year. They may be shown in Eastern tack, but far more often Western-style in seventeen performance specialties including working cow-horse classes, calf roping, dally team roping, trail riding, and pole bending (a timed slalom-style race). At the same time, the Quarter Horse's original role as a racehorse is not forgotten. More than a hundred tracks in the western U.S. conduct Quarter Horse races over short distances and offer some of the richest purses in the racing world: $1 million to the winner of the All-American Futurity at Ruidoso Downs, New Mexico (the capital of Quarter Horse racing). To date, the fastest time recorded over the customary quarter-mile/0.4 km is 21:02 seconds (a blistering 46 miles per hour/74 kph). The most famous, highest-earning sprinter is Dash for Cash, now at stud.

Side-saddle classes are enjoying a renascence in America, after having practically disappeared from the horse show scene. This stylish rider is Joy Carrier, an accomplished equestrienne astride as well. She was the first woman jockey to win the Maryland Hunt Cup (in 1980 and 1981 on Cancottage).

Quarter Horse owners seem to thrive on competition and appreciate awards, for there are many of them. Champions abound. A sufficient number of points earned in performance events qualifies a horse for the Register of Merit. To win a championship title, the horse must earn a specified number of points at halter as well as in performance. The annual World Championship in Oklahoma City sets attendance records every year, a tribute to this engaging, typically American, remarkably sporting animal.

Almost any horse can be entered in a horse show somewhere and find a class or classes suited to its abilities. But when one speaks of a "show horse," the image that comes to mind is that of the American Saddlebred which, along with the Tennessee Walking Horse, was developed on plantations in Kentucky, Tennessee, and Missouri to provide a comfortable, elegant means of transportation either under saddle or in light harness. Its official foundation sire was Denmark, a Thoroughbred racer; but the breed has become quite different in appearance and action. Short-backed, high-headed, with a long, tapering neck, the Saddlebred picks his feet high off the ground and has a distinctive way of moving. The Three-Gaited Saddle Horse (who wears his mane roached and the top of his tail clipped) produces the three natural gaits (walk, trot, canter) with a high degree of elevation and cadence. The Five-Gaited (usually heavier, with a long, flowing mane and tail) is trained to produce two additional "artificial" gaits: a slow, syncopated, four-beat stepping pace, and a fast rack. The latter is a spectacular, smooth, extended movement in which each foot strikes the ground at equal intervals in a streak of speed. It is tiring for the horse, but thrilling to the rider and spectators. No other breed performs it with such brilliance.

The Paso Fino, an elegant, ancient Spanish breed recently accorded a horse show division of its own, also produces spectacular gaits in the show ring, natural to it alone: an animated, collected walk; the Classic Fino (an evenly spaced, four-beat lateral gait, fast and flashy); the Paso

Corto (similar, but with moderate speed and extension); and the Paso Largo (collected, bold, and animated, with longer extension and greater speed); a smooth canter; and a slower-cadenced lope.

Ribbons and trophies are an end in themselves for owners of such "show horses," resulting in the same distinction between the show and working varieties of some breeds as exists between a champion show collie and a working sheep dog. A champion conformation show hunter is seldom seen in the hunting field, if only to avoid a blemish that might compromise his career. He'd probably be unable to stay the distance anyway, because show judges like their hunters plump, while fox hunters keep them lean and fit.

Showmanship is most evident in the Saddlebred division. The horses are groomed with the greatest care to enhance their glamourous appearance (often with the aid of hair dye and tail wigs); their rather fancy trappings gleam; their riders wear dapper Kentucky jodhpurs, short boots, a flared jacket nipped in at the waist and perhaps lined with bright satin. Nor would a Saddlebred show horse survive a hard day's work on a plantation. His feet are permitted to grow to an exaggerated length, and weighted shoes increase his high action.

Little girls and ponies seem to have an affinity for one another. Children of riding parents may be taught to ride almost at the same time they learn to walk. But her mother's hand may not be necessary to support this child as she enters the ring for a pony class. Experienced ponies can be incredibly indulgent and understanding with tiny tots.

The Equitation Division (subdivided into Hunter, Saddle, and Stock Seat), for riders under eighteen years of age, is another in which competition is extremely keen and entries so numerous that the National Maclay (Hunter Seat) Finals have sometimes had to start at 3 o'clock in the morning in order to fit them all in. Hunter Seat is, of course, most important, because there are no FEI competitions for Saddle Seat or Western riding, and no Olympic event. The rider, not the horse, is judged. But it's not enough to be a good rider in order to win, as strategy, showmanship, a suitable mount, and the judge's personal preference in equestrian style also are involved. Many winning rounds of top jumper riders would be placed at the bottom of the scorecard by a Hunter Equitation judge. The competitors usually are accompanied by a trainer who helps them school their horse and advises on show-ring strategy as the class proceeds. Together they plan their season's campaign with the goal of reaching the finals and winning one of the medals awarded to the young riders with the most points each year in certain Equitation events. While no prize money is permitted, glory is not the sole reward: the annual leaders are sometimes invited to train at the U.S. Equestrian Team headquarters, and quite a few have eventually made the team. Bill Steinkraus, Frank Chapot, George Morris, Mary Mairs, Bernie Traurig, and Conrad Homfeld were all Maclay Medal winners in their early teens before being selected to represent the United States in international show-jumping events.

With hundreds of horse shows scheduled throughout the year, it is a prosperous industry for horse show managers, announcers, and sup-

257

pliers; a full-time activity for many professional horsemen and women; and an opportunity for horse dealers to display their wares and for riders and trainers to demonstrate their skill.

Many horse shows are also highlights of the social season: the elegant National in New York (which in 1983 celebrated its centenary), the shows in Harrisburg, Pennsylvania (far less formal), Toronto (during the Royal Winter Agricultural Fair), Devon, Pennsylvania (more intimate but prestigious), Kansas City (the American Royal), San Francisco (with social status to match the city's opera), Washington, D.C. (traditionally attended by the President), and Palm Beach. England's most select shows are London's Olympia and the Horse-of-the-Year Show at Wembley. Completing the international circuit are the Paris Bercy show (in a spectacular futuristic new stadium), the Rotterdam Horse Show (in the presence of the Queen of the Netherlands), and the Dublin Horse Show (with a week of nightly balls). But the vast majority of horse shows are local affairs which provide a pleasant diversion for horses and riders of modest ability, an occasion to see old friends and make new ones who share a passion for horses.

ENDURANCE RIDING

In endurance riding, it is not only a question of "How fast?" but of "How fast, how far, without impairing soundness?"

Long-distance rides by individuals seeking to set a record or win a wager have long existed. The U.S. Cavalry used to test its horses in five-day 300-mile/480 km treks carrying weights of 200 pounds/90 kg or more. These were undoubtedly the inspiration for endurance riding as a sporting activity, which originated in America, spread to England in the 1960s, to Continental Europe in the 1970s, and in 1985 was recognized by the FEI as an official international equestrian sport.

It is a competition in which the horses are required to cover 25, 50, 75, or 100 miles/40, 80, 120, or 160 km in a single day (sometimes in two or three), within a time limit based on a speed of 5 to 9 miles an hour/8 to 14.4 kph (but often requiring a speed of 15 mph/24 kph or more to win). There is no minimum time limit, as in the equally fast-growing, more informal sport of competitive trail riding, which is designed to discourage excess speed and the abuses arising from it. Speed is not, however, the sole criterion of endurance rides. The horses' condition is checked at regular veterinary posts (P&R—Pulse and Respiration) along the way as well as at the finish, when they are examined for signs of soreness, lameness, dehydration, and respiratory or cardiac stress. The winner must be perfectly sound as well as fast. A special award is presented to the horse in Best Condition among the first ten finishers; a prized token of a belt buckle or a pin is given to com-

This little boy in saddle-seat attire proudly displays his ribbons. Were he in England or Canada, he could be even prouder, for red ribbons there denote first prize. AHSA awards range from blue for first, red for second, yellow for third, to white, pink, green, purple, brown, gray, and light blue.

259

petitors who have succeeded in completing the ride, which is in itself an achievement.

It takes a very sound, fit horse, a considerate, fit rider, careful planning, even the collaboration of a "pit crew" to cross the finish line. As much as four or five months is spent in conditioning for a ride, not unlike the three-day eventers' training program. Horse and rider form an intimate partnership. The rider has to know his horse so well that he can recognize the slightest sign of fatigue or discomfort and save strength for the most taxing portions of the trail and the final run-in. Unlike competitive trail riders, he (very often she) is permitted to dismount, and many do so in order to lead their horses through scary stretches or downhill; they also "tail" up steep rises, literally hanging onto the horse's tail.

Although any breed of horse is eligible (even ponies and mules), Arabian and Thoroughbred horses or crosses predominate and excel in the major events. Morgans, Quarter Horses, and other Western breeds do well depending on the terrain, which varies widely. In the western U.S. it consists of forest trails, prairies, rocky mountain slopes; in the East, of woods and fields, and National Park trails. The most world-famous endurance ride, the Tevis Cup (now called the Western States Trail Ride), which was founded in 1955 by Wendell Robie, the "father of the sport," follows a route once used by Pony Express riders from Tahoe City, Nevada, to Auburn, California, during which conditions range from 100-degree/38 C. heat in El Dorado Canyon to icy wind and snow over Sierra Nevada mountain passes.

This renowned event is the Kentucky Derby, one might say, of American endurance riding; the Old Dominion Ride in Virginia, its Preakness. In England, the seventy-five-mile/120 km, two-day Golden Horseshoe Ride would be its Ascot Gold Cup. The richest of all is the recently inaugurated Purina Race of Champions; the most international, the FEI-approved North American Open Championship. Almost a "national event" is the Great Two-Day Endurance Race in Queensland, Australia, which covers 200 miles/320 km the first day and 50 miles/80 km the next.

Throughout the year there are many less demanding endurance rides and an increasing number of competitive trail rides, the principal distinctions between them being speed and distance: the former covering twenty-five to one hundred miles/40 to 160 km a day, the latter fifteen to forty miles/24 to 64 km; the former at the fastest possible speed without impairing soundness, the latter within a minimum as well as a maximum time limit, with penalty points for completing the ride too soon. Competitive trail rides are not races. Winners are determined according to points awarded for Soundness (40%), Condition (40%), Manners (15%), and Way of Going (5%), scored by judges along the way as well as at the finish. Among numerous other awards,

The "shotgun start" (all-at-once) of a ride-and-tie race in California, where this novel, recent equestrian sport originated. A team of two riders races over a distance partly on foot, partly on horseback, alternating the roles of rider and runner.

Horsemen have invented many ingenious sports in which men and horses form a team. One of the most picturesque is ski-joring, in which the horse is driven in long reins by a skier, as shown here at St. Moritz.

there is one for Horsemanship. Less stressful than endurance riding, it is more of a weekend sport; many competitors start out in competitive trail rides and move on to endurance.

An amusing variation is the ride-and-tie race. Devised as a promotional event, it has become a popular sport with more than 350 races held each year in America and Europe. It is a race with one horse and two riders. At the start, one team member mounts the horse, rides a predetermined distance decided on between the teammates, ties the horse, and then sets off running. The other team member starts the race on foot, runs to where the horse has been tied, mounts it and rides past his teammate to the next tie spot and sets forth on foot again —and so forth, until the horse and both riders have crossed the finish line. At least five changes are required in the Championship event, but the contestants can schedule them as they like.

All of these related sports have been growing fast. There are already 550 annual endurance rides, hundreds of competitive trail rides, and ever more enthusiasts attracted by the challenge and the generous, friendly atmosphere of these (still) exemplary amateur equestrian activities.

VAULTING

Is vaulting (*voltige* in countries where the French terminology is used) an equestrian activity or a gymnastic discipline? The FEI chose the first definition by recognizing it as an official international equestrian sport in 1985, even though the horse is not ridden in the usual sense, nor do vaulters resemble horsemen.

Instead of breeches and boots, they wear leotards and soft-soled gymnastic slippers as they perform a variety of gymnastic exercises on the back of a trotting or cantering horse that is controlled by a longe line held by a "longer" standing in the middle of a circle at least 43 feet/13 m in diameter. Instead of a saddle, the horse wears a leather vaulting surcingle with a ring on top to which a strap is attached; instead of stirrups, there are hand grips on either side of the surcingle and loops farther down to hold the vaulter's feet during spectacular Cossack-style figures.

Long a practically obligatory feature of the circus, vaulting is certainly a much older activity than modern gymnastics performed on a leather "horse" in a gymnasium. Ever since the days of the Roman Empire, it has been used to school riders to develop balance, rhythm, courage, and sensitivity to the horse's movements. It is part of the curriculum of most cavalry schools and many riding academies. In the early twentieth century, it became a competitive cavalry sport and as such was included in the Olympic Games during the 1920s.

Modern vaulting is still a predominantly amateur sport for youths,

United States vaulting champion Jeanette Boxall performs the "Flag" movement on Boris during the World Vaulting Championship at Bulle, Switzerland, in August 1986, where she was the Women's Reserve Champion.

although there are professional vaulters as well as adult enthusiasts. It is most widespread in countries where gymnastic arts as well as horse sports are most appreciated: in Germany more than anywhere else, but also in France, England, Switzerland, Sweden, Spain, Eastern Europe, and the United States (especially in California). In addition to informal club events, there are official national and international competitions for teams composed of eight members (plus a reserve member), all boys or girls under eighteen years of age; competitions for individuals and pairs (Pas de Deux) are open to vaulters over sixteen, with no upper age limit.

The competitions consist of six compulsory exercises performed individually as the horse circles around the arena: the basic seat, the flag, the mill, the flank, the free stand, and the scissors. Then the team presents a five-minute freestyle composition of its own, usually to music, to display its technique, teamwork, and creativity. As many as three vaulters may be on the horse at once during the performance of dynamic, coordinated figures and beautiful, sometimes daring static poses that are held for at least three strides.

Judging is based on technique, essence, form, scope (elevation and amplitude of movement), difficulty, security, balance, and consideration for the horse.

Theoretically, any sound, robust horse six years old or over, with a good disposition, can be used as a vaulting horse, although—for once—the Thoroughbred is not ideal. At vaulting competitions one sees Quarter Horses, Morgans, and Appaloosas; Percherons excel among the heavy-horse breeds. Gentle ponies are a safe choice for beginners; in Germany, retired dressage horses are often used, for they are trained to flex their body moving around the circle instead of leaning over. It takes only one horse to "mount" a team. In fact, it takes only one horse to start a vaulting club—an economic factor that gives this artistic, athletic sport a great advantage over most other equestrian activities.

GYMKHANA AND PONY CLUB GAMES

Is anything in the world of sport more appealing than the sight of little children riding ponies? From pony show "lead classes" for the tiniest of tots, to pony races, gymkhana games, and more adult-style Pony Club competitions for teenagers (the age limit being seventeen, leading on to Associate membership until age twenty-one), it is enchanting to observe the expressions on their faces: self-confident or shy, exhilarated or intimidated, set in determination, glowing with pride, beaming with joy. No horse show nerves here! It's all for fun, and the children and ponies seem to be having the time of their lives.

Gymkhana games were adopted and adapted by British officers in India (hence the Hindu name) and brought back by them to England.

263

Now it is more often an activity for children, a feature of a local horse show, or an occasion in itself. Many of the games are team races: relay races, pole bending, potato races; others are individual, like the ball-and-bucket race, egg-and-spoon, apple bobbing, and water-glass race—the variety is limited only by the imagination of the organizer, very often a riding school or Pony Club.

The Pony Club is a largely voluntary organization founded in England in 1929 as a junior division of the British Horse Society, with the goal of developing succeeding generations of well-trained, responsible riders and future fox hunters. The U.S. Pony Clubs, Inc., created in 1953 in the image of its British counterpart, comprises some 420 member groups, often affiliated with a hunt club, and the movement has spread to twenty-two other countries, including France, Australia, and New Zealand.

During Pony Club games, it's not the pony's job to reason why (why his young rider is leaning over his neck to spear an apple in a tub, or carrying a glass of water in her hand), but often to stand quietly, ready to race over the finish line after his little rider has accomplished the strange things required by the rules of the game.

Horse care and horsemanship are stressed, but fun is not forgotten. Throughout the years, the gymkhana games have been supplemented by modified versions of major equestrian competitive disciplines for older children: hunter trials and point-to-points, polo, jumping, vaulting, fox hunting, dressage, even a variation of the Olympic Pentathlon, called the Tetrathlon, with four events: riding, shooting, swimming, and running. Young riders progress through proficiency tests from classifications D to A. Regional team "rallies" during the year conclude in National Finals. In England, the climax of the gymkhana year is the Prince Philip Cup at the Horse-of-the-Year Show. In 1985, Prince Philip donated a similar perpetual trophy to reward the top Pony Club–mounted games team of the United States, inaugurating a new, delightful highlight event of the National Horse Show.

Many future equestrian stars began their riding education in a Pony Club, and scored their first wins in an egg-and-spoon race, such as two-time World Champion three-day eventer Bruce Davidson and his teammate Tad Coffin; USET jumper-riders Melanie Smith and Buddy Brown; champion American steeplechase jockey Tommy Skiffington.

While older children at advanced levels are more often mounted on small horses, the youngest competitor in a game of Musical Chairs may be riding a pony twice as old as he is. Cheer the child, but do not forget the pony. Some of these wise, experienced, little fellows are unsung heroes who make an inestimable contribution to the horse world in their modest way, by teaching children good horsemanship and good sportsmanship, preparing future generations of riders or merely horselovers to support and perpetuate the impressive range of equestrian sports.

Little children like these seem to know instinctively what many city-bred adults forget or never learn—that horse and man together can experience not only an incomparable sporting partnership, but also an almost mystical rapport that is unique among our relationships with other living creatures.

264

267

1: Bob Langrish. 2–3: Magnum. 4: Ian Berry/Magnum. 8: Douglas Lees.

Flat Racing
11, 12–13: both, Cappy Jackson. 14: top, Baltimore Museum of Art; bottom, courtesy American Heritage. 15: Kay Chernush 1985. 16: top, courtesy William Steinkraus; center, UPI; bottom, New-York Historical Society/American Heritage. 17: top, courtesy William Steinkraus; bottom, New York Racing Association. 18–19: Gerry Cranham. 20: Gerry Cranham. 22: Raymond Woolfe. 25: Richard Kalvar/Magnum. 26 & 28: both, Ian Berry/Magnum. 30: top, William Strode; bottom, Bob Langrish. 32: William Strode. 33: Ian Berry/Magnum. 34: William Strode. 36–37: Magnum. 39: top, Richard Kalvar/Magnum; bottom, Paul Fusco/Magnum. 41: Magnum. 42: Mike Roberts. 44: top, Kay Chernush; bottom, Magnum. 46: Paul Fusco/Magnum. 47: Raymond Woolfe. 48: William Strode. 49: Kit Houghton. 50: Ed Byrne. 51: Paul Fusco/Magnum. 52: Raymond Woolfe. 53: Alix Coleman. 54: Magnum. 55: Richard Kalvar/Magnum. 57: Kit Houghton. 58: Magnum. 59: Kit Houghton.

Steeplechasing
61: Kit Houghton. 62: Alix Coleman. 64–65: Ed Byrne. 66: top, UPI; bottom, courtesy William Steinkraus. 67: both, UPI/Bettmann Newsphotos. 69: both, Bob Langrish. 70: Paul Fusco/Magnum. 72: all, Mike Roberts. 74–75: Kit Houghton. 76–77: Magnum. 79: Ian Berry/Magnum. 81: top, Rick McIntyre; bottom, Richard Kalvar/Magnum. 82: Dave Hartley/Rex Features. 83: Sue Maynard. 85: Kit Houghton. 86: Mike Roberts. 87: Richard Kalvar/Magnum.

Show Jumping
88: Max Ammann. 89: Bob Langrish. 90–91: all, Max Ammann. 92: Sandra Langrish. 94: top, Werner Ernst; bottom, Findlay Davidson. 95: Findlay Davidson. 96: top, Ian Berry/Magnum; bottom, Magnum. 97: Magnum. 98: Findlay Davidson. 99: top, courtesy William Steinkraus; bottom, Paul Fusco/Magnum. 100–101: both, Bob Langrish. 102 & 103: both, Kit Houghton. 104: top, Ian Berry/Magnum; bottom, Bob Langrish. 105 & 106: both, Bob Langrish. 107: Kit Houghton. 108: Kit Houghton. 109: Bob Langrish. 110: Karl Leck. 111: Magnum. 112: courtesy William Steinkraus. 113: Bob Langrish.

Dressage
114: both, Max Ammann. 115: Kit Houghton. 116: Karl Leck. 118: Alix Coleman. 119 & 120: both, Bob Langrish. 121: Kit Houghton. 123–125: all, Findlay Davidson. 126: Richard Kalvar/Magnum. 127: Karl Leck. 128: Kit Houghton. 129: Cappy Jackson. 130: top, Findlay Davidson; bottom, Bob Langrish. 131: Werner Ernst.

The Three-Day Event
132–133: all, Max Ammann. 134: both, Ian Berry/Magnum. 135: Sandra Langrish. 136: Ian Berry/Magnum. 137: Bob Langrish. 139 both, 140, 141 both, and 142 top: Kit Houghton. 142: bottom, Findlay Davidson. 144: Mike Roberts. 145: Kit Houghton. 146: Bob Langrish. 147: Kit Houghton. 149: top, Alix Coleman; bottom, William Strode. 150–152: all, Kit Houghton. 153: Paul Fusco/Magnum.

Polo
154: both, National Museum of Polo. 155: David Lominska. 156: Kit Houghton. 157: Mike Roberts. 158–159: Bob Langrish. 160: Jeffrey Blackman. 161: top, Linda Schwartz; center, Mike Roberts; bottom, Kit Houghton. 162: Transatlantic Films. 163: Ricardo Motran. 164: Mike Roberts. 165: Janet Keeler-Lominska. 166: Transatlantic Films. 167: Jeffrey Blackman. 168: David Lominska. 169: Kit Houghton. 170–171: all, David Lominska. 172: Ricardo Motran. 173: David Lominska. 174: Kit Houghton. 175: Alix Coleman. 176–177: both, David Lominska.

Rodeo
178: Jeffrey Blackman. 179: James Fain. 180: Wyoming State Archives/American Heritage. 181: University of Oregon Library/American Heritage. 182: top, Paul Fusco/Magnum; bottom, Sue Maynard. 183: James Fain. 184–185: Jeffrey Blackman. 186: top, James Fain; bottom, Jeffrey Blackman. 187: Transatlantic Films. 188 & 189: both, Jeffrey Blackman. 189 bottom, 190–191, and 192: both, James Fain. 193: Sue Maynard. 194: Bob Langrish. 197: Alix Coleman. 199: James Fain. 200: Alix Coleman.

Combined Driving
202: both, Max Ammann. 203: Findlay Davidson. 204–205: all, Ian Berry/Magnum. 206: top, Mike Roberts; bottom, Bob Langrish. 207: Ian Berry/Magnum. 208: Werner Ernst. 209–213: all, Ian Berry/Magnum. 214: Cynthia Mathews. 215–216: top, both Bob Langrish. 216 bottom, 219 both: Findlay Davidson. 220: Cynthia Matthews. 221: Bob Langrish.

Harness Racing
223: top, private collection/American Heritage; bottom, UPI. 224: private collection/Laurie Platt Winfrey, Inc. 225: top, UPI/Bettmann Newsphotos. 225: middle and bottom, United States Trotting Association. 226–227: Richard Kalvar/Magnum. 228: Richard Kalvar/Magnum. 229: Paul Fusco/Magnum. 230: Magnum. 232–233: Paul Fusco/Magnum. 235: Richard Kalvar/Magnum. 236–237: all, Paul Fusco/Magnum. 238: United States Trotting Association. 239: Kay Chernush. 240: top, Richard Kalvar/Magnum; bottom, United States Trotting Association. 241: United States Trotting Association. 242: Magnum.

Other Equestrian Events
245: Peter Harding, courtesy *Horse and Hound*. 246–248: all, Douglas Lees. 250–252: both, Kit Houghton. 253: Douglas Lees. 254: Alix Coleman. 255: Paul Fusco/Magnum. 256–257: both, Alix Coleman. 258: Paul Fusco/Magnum. 261: top, Buddy Mays; bottom, Mike Roberts. 263: Lynne Nelson/American Vaulting Association. 264: Alix Coleman. 265: Kit Houghton.

The type in this book was set in Bodoni on a Compugraphic MCS8400 by Arkotype Inc., New York, New York.
The book was printed and bound by Toppan Printing Co., Ltd., Tokyo, Japan.